THEODOR FONTANE

THEODOR FONTANE

Literature and History
in the Bismarck Reich

Gordon A. Craig

New York • Oxford

Oxford University Press

1999

Oxford University Press

Oxford   New York
Athens   Auckland   Bangkok   Bogotá   Buenos Aires   Calcutta
Cape Town   Chennai   Dar es Salaam   Delhi   Florence   Hong Kong   Istanbul
Karachi   Kuala Lumpur   Madrid   Melbourne   Mexico City   Mumbai
Nairobi   Paris   São Paulo   Singapore   Taipei   Tokyo   Toronto   Warsaw

and associated companies in
Berlin   Ibadan

Published by Oxford University Press, Inc.
198 Madison Avenue, New York, New York 10016

Oxford is a registered trademark of Oxford University Press

Library of Congress Cataloging-in-Publication Data
Craig, Gordon Alexander, 1913–
[Über Fontane. English]
Theodor Fontane : literature and history in the
Bismarck Reich / Gordon A. Craig.
p.   cm.
Includes bibliographical references and index.
ISBN 0-19-512837-0
1. Fontane, Theodor, 1819–1898.   2. Authors, German—19th
century—Biography.   3. Germany—History—19th century.
4. Prussia (Germany)—History—1789–1900.   I. Title.
PT1863.F66   C7313   1999
833'.8—dc21
[B]   98-47520

1 3 5 7 9 8 6 4 2

Printed in the United States of America
on acid-free paper

To the memory of
Daniel Marcus Davin
Arthur Spring-Rice Pyper
Jerome Blum

———————

In midst of all inconsequential things,
I find myself remembering other springs.

CONTENTS

INTRODUCTION

In his remarkable series of essays *The Spirit of the Age*, William Hazlitt wrote:

> A really great and original writer is like nobody but himself. In one sense, Sterne was not a wit, nor Shakespear a poet. It is easy to describe second-rate talents, because they fall into a class and enlist under a standard; but first-rate powers defy calculation or comparison and can be defined only by themselves. They are *sui generis* and make the class to which they belong. I have tried half-a-dozen times to describe [Edmund] Burke's style without ever succeeding: its severe extravagance, its literal boldness, its matter-of-fact hyperbole, its running away with a subject and from it at the same time, but there is no making it out, and no example of the same thing anywhere else. We have no common measure to refer to, and his qualities contradict even themselves.[1]

These words are worth bearing in mind when we think of Theodor Fontane. There are nineteenth-century German writers whom we would rank higher: Goethe certainly, who had the ability to do everything anyone else did just a little bit better; and Heine, who had no equal as a prose writer and whose satirical gifts recall those of Juvenal; and any number of lyricists whose talents were truer and fuller than

Fontane's. Even so, the products of Fontane's pen were so original and so diverse that their author's stature is as undeniable as his defiance of classification. There is no one like him. No writer in his time had a range as great as his, including as it did political journalism of the highest quality, ballads, songs, historical poems and *vers d'occasion*, a unique kind of travel literature, military history and historical essays on Prussian, English and Scottish history, extensive writings on the theater, novels that have been described as the most completely achieved of any written between Goethe and Thomas Mann, and a volume of correspondence that marks him as one of the most entertaining letter writers in German literature.

Nor does such a listing of categories succeed in giving a true sense of the uniqueness of his work. Anyone who picks up a volume of *The War against France* or *Wanderings through the Mark Brandenburg* with the expectation that it will conform to conventional nineteenth-century military or travel literature will be happily surprised, in the former case by the clarity and essentially literary quality of the style, which makes technical detail and complicated maneuvers comprehensible to the general reader, by the masterful description of the historical and political context and of the terrain in which the hostilities take place, by Fontane's eye for the critical turning points in battle and his dramatic re-creation of individual passages of arms, by his freedom from narrow national partisanship, and—above all—by his insistence upon entering into the minds and attitudes of the soldiers on the other side of the hill. It is these qualities that have assured the survival of his military histories, while the professional studies of the time, written by people who refused to believe that a mere civilian was capable of writing about their métier, have long since sunk into oblivion. Similarly, one can say of the *Wanderings* that there is no example of the same thing anywhere else—a kind of travel literature that enchants the reader with its mixture of description, history, and anecdote, that is studded with brilliant set pieces, like the story of the execution of Katte, the friend of Frederick II's youth, at Küstrin, and that is written in a style that varies between the circumstantial and the playful, *Sachlichkeit* consorting easily with *Plauderei*.

In his splendid biography, Hans-Heinrich Reuter has written that Fontane's greatest gifts were his power of acute observation, his critical capacity, and his sense of history, and that it was these, gradually developed and mutually self-supporting, that comprised his originality and determined the character of his finest work.[2] More will be said of all these qualities in the chapters that follow, but—since the author of these pages is himself a historian—the emphasis will fall upon the third, Fontane's affinity for history, which he came to naturally and which was his strongest passion.

At this point, I should confess that the genesis of my own admiration of Fontane was very belated and that, to the best of my recollection, I had neither heard his name nor read a page of his work until 1938, when I was twenty-five years old. This still seems a bit odd to me, for during my training in history at the university I had a strong interest in German literature, and I can only attribute it to the fact that, in American universities in the 1930s, departments of German literature did not pay much attention to the nineteenth-century novel. Beyond the *Laokoon* and the *Hamburgische Dramaturgie*, and the writings of the Weimar *dioscuri*, and the Romantics, a great wasteland extended in which Schopenhauer and Wagner and Nietzsche were rumored to dwell but which was apparently forbidden territory for novelists, who had to go to Russia or France or Great Britain in order to ply their trade. It was not until I came back to Princeton from Oxford as a graduate student in history that I discovered that this view was exaggerated. At that time, my *Doktorvater* Raymond James Sontag gave me a book by Ernst Kohn-Bramstedt,[3] and I heard for the first time the names of Gustav Freytag, Friedrich Spielhagen, Wilhelm Raabe, and Theodor Fontane.

Kohn-Bramstedt was a confirmed believer in the importance of the novel of society as a historical source, a belief that he emphasized at the outset:

To what extent can one rely on literature in depicting society? What likelihood is there that the social novel will help to a better understanding of society? By means of particular instances and sequences of events it can portray the specific character of social situations or of social types and illustrate even the smallest features of everyday life. Today a serious social novel implies just as exact an empirical knowledge of its subject as does a scientific sociological analysis.

Although, in contrast with science, the novel does not verify its results with the aid of a statistical method, it works with a combination of observation and intuition, involving the risk of inaccuracy, but conferring the advantage of a greater approximation of life.[4]

Had I been further advanced in my historical studies, I might have considered that statement as exaggerated or even dogmatic. But I was at the time under the spell of the great French and English social novelists and inclined to believe that Kohn-Bramstedt was right. And in any case, I was curious about the work of these German writers of whom I had never heard. What Kohn-Bramstedt had to say about their novels and the light that they threw on the manners and morals of nineteenth-century German society was both interesting and illuminating, and I sat down to read Freytag's *Soll und Haben*, Spielhagen's *Sturmflut*, and Raabe's *Pfisters Mühle* with enthusiasm and profit. Indeed, I learned more from them about early industrial development in Germany and the social consequences of the new capitalism and the financial collapse of 1873 than I had from any historical account that had yet come my way.

Of all these new discoveries, however, it was the novels of Theodor Fontane that seemed to me to focus most consistently upon the problems that had fascinated Dickens and Trollope and would later challenge the imagination of Proust—the decline of the aristocracy, the insidious effect of parvenuism on the middle class, and the general deterioration of values that flowed from all of this. As an apprentice historian, I was already working hard on the Bismarck and Wilhelmine periods, and from the beginning Fontane's novels struck me as an indispensable source of material, and one that could be read with the keenest intellectual and aesthetic enjoyment. I was captivated by their economy, their artful construction, and their urbanity, humor, and felicity of phrase, but no less by their author's skill in laying bare the essentials of social reality and class conflict by his delineation of his characters as social types responding to the problems of their time in typical ways.

In short, I admired the historian in Fontane more than the artist, of whom I was, of course, incapable of making any very sophisticated judgment. And yet, as I turned to his earlier works—the ballads, and the book on Scotland, and the wonderful *Wanderings through the*

Mark Brandenburg, and the war books, all works in which his historical gifts were more directly manifest than in the novels and which I read with enthusiasm and gratitude (rightly so, for what would my own book on Königgrätz have become had I not read Fontane's *German War of 1866?*)—I began to understand that Fontane was a gifted historian because he was a great artist, often arbitrary in his handling of the material the professional historians brood over endlessly in their search for accuracy, but more searching and incisive for all of that, intent on looking into history rather than on photographing it, and sometimes succeeding, despite a proneness to small mistakes of fact, in giving a more truthful picture of the past than his academic colleagues.

Fontane was himself not unaware of this. At the end of a dreary Sunday in London in 1856—a time when he was serving as press attaché to the Prussian envoy Graf von Bernstorff, doing work that did not challenge his talents, homesick and separated from his wife and son, and with only a handful of friends—he wrote in his diary:

> Simpson's on Drury Lane. Mutton as usual. I can't stand it. I would give a *Reichsthaler* for a portion of green peas and beets or a bowl of sour milk. My stomach is done for, and it is an eternity till Christmas [when he would have home leave]—Café Divan. . . . Read Macaulay—the ever closer approach to the abyss, Tyrconnel in Ireland, the overthrow of the Hydes (Lord Clarendon, the viceroy of Ireland, and Lord Rochester, the First Lord of the Treasury)—all marvellous! Perhaps more of a work of art than a work of history in the common sense, but all the greater on that account.[5]

It is not unlikely that the lonely writer, putting his cares aside by burying himself in his oldest passion, history, recognized in Macaulay a kindred spirit and an example of that felicitous combination of history and literature that would characterize his own future work.

THEODOR FONTANE

1

History

Theodor Fontane's first published prose work was a story called "Sibling Love."[1] He tells us in his memoirs that on 19 December 1839, shortly after his twentieth birthday, he had gone to the local district physician, Dr. Natorp, for an oral examination in botany and related subjects and that Natorp had certified his promotion from apprentice to assistant apothecary. On the way back to Rose's pharmacy where he was employed, Fontane stopped off at the Heureuse Konditorei in the Kölln Fish Market to look at the *Berlin Figaro*, his favorite journal, and discovered his story in its pages. He had already had some poems published in the paper, but their appearance had never had the same effect upon him, he wrote, "perhaps because they were so short; but here, these four columns with the 'To be continued' at the bottom, that was marvelous. By everything that this afternoon had brought me, I was as if stunned, and had every reason to be so. In little more than half an hour I had been promoted by Natorp to a 'Herr' and by Heureuse to a writer of stories."[2]

It is perhaps significant that he says nothing about the story itself. Certainly anyone who reads it in the hope of discovering some sign of the great novelist to come will be disappointed. The theme is provocative enough, and has appealed to other writers, including Fontane's admirer Thomas Mann, in his unpleasant little story "The Blood of the Volsungs," but Fontane exploits none of its possibilities. His story is about Clärchen, a young woman who lives, in straitened circumstances, with a brother who has been blind from birth but has apparently reached man's estate without developing any talents except an extraordinary self-pity and the ability to play melancholy songs on a lute. The preacher in the local cloister church becomes interested in the pair, visits them frequently and has long talks with the brother, and gradually falls in love with Clärchen, and she with him. When the brother discovers that they intend to marry, he submits the lovers to every kind of moral blackmail and, when they persist in their plans, says that he never wishes to see them again. The parting, for he is true to his word, proves too much for his sister, who after a year of marriage becomes persuaded that God may have intended that her love should be reserved for her brother and becomes fatally ill. The preacher prevails upon the brother to give up his obduracy and come to her deathbed, where the siblings are reconciled. In death, her love makes the two men close friends for the rest of their lives. Indeed, they die within hours of each other, "and there above they found their faithful and true loved one and stilled their hot longing and forgot all the pains of separation in their blessed reunion with their Clärchen." Although the theme of incest, which was to occupy Fontane on later occasions, is touched upon here, the mawkishness of this tale, and of the interspersed verses that accompany it, is equaled by the lameness of its plot and the inertness of the style in which it is told, and Clärchen and her brother are both so colorless that no one could have predicted that their creator had a future as a writer.

Yet "Sibling Love" was certainly no worse than hundreds of other stories written and published in Germany in its time, and may indeed be described as a characteristic product of its age. Two years before its publication, the leader of the Young German movement, Karl Gutzkow, had written in his journal *Das Telegraph für Deutschland* that "the present generation of German writers seems destined only to open the way for a future one; great things will not develop out of it; it will have to fill the trenches over which another race advances to victory." He attributed this circumstance to the fact that contemporary writers had to contend with the suspicion of literature that dominated established bureaucracies, the illogic and lack of principle of the press laws, the crude pretentiousness of popular criticism, the timidity of the publishing industry, the pervasive mysticism and materialism, and, above all, "the ice-coldness of our daily experience,"[3] that is, the fact that nothing exciting ever happened. In the daily lives of young writers there were simply too few things that helped them grow, and too many that cabined, cribbed, and confined them. The atmosphere in which they lived stifled talent, and the models that were available to them were antiquated, tradition-bound, and uninspiring.

In Prussia this was true not only of the provinces but also of Berlin, which in the late 1930s, in contrast to the capitals of other great nations, was a mere residential city, dominated by its court, its bureaucracy, and its military establishment, with a population that was predominantly lower middle class, with neither a self-confident bourgeoisie nor a sizable proletariat to challenge conventional ways of thinking, and with a heterogeneous class of actors, scribblers, and pseudo-intellectuals who congregated in its many cafés and pastry shops to read the newspapers or formed literary clubs and read their latest works to each other. Even the young assistant in Rose's pharmacy, dreaming of becoming an independent writer one day, was vaguely aware that this might not be the best place in which to achieve his dreams. In one of those miscellaneous pieces that he began to submit to newspapers, he wrote in 1842:

> There was a time when Berlin seemed destined to be Germany, to rule the world; the presentiment of this great destiny penetrated the hearts of its best men. But that time has passed, and the mission has been thrown into the rubbish bin, and anyone who still believes in it is a child. . . . Formerly over-confident, the Germanic Gascon, now it is modest and discomfited. Formerly giving itself airs as the leader of the spiritual power of Germany, now it runs around naked and unashamed as the promoter of the most reckless and outrageous stock-jobbery. . . . A foreigner who has lived here for a short time can say, "Berlin is a great city, a *Residenzstadt*; and as such it provides a mass of amusing ways to pass the time." That, however,

is all that we can attribute to Berlin; of a genuine amusement and
one that lasts, there can be no question. That is due to the complete
lack of public life. Mere being together, talking together, sitting
together, dancing together is far from being public life. A public
life, a *Volksleben*, can only exist when the population is penetrated
by a distinct character, as, for example, in Vienna or Paris. . . . Berlin
is hardly more than a colony . . . in which all inclinations and opinions are contradictory, . . . and the *inner* unity, which in the case of
a true *Volksleben* is mirrored in every face, is conspicuously absent.
The heartless mania for making pitiless wounding witticisms about
everything that people hold sacred comes in large part from this
condition.[4]

For a time, the would-be writer felt that his talent might flourish
elsewhere than in Berlin, and he seriously considered making his career in Leipzig or Dresden, where he worked as a pharmacist after
leaving Rose's. In both cities he made friends but in the end found
the atmosphere no livelier than that in Berlin, to which he returned in
1844 for his military service. In Leipzig and Dresden he became for
a time interested in politics and became a critic of King Frederick
William IV of Prussia and his increasingly conservative course. But
this was backed by no real energy. At no time in his life did Fontane
become interested enough in politics to give it more than superficial
attention, and his own political position was always marked by con-
tradictions and great lability, given his distrust of parties. Above all,
aside from some poems in the Herwegh manner and a few not very
profound articles in newspapers, nothing much resulted from his intermittent political activity, nor did it bring him any closer to his goal
of becoming a real writer, that is, one who produced works of art.[5]

Finding nothing to challenge him in the present, Fontane therefore
turned increasingly to the past. Since politics provided no inspiration
for his muse, he sought it in history.

I

Fontane came to history naturally and never lost his passion for it. In
a letter written to Theodor Storm in 1854, he said that even when he

was a child in Swinemünde, it was his favorite subject. His interest was stimulated by his father's encyclopedic knowledge of the campaigns of Napoleon Bonaparte and the delight he took in telling tales about the emperor and his marshals Ney and Lannes and "le premier grenadier de la France," Latour d'Auvergne.[6] He told Storm that, when he was ten years old and was asked what he would like to become when he was grown up, he said stoutly, "Professor of history!" When he was twelve, he added, he was already

> an ardent newspaper reader, fought with Bourmont and Duperre in Algeria, participated four weeks later in the July Revolution and wept when it was all up with Poland after the battle of Ostrolenka. ... And then I went to the Gymnasium. As a thirteen-year-old third grader, and a mediocre student to boot, I had such a reputation in history that the first-graders took me on walks and allowed themselves to be—I can't think of any other way of putting it—crammed by me for exams.

His stock-in-trade was mostly names and dates, he admitted, but there was one occasion when he astonished his auditors with a highly colored description of the battles of Crécy and Poitiers.[7]

Fontane continued to play with the idea of making history his career until the midforties, but nothing came of it. Instead, he went to Berlin in 1833, lived with an uncle, and attended the Klodensche Gewerbeschule. Six years earlier Bettina von Arnim had wanted to send one of her sons to this school, which, she told her husband, was attracting more and more children from families "of our class," but Achim von Arnim was not persuaded, writing that the trade school, which had no classes in Greek or Latin, could not provide a first-class education.[8] The young Fontane was by his later admission so given to truancy that his example is useless for testing Arnim's opinion. About all we know about his record is that he continued to impress people by his historical knowledge. Seeking to escape his school chores, which included the writing of a "German essay on a self-chosen theme," he spent a Sunday afternoon in 1833, trudging from Berlin to the village of Löwenbruch three miles south of the city, where he had family friends. On the way he was reminded that twenty years earlier, Bülow's army, composed mostly of Landwehr, had marched under streaming rain in the same direction and, in the fields around the Großbeeren churchyard, had fought the great battle in which Oudinot's forces were driven into retreat and Napoleon prevented from reentering Berlin. He remembered also that on 14 August 1813, his mother, still a girl, had gone out with other women to tend the wounded left on the stricken field and that the first unfortunate she came upon was "a very young Frenchman who—with hardly a breath left in his body—when he heard his own language being spoken raised himself up as if transformed. Then, with one hand holding the beaker of wine and the other my mother's hand, he was dead before he could drink." That would be a good theme for the essay, thought the student Fontane, and when he got back to Berlin he wrote it and for once received a "Very good" from his teacher, instead of the usual *"Vidi* [Seen]."[9]

Three years later, Fontane graduated from the trade school and, following his father's footsteps, became an apprentice in Rose's pharmacy in the Spandauerstraße next to the St. Nicholas Church. His passion for reading newspapers did not diminish, and he spent much of his free time in establishments that provided them for their patrons, mostly in the Konditerei Anthieny in the northeastern part of town but occasionally in the grander cafés like Stehely on the Gendarmenmarkt and Sparnapagni on Unter den Linden. The literary and political discussions that he heard in these places were probably the real cause of his determination to become a writer, and he started to experiment in various forms. Gradually he concentrated on what he considered to be his greatest strength and began to write historical verse. Thus, in the wake of the doleful "Sibling Love," he composed a poem on the battle of Hochkirch that was inspired by Chamisso's "Salas y Gomez," an epic called "The First Love of Henri IV," and his first ballad, "Retaliation," which dealt with the guilt, triumph, and end of Pizzaro.

Crucial in the development of his poetry was the fact that during his military service in 1844 he became fast friends with Bernhard von Lepel, an officer in the Kaiser-Franz-Regiment in Berlin who also had literary ambitions. Lepel was a member of a literary club called the Tunnel Over the Spree. Founded in 1827 by the Berlin wit M. G. Saphir, it was a kind of personal bodyguard to support him in his endless feuds and to supply material for his paper, the *Berlin Express*, Originally dominated by a rowdy group of law students, young businessmen, actors, journalists, and lieutenants with an interest in the arts, the club had with the years become both more respectable and more conservative. In Fontane's time, it included such notables as the epic poet Christian Friedrich Scherenberg, the reader to the king Louis Schneider, the lawyer Wilhelm von Merckel, the painter Adolf Menzel, the art historian Franz Kugler, Rudolf Löwenstein, the editor of the new satirical journal *Kladderadatsch*, the military publicist Max Jähns, the artist and illustrator Theodor Hosemann, the Swiss philosopher Max Orelli, and the writers Felix Dahn, Paul Heyse, and Theodor Storm, who met periodically to read and discuss new verse and prose written by fellow members.[10]

There was a strong dilettantish cast to the Tunnel, and very few of its products—aside from Fontane's ballads and the much anthologized "The Heart of Douglas" by Moritz Graf von Strachwitz, a Silesian poet who died in 1847—have survived the test of time. The members took themselves very seriously and exercised their critical function with an energy that bordered sometimes on the ferocious. Alexander von Ungern-Sternberg, a highly regarded author of novels and stories of social criticism, found their pretensions faintly comical and refused membership because he said he would not submit his work to "students and soldiers who with the proven German philistine attitude would assure me that my stories were worthless," an opinion that might get out and lead booksellers to cut his royalties.[11] But this was an exaggeration from a writer whose novels might have profited from criticism, and in general the Tunnel gave a fair and often helpful hearing to new works.

This was certainly true in the case of Fontane. He was proposed for membership by Lepel in 1844 and began to attend meetings regularly after the conclusion of his military service. Apparently, his first presentations did not impress the membership, and every now and then they were inclined to feel that his later ones were frivolous or in violation of the society's prohibition of political themes. This would almost certainly have been true of his charming poem in 1848 urging his fiancée, Emilie Rouanet, to join him in exchanging the depressing political atmosphere of Berlin for that of the Cordilleras, where

Ohne Wühler dort und Agitator
Frißt uns höchstens mal ein Alligator. . . .
Und dem Kreischen nur des Kakadu
Hören wir am Titicaca zu.

But in 1846, when Fontane read his ballad "The Old Derffling" to
the Tunnel, his reception must have been very much like that accorded
to the poet Hansen-Grell in the Kastalia chapter of his novel *Vor dem
Sturm*: his audience's enthusiasm far outweighed their criticism;[12] and,
on 18 April 1847, the reading of "The Old Ziethen" and two other
ballads about Seydlitz and Schwerin was an extraordinarily great success.[13]

He was encouraged, therefore, to stick to this vein and to develop
it, a process that was facilitated in 1848 (when he had run out of
Frederician marshals to write about) by his discovery of *Reliques of
Ancient English Poetry*, a collection of ballads, sonnets, historical
songs, and metrical romances published by Thomas Percy, later bishop
of Drumore, in 1765, and *Minstrelsy of the Scottish Border*, three
volumes of ballads compiled by Walter Scott and, after some heavy-
handed editing by him, published in 1802–1803. Fontane fell upon
these with delight, and they became his favorite reading and his
greatest resource, determining, as he wrote later, his taste and direction, and providing him with a source of deep enjoyment for the rest
of his life.[14]

His skill in exploiting these sources soon brought his work to the
attention of a wider audience than the Tunnel. His poems were printed
and in time established themselves in the popular consciousness, so
that even today, when he is chiefly remembered as a novelist, Fontane
is well represented in popular anthologies of poetry, like Ludwig Reiners's *Eternal Spring*,[15] which in its 1958 edition had forty of Fontane's poems, including the ballads, "The Old Derffling," "Archibald
Douglas," "John Maynard," "Jan Bart," "Herr von Ribbeck auf
Ribbeck im Havelland," and the marvelous "Gorm Grymme," with
its chilling conclusion, telling how, after the death of King Gorm's
only son, his queen

. . . gab ihm um ein Mantel dicht,
Der war nicht golden, nicht rot,

Gorm Grymme sprach: "Was niemand spricht,
Ich sprech es: Er ist tot."
Er setzte sich nieder, wo er stand,
Ein Windstoß fuhr durchs Haus,
Die Königin hielt des Königs Hand,
Die Lichter loschen aus.[16]

[Gave him a thick mantle,
It was not golden or red.
Gorm Grymme said, "What none will say
I'll say it: He is dead."
He sat him down then, where he stood.
A gust of wind blew through the house.
The Queen took the King's hand.
The lights went out.]

We should perhaps at this point ask why it was that Fontane had such great success with his ballads. This method of telling a dramatic story in short stanzas with a striking or dramatic conclusion had, of course, been popular in Germany ever since the eighteenth century, encouraged in the first instance by Herder's interest in folk songs and attracting such poets as Goethe ("Der Erlkönig") and Bürger ("Lenore") in the Storm and Stress era and, in the Romantic period, Chamisso, Brentano, Eichendorff, and Uhland. In Fontane's day, both before and particularly after the 1848 revolution, interest in the ballad revived because, in an apparently inert society with nothing in particular to look forward to, people took refuge in stories about their past triumphs or, failing that, about dramatic events in the remote history of Germanic peoples, the Danes and the Norwegians, the English and the Scots. In this climate, Fontane's insatiable interest in history stood him in good stead, as did his sense of the popular temper. In a letter to a friend in April 1850, he wrote, "The far away has charm, and precisely from the vantage point of the mixer of pills, clinging to the Percies and Douglases is psychologically correct."[17]

Fontane was, of course, not the only aspiring writer who sought to exploit popular interest in the past. His friend Christian Friedrich Scherenberg wrote large epics about the battles of Ligny and Waterloo and had the honor of having the latter read to the king by Louis Schneider at one of the periodic literary teas in the castle, and even in the Tunnel Fontane was not the only composer of ballads. His greater success in the genre came less from his superior poetic gift than from his deep reflection on its requirements. In the first place, he was well versed in the work of his German predecessors, and before them in the rich store of medieval *Volk* ballads, which he once said was the necessary basis for any understanding of what a ballad was and how it was constructed. In his view, ballads had to be composed—that is, written according to a logical scheme—but must, at the same time, appear to be natural and free of any literary artifice. Success depended also on the skillful use of suggestion, omission, and abrupt transitions, on mastery of the art of repetition, refrains, and leimotiv, on an ability to create effects with a minimal use of means, and, above all, on color.[18] His own attention to such requirements is apparent even in his earliest ballads, which showed, in addition to great verbal and metrical facility, a remarkable ability to combine highly sophisticated symbolic techniques with the artless diction that the ballad required.

Thus, in what was almost his first ballad, ''The Old Derffling,'' which dealt with the life and death of the victor at Fehrbellin, he took as a leitmotiv the fact—if it is a fact, and not merely the invention of enthusiastic biographers—that Derfflinger had been a tailor in his youth, an occupation from which he had run away to serve with the Swedes in the Thirty Years War. Fontane scattered images taken from the tailor's trade throughout the poem, as if to emphasize the consistency and coherence of the old hero's life and the admirable simplicity of his character.[19] Thus, as a soldier,

> Er war der flinke Schneider
> Zum Stechen wohl geschickt.
> Oft hat er an die Kleider
> Dem Feinde was geflickt.
>
> [He was the nimble tailor,
> Adept at making holes in things,
> And he had often put patches
> In his enemies' clothes.]

and, when he died, well stricken in years,

Er sprach: "Als alter Schneider
Weiß ich seit langer Zeit,
Man wechselt seiner Kleider—
Auch hab' ich des nicht Leid.

Es fehlt der alte Hülle
In Breite schon und Läng',
Der Geist tritt in die Fülle,
Der Leib wird ihm zu eng.[20]

[He spoke, "As an old tailor,
I've known for a long time
That one changes one's clothes—
And I'm not sorry about that.

The old clothes are lacking
Already in breadth and width.
The soul gains in fullness,
The body becomes too tight for it.]

Fontane used a similar technique in his ballad about Jacob Keith, the Stuart supporter who had to go into exile after the failure of the 1715 rising and who had then served in the Spanish and Russian armies and the Russian diplomatic service before becoming one of Frederick's field marshals. Fontane had the happy idea of portraying Keith as a player forced by circumstance to wander from theater to theater.

Ein Kunst- und Wanderleben
Hob an; von Land zu Land:
Gastrollen tätst du geben;
Der Degen in dem Hand.

Du spieltest alle Rollen,
Den Höfling selbst, mit Glück,
Doch schöpfen aus dem vollen
Ließ sich das Ritterstück.
Das war dein Fach, das Kühne,
Der Mut bis an den Tod,
Und manche schlechte Bühne
Halfst du aus arger Not—

[And so began, from land to land,
A life of art and wandering,
And you gave guest appearances
With your sword in hand.

You played all roles excellently,
That of the courtier too,
But pieces about chivalry
Gave you the greatest scope.
Daring was your profession,
Courage in the face of death,
And many a poor theater
You helped in the worst of times.]

until he came in the end to the theater of the master director Frederick and played his greatest roles at Roßbach and at Hochkirch, where he fell.[21]

These strokes of creative imagination distinguished Fontane's ballads from those of his competitors, and they also explain what he meant when he warned poets who took medieval ballads as their models that they must bring something of themselves to this process and not simply try to make a perfect copy of the older form. In a correspondence with Pol de Mont, a professor in Antwerp who was a specialist in ancient Nordic poetry, Fontane wrote in 1887 that the ballad had not yet completed its evolution and that one should not fasten upon any of its diverse forms as a model for imitation. In writing ballads, he added, we may make "borrowings" from the old *Volk* ballads, but the important thing is our own contribution. We must invest the tone of the old ballads with material from our own world and, alternatively, gave the material of the old ballads a new, or at least greatly altered, sound. It is best, he added, "if we refurbish *both* and hold the old ballad in our ear merely as the echo of memory."[22] Fontane's fidelity to these principles accounted for his staying power as a writer of ballads and the extraordinary success that he had not only with ballads like "Archibald Douglas," read at the anniversary meeting of the Tunnel in December 1854, but also with "John Maynard" and "Jan Bart," and others written thirty years later when the interest and taste of the time were vastly different. In the Bismarck period, an age that loved dramatic declamation, it was not unusual for a new Fontane ballad to be read by professional actors as part of a theatrical performance. In January 1880 Fontane wrote to his old friend Mathilde von Rohr:

> Last week, in No. 2 of the *Gegenwart*, I published a poem, ''The Bridge on the Tay,'' in which I handle in the ballad manner the frightful railway accident near Dundee. Perhaps it has come to your attention; if not, I'll send it to you. . . . It has made a kind of sensation here, perhaps more than anything I have written. Sunday fortnight [Richard] Kahle will recite it at a Singakademie concert.[23]

Fontane's colleagues in the Tunnel in the 1840s might have had some difficulty in identifying ''The Bridge on the Tay'' as a ballad, but, although the form was greatly changed, the echo of memory, of which Fontane had spoken, was there.

Fontane's longtime reputation as a poet, therefore, justified the decision he had made in the 1840s to seek to establish himself as a writer by means of historical verse. At the time, however, there was one serious drawback: it was difficult to make money at it. Later on, there would be collected editions of his poems and the royalties that went with them. In the late 1840s that was not true. He calculated once that he could not count on selling even one of his best ballads for more than 2 reichstaler, 7½ silver groschen.[24] And when his six patriotic ballads about Derfflinger and the Frederician marshals appeared in Louis Schneider's *Der Soldatenfreund*, he received an honorarium of half a groschen per line, for a grand total of 4 taler, 20 groschen.[25] Indeed, publishers and booksellers like A. W. Hayn seemed to operate on the principle that the art of poetry depended on the poet's lack of adequate nourishment.[26]

This was all very daunting for Fontane, who wanted to give up pharmacy and to get married. There was always the possibility that he might secure a salaried job as a writer with a government department, but his chances in that direction were compromised to some extent by the extreme conservatism of the government after the suppression of the revolution of 1848 and Fontane's reputation for liberal ideas. It is true that he had done nothing very alarming during the revolution. His sympathies were undoubtedly with the people of Berlin, but, true to his propensity for seeing everything through historical spectacles, he seems to have believed that the best contribution he could make to their cause was the writing of a historical drama to be called "Charles Stuart," which would deal with the English Revolution by focusing on the weakness of the king and Cromwell's consciousness of guilt.[27] In the end, the materials proved to be too rich and the problems of causation and responsibility too complicated for him, and he abandoned the project and turned to the writing of political articles for the *Dresdener Zeitung*, in which he was critical of royal policy and the signs of growing reaction.[28] These were for the most part temperate and well reasoned, but they were enough to attract unfavorable attention in high places, and Fontane became so discouraged that he considered leaving Berlin and offering his services to the beleaguered troops of Schleswig-Holstein, hard-pressed by the Danes and abandoned by their German allies.[29]

How he thought this adventure could relieve his situation is not clear. In any event, thanks to the intervention of friends in the Tunnel, he was able to find employment as a writer of feuilleton pieces for two government papers of moderate views, Werner Hahn's *Deutsche Reform* and Wilhelm von Merckel's *Literarische Cabinet*, and this enabled him in August 1850 to marry his fiancée. But in the following January, when Otto von Manteuffel became minister president, Prussian policy became more rigidly conservative, and Fontane once more found himself with no regular income. He searched desperately for a new occupation without success, and finally, in October 1851, decided that his family took precedence over his liberal principles and wrote a letter to the *Adler-Zeitung*, a quasi-government publication, promising to send them a commemorative poem for the king's birthday and using the occasion to request employment as a writer on English affairs.[30] When this had positive results, he wrote ruefully to his friend Lepel:

> Today I sold myself to the reaction for thirty pieces of silver a month and am once more a salaried *Scriblifax* (in verse and prose) in the *Adler-Zeitung*, resurrected from the late lamented *Deutsche Reform*. These days one cannot survive as an honest man. I am making my debut with octaves in honor of Manteuffel. Content: Minister President crushes the (inevitable) dragon of revolution. Very nice![31]

II

However bruising to the ego, this small gesture to conformity gave
Fontane the security he needed in order to pursue his own writing
while being paid for what he considered to be hackwork comparable
to an apothecary's filling of prescriptions.[32] But, *Brotarbeit* or not,
journalism brought him the opportunity to travel. In the summer of
1852, with a subvention from the king, Fontane went to London as a
correspondent for the *Adler-Zeitung* but with a free hand to choose
the subjects of his reportage. Three years later, in the middle of the
Crimean War, relations between the British and Prussian governments
were strained because of Prussia's neutrality in the conflict, and Fontane was sent back to London as a reporter on English politics and
press opinion. It was not the happiest of assignments, for he was too
objective and too sympathetic to his English hosts to write the kind
of reports that the Manteuffel government desired, and there were
continuous difficulties between him and the bureaucrats in the press
section in Berlin.[33] He was happy, therefore, when his official reporting duties came to an end in March 1856 and he was made an attaché
for literary and cultural questions and a semiofficial correspondent to
the Prussian press. The significance of his residence in England, which
lasted until 1858, was that, aside from deepening Fontane's knowledge
of a country other than his own, it weaned him away from the belief
that poetry was the highest form of literature, a product in part of his
membership in the Tunnel, and made him a prose writer, a turning
point in his career that was signaled in 1858 by the appearance of his
book *A Summer in London.*

The English experience also deepened Fontane's historical sense
and broadened his historical interests, but, to the extent that it did so,
it militated against the success of his political reporting. Charlotte
Jolles has written of the great opportunity that his sojourn in the home
of modern politics gave to Fontane to develop his knowledge of the
arts of political journalism, an opportunity that was enhanced by the
presence in England of a master of the art, in the figure of Lothar
Bucher, who was later to be the most brilliant figure in Bismarck's
press bureau. At the time, Bucher, in exile because of his political
activities in 1848, was writing articles for the liberal *National-Zeitung.*

If the two writers were in a sense competitors, however, Fontane never came close to developing Bucher's skill in tailoring his style and his argument to the needs and interests of his readers and making the values that his political masters wished to implement comprehensible and desirable to them. The fact of the matter was that Fontane wrote for himself rather than for his readers and was always thinking of what he could learn about the subject he was writing on. Nor was he interested in conjecture or in possibilities or in contingencies that had not yet arisen; he preferred things that were true and had demonstrable origins and effects. His were the gifts of analysis rather than those of advocacy. He thought, in short, like a historian rather than like a politician. This explains why his masters in Berlin were always complaining about the irrelevance or abstraction of his political articles and the prolixity of his feuilleton pieces and his failure to make concessions to popular interest.[34]

In his heart Fontane probably admitted the justice of these criticisms. The fact was that he was happier when working on historical subjects, like his studies of the English press,[35] than when describing the daily events of British life or the crises of party politics. In this sense, his last years in England were years of frustration. He was increasingly critical of English life and culture. He had always hated the food, which he found unimaginative, rarely "cooked with love," to use the German phrase, and potentially ruinous of his health. Although he had made many friends, having enjoyed evenings in their homes and been admitted to their social clubs, including one that had some similarity to the Tunnel, he increasingly felt that English culture was superficial, providing only rare opportunities for deep and extensive discussion of important subjects, like history, philosophy, and art. Above all, his life in England, and the incessant demands that his position imposed upon him, gave him no opportunity to express himself as an artist. His diary during the London years reflects all of these feelings. For the most part a matter-of-fact and even laconic account of his daily life and doings, its most interesting pages are those in which he lets himself go on subjects that really interest him—the history of the English stage, for example, and the differences between popular theater in Germany and in England[36]—or when he writes about historical projects that he intends to complete when he gets home. Thus, on 19 August 1856, he wrote: "Made a plan. 'The

Marches. Their Men and their History. Collected and edited for the sake of the Fatherland and future literature by Th. Fontane.' The contents themselves I would present alphabetically. If I could get to the point of writing *that* book I would not have lived in vain and could lay my bones to rest.''[37] Again, on 4 June 1857, he wrote: ''Planned a book: 'Stories of Brandenburg,' for example: the false Waldemar, the Hussites before Bernau, the beautiful *Gießerin*, the White Lady, the old noble families and their sagas, Derffling, Agnes von Borck, . . . the electoral castles, Rheinsberg, Kohlhaas, the Prince von Hessen-Homburg, etc.''[38] Charlotte Jolles has written that in Fontane's last London years the yearning after artistic expression was constantly on his mind and that he suffered from his inability to satisfy it. ''Only his trip to Scotland gave the writer a certain satisfaction.''[39] It did so, of course, not only because it allowed him for a brief period to immerse himself in history without any distraction, but also because it strengthened his resolve, as he returned to Germany, to focus and actualize the projects that had gnawed at the fringes of his mind during his journalistic career.

Indeed, the English years can be seen as a useful and necessary prelude to the longer period during which his principal work was historical. When he returned to Berlin in January 1859, his first problem was to find an occupation that would support him and his family, and for a short time he was captivated by the idea, which originated with his friend Paul Heyse, that he might, if he played his cards right, secure a position at the court of Ludwig II of Bavaria, which would enable him to live as an independent writer.[40] It is amusing to speculate about what his life would have been like if anything had come of this. He might even have become a colleague of Richard Wagner, who came to Munich at Ludwig's invitation in the early 1860s: and, given Fontane's low opinion of Wagner's music, that might have had explosive results. But, although Fontane went to Munich in March 1859 and had two audiences with Ludwig, during which he read his poems to the king and was quizzed about them and about Scotland and his work in England, nothing positive emerged, perhaps because of the distraction caused in Munich by the onset of the Italian War.[41] Fontane himself had by then developed strong misgivings about a move to Bavaria, whose pronounced Catholic atmosphere would hardly have been congenial to his tastes and temperament.[42]

Instead, he took a position at the *Kreuzzeitung*, the paper of the most rigidly conservative Prussian nobility although, in its editorial practices and in the freedom it allowed its staff, remarkably open-minded. This job, like the one he took as theater critic for the *Vossische Zeitung* in 1870, gave him the time to do the things he wanted to do. In the first instance, these were the extensive researches by foot that led in the end to the four volumes of the *Wanderings through the Mark Brandenburg*, the first fruits of which appeared as articles under the general title "Scenes and Stories from Mark Brandenburg" in Cotta's *Morgenblatt* in 1860.[43] Then, as Bismarck's policy unfolded in the years after 1864, came the three remarkable war books, and, after them, the great essays, like those on the cavalry commanders in national history[44] and the relationship between the Mark and Berlin and the development of Berlin character.[45] And then, starting in 1878, came the historical novels and stories, *Vor dem Sturm, Schach von Wuthenow, Grete Minde,* and *Ellernklipp.* It was only when he turned to the social novels of his last period that the emphasis on history was relaxed, although none of the novels is entirely free from historical pastiches and references. This was so because Fontane was part of all his characters, and history came naturally to them as it did to him.

Thus in the charming scene in the last of the novels, when Dubslav goes to Rheinsberg to cast his vote in the Reichstag election in which he himself is the conservative candidate for the district seat, he refuses to sit around and wait for the results. Instead, he proposes to a few friends of his age and political conviction that they take a boat and cross to the other side of the lake, where they can see the statue of Prince August Wilhelm, the second son of King Friedrich Wilhelm I, and study the French inscriptions on the tablets on its base, with their references to Prussian heroes in the Seven Years War. "Such a recapitulation," says Dubslav, "always strengthens one historically and patriotically, and our rear-area French also regains strength."[46] Like his creator, Dubslav believed that, whatever the circumstances, history was always edifying.

III

Fontane lived in an age in which the art of history became at once more scientific and more professional. Under the leadership of German scholars like Niebuhr, Gregorovius, and Ranke, historians learned to pay more attention to the nature of the sources of historical knowledge and were less willing to accept the authority of legend, tradition, and conventional wisdom. Theories of causality and generalization, once employed so loosely by writers, now became the object of anxious scrutiny; a new historical method was devised to promote a more faithful interpretation and understanding of the past; and the written document, scientifically interpreted, became the primary instrument of truth. The free and easy methods of historians like Schlosser and Gervinus, more future-oriented than bound to the past, now fell into disrepute.

The new scientific methodology was propagated by the universities, which trained their students in the new methods and in time placed them in university chairs of history. This soon became the accepted and normal method of becoming a historian, and it amounted to a professionalization of the discipline. Anyone who went to the university and took the required number of courses and examinations and wrote the required doctoral and habilitation dissertations and served the usual number of years as an assistant to a professor and then became a professor himself, was considered and considered himself to be a professional historian. Writers of history who did not have the benefit of academic training were regarded as amateurs.

This system has perpetuated itself, both in Germany and in the Anglo-Saxon countries, until the present day. It should be noted that it has little to do with talent. It would not be difficult to name half a dozen so-called amateur historians at any one time who have talents and records of achievement equal to those of the most distinguished holders of academic chairs, and there is not the slightest doubt that by far the greatest number of academic positions in history are filled with earnest dullards. There is a rough justice in the fact that the latter enjoy the prestige that still clings to the title professor; the amateurs have to make do with the royalties that come from the greater sales of their books. In the nineteenth century, it was the rare academic historian who had the courage to break with the heavy and footnote-laden style favored by his colleagues and vie with the amateurs for popular favor, although Mommsen did so in his great *Roman History* and Droysen in his *Alexander the Great*, and although Burckhardt once wrote, when he was working with Kugler in Berlin in 1847–1848, ''At the risk of being considered unscientific by the population of pedants, I am firmly resolved from now on to write in a *readable* fashion. . . . Against the sneers of the contemporary scholarly generation, one must arm oneself with a certain scholarly indifference, so that one will perhaps be bought and read, and not merely be the subject of bored note-taking in libraries."[47]

In this scheme of things, Theodor Fontane was clearly an amateur, and it is plain enough that he was made to feel it on occasion. Hence his exasperated remark that two anecdotes about Frederick the Great were worth all the state papers of his reign, which was surely not meant to be taken literally, and his frequent sallies against academic historians. In February 1862, a Professor J. A. E. Preuß wrote to the *Vossische Zeitung* to correct Fontane's assumption in an essay in that paper that Johann Christoph Schadow had been born in Saalow. Fontane wrote to thank him, and, as he informed the publisher Wilhelm *Hertz*:

> Preuß answered my letter at once and wrote almost four full pages. One couldn't ask for more than that. The letter included lots of things that were true—some of them with a bitter aftertaste—and held to a line half way between friendliness and goodwill on the one hand and a consciousness of superiority on the other. Personally, I feel not in the least offended; but in general and in principle I deplore the fact that for these "men of research" no compromise, no recognition of *mutual* rights seems possible. While we on our side are ready at any moment to be just and to show all possible respect to "research" (even if from time to time it is dry and leathery enough and likewise, in its results, subject to correction at any time), the old professor with his hair in a braid [*Zopf-Professor*] cannot conceive of the idea that the free *artistic* handling of material, for the sake of the artistic, has a right to existence, even if the strict historical truth is violated in the process.[48]

One might ask here how much violation of the truth is to be permitted the artist. Fontane, who was recognized for his poetry sooner than for his other writings, was sometimes accused of writing history as if it were a ballad, and there is some truth in this. As in the case of the ballad, he believed that the historian should not merely attempt to reproduce the past but bring something of himself to it. That, it might be noted, he will do in any case, but when he does it consciously he runs the risk of seeking to improve and embellish the truth for the sake of the story. The art of writing ballads, as Fontane had written to Pol de Mont, also involved the skillful use of leitmotivs and omission. In the writing of history, this was also questionable. It might be argued that in Fontane's brilliant essay "The *Märker* and the Berliner and How *Berlinertum* Developed," he was a bit heavy-handed in his argument that Berlin temperament and speech were the result of the style of Frederick William I's *Tabakskollegium*, refined at the court of Frederick the Great and transmitted to Berlin by the veterans of his wars who settled there. The omission here, the failure to do justice to the importance of French, Slavic, and Jewish influences, weakens the article as a whole.

But these faults—if that is what they were—were occasional and never fatal, and they were offset by the great virtues of Fontane's historical writing. He was an inveterate reader of history. He knew the classical historians well enough to cite them comfortably; during his English years he whiled away lonely evenings at the Café Divan reading Macaulay and Lecky;[49] he was on friendly terms with Ranke and corresponded with Droysen. He respected their work while occasionally criticizing their style, and he sought in all his major works to emulate their energy and scrupulous attention to the laws of evidence. In his own work, he showed imagination, persistence, and thoroughness in his search for and exploitation of sources. Pierre-Paul Sagave has described how conscientiously he labored, during the composition of his novel *Schach von Wuthenow*, to reproduce the geographical reality and the social relationships of Berlin in 1806, the reciprocal influences that passed between the court and the upper class, the condition and intellectual atmosphere of the officer corps, and the character and personal foibles of the historical figures who appeared in his story, and how solidly the novel was based upon his research in contemporary historical literature and in the pamphlets, fly sheets, legal briefs, and eyewitness reports inspired by *l'affaire Schach*.[50]

In time, Fontane learned to tolerate, and even to profit from, the criticisms of the *Zopf-Professoren*, just as he later, when he turned to military studies, learned to put up with the condescension of the General Staff historians. He came to see that in both cases he was confronted with *Ressortpatriotismus*, the attempt of insiders to protect their turf against interlopers. He didn't mind being considered an interloper because he knew that he was doing something that no one else, least of all his critics, was doing. Instead of becoming involved in scholarly controversy, so dear to the German heart, he therefore went about his business, which was the writing of *The Wanderings* and the impressive war books, which will require our attention in due course.

2

Scotland

It is generally recognized that Scotland has always exercised a strong fascination on the minds and sentiments of the Germans. It may be that this has its origins in a sense of common roots, for both are characteristically northern peoples, and between the sixth and eighth centuries Germans—Angles from England (but originally from Holstein and adjoining lands) and Frisians—fought against the native Britons and Picts and Scots for the domination of Galloway and Midlothian and were eventually absorbed through alliance and intermarriage by their more numerous antagonists.[1] It may also be noted, although perhaps at the risk of unwise generalization, that there is a temperamental similarity between Scots and Germans, and it is possible to describe both of them as riven peoples, combining and seeking to reconcile within themselves the virtues of piety, thrift, moral conscience, and common sense on the one hand, and romanticism and intemperance on the other, both of them having, moreover, a tendency to glamorize the past at the expense of the present, both of them given to dualism and contradiction in their thinking (the similarity of what has been called the Caledonian Antysyzygy and the concept of *Zerrissenheit* offers a rich field for study),[2] and both seeming to be constantly harried by uncertainty about their own identity.[3]

In addition, the Scottish landscape, with its dramatic combinations of mountain and glen, cliff and sea, gray sky and somber heath, evokes a strong emotional response in German hearts, a fact attested to both by Felix Mendelssohn-Bartholdy's Hebrides Overture and Scottish Symphony and, in an earlier period, by the vogue of Ossian, who, Goethe wrote,

> drew us to the ultimate Thule, where we then, wandering on gray unending heath among moss-covered gravestones that stared out at us, gazed at the grass around, torn by a ghastly wind, and at the beclouded sky above. Only by moonlight did this Caledonian night become day. Long dead heroes, maidens whose beauty had long since faded, hovered about us until at last we thought we saw the spirit of Loda in his true and fearful shape.[4]

Real German wanderers on that moorland were sometimes enchanted to find clumps of a kind of heather that, back home in Holstein, was known as *Edelheide* or Erika, an experience that could not but strengthen the feeling of kinship.[5]

Finally, there was always Scotland's violent and turbulent history, a record of feckless gallantry and lost causes, in which the Bannockburns were always outnumbered by the Floddens and Cullodens. This dark chronicle of twisted loyalties and wanton treachery, of conspiracy and betrayal, of lust for power and brutal murder (Duncan meanly slaughtered in the keep of his host and vassal Macbeth; the Red Comyn cut down before the altar in Dumfries by Robert the Bruce; James III, the "Fiddler King," slain by an unknown cleric after his defeat at Sauchieburn; Darnley, escaping the explosion in Kirk o'Field, only to be caught and strangled by the Douglases; Moray, Mary Stuart's ambitious half brother, shot from ambush by a Hamilton in the streets of Linlithgow)—all this could not but appeal to Germans, whose own early history was richly peopled by ambitious kings and desperate men, like the Quitzows and Götz von Berlichingen.

This attraction would hardly have been so strong without the achievement of Walter Scott, who cast a veil of romance over the blood feuds and brutalities of the Scottish clans and made them the background for a series of narrative poems, stories, and novels that took Europe by storm in the first decades of the nineteenth century and left few members of the educated classes unaffected. In an age in which statesmen still read works of literature, Metternich was affected as deeply by Scott's first novel, *Waverley*, a tale of the 1745 rising, as he had been by *The Sorrows of the Young Werther*; while in France, where Scott's novels were translated in the 1820s, the young Hector Berlioz wrote his Op. 2, the concert overture "Waverley," in 1827, scribbling on the manuscript the couplet

While dreams of love and lady's charms
Give place to honour and to arms!

To this enthusiasm Germany was far from being immune, and Goethe's praise of Scott ("I am discovering in him a whole new art that has its own laws")[6] was excelled by the emotional intensity of the reading public's surrender to the charms of Flora MacIver and the fortunes of her naive lover. Ludwig Tieck once boasted to Eckermann that he had brought the first copy of *Waverley* into Germany in 1818.[7] Less than ten years later, Wilhelm Hauff wrote that sixty thousand copies of Scott's novels were circulating in Germany, turned out by "a translation factory based on teamwork" in Scheerau, and many of these copies would, of course, have been in lending libraries, like the one in Bremen that in 1829 had twenty-two titles by Scott.[8]

If what Tieck said was true, his service to German readers occurred one year before the birth of Theodor Fontane, a fact that is worth noting, for Fontane, in his youth and early manhood, became one of Scott's most avid readers. As late as 1868, after reading *The Tales of a Grandfather*, he wrote of their author:

He wrote these stories, which are a poetic representation of Scotland's history, fifty years ago for his seven-year-old grandson. . . . The grandson probably made little out of them at that time or even

later. But the great poet of *Waverley* wrote them, at a different re-
move, for a babe in swaddling clothes who had just been born in
the Lion pharmacy in Neuruppen and lay in his cradle.[9]

Fontane was to become, among German writers, the one who was
most devoted, and most loyal, to the myth of romantic Scotland that
Scott inspired. It is not too much to say, indeed, that this passion for
Scotland not only influenced all of his early work as a writer but
actually helped to shape his literary career, which might have been
quite different without it.

                                I

Fontane's first Scottish poems were written and read to the Tunnel in
1846. They had their origins in an experience that occurred during
Fontane's year of military service. Invited by a friend to accompany
him on a brief trip to England, he applied to his colonel for two weeks
of leave and, rather to his surprise, was granted it. A few days later,
in the great Tudor museum in Hampton Court, he came upon a small
portrait by an unknown artist of Mary Stuart, the beautiful and unhappy Queen of Scots, painted as a nun in a convent, with a characteristically melancholy and uncommonly appealing expression.
Whether or not it was truly a portrait of the queen was a matter of
conjecture, but there were no doubts in Fontane's mind. Many years
later, he wrote: "In my *Schwärmerei* for the beautiful queen—an enthusiasm from which, as in the case of many another, I have somewhat
receded—I took everything, because I wanted to, on loyalty and faith
and was completely bedazzled to have seen this 'lovely one,' at least
in a portrait."[10] Fontane was, of course, familiar with Mary's life and
tragic end, at least in the version that Schiller had given to the world
in his drama "Maria Stuart," and like most educated Germans he
already had—thanks to Walter Scott—a romantic interest in Scotland.[11] The encounter at Hampton Court must have come as a shock
of recognition and, since he was a practicing poet, a challenge to tell
Mary's story in his own way. After his military service was ended,
he began to read Friedrich von Raumer's *Beiträge zur neuern Geschichte*, the first volume of which had been published in 1836 under

the title "Queens Elizabeth and Mary Stuart."[12] At the same time, he began a series of poems that were inspired by his visit to England in 1844.

Chief among these were four about Mary and one about her grandson, Charles I, all of which Fontane read before the Tunnel in 1846 and 1847. At a meeting of the circle in October 1846, he paired the last of these with some verses on Oliver Cromwell under the title "Two Last Nights." This is interesting not only for the poet's attempt to imagine what Charles's thoughts might have been in the last hours before his execution but also because it indirectly violated the Tunnel's prohibition against poems about current political events. It would have been an unimaginative listener who did not find himself, as Fontane described Charles I's self-reproaches, thinking of the political vacillations of King Frederick William IV of Prussia, who began his reign in 1840 with an eloquent appeal to his people that seemed to augur progress toward civil rights and parliamentary government but then retreated to an insistence that the power vested in him by God forbade constitutional concessions.[13] The implied comparison was manifest in the condemned Stuart king's description of himself as

. . . schwankend zwischen Sucht zu herrschen
Und zwischen Lust, dem Volke zu gewähren.
Ich hieß Tyrann, wenn ich den Zügel straffte,
Und Schwächling nur, wenn ich ihn nachgelassen.
Der Mensch in mir befehdete den König;
Der eine riet: den Strom zurückzudrängen,
Der andere: sich ihm mutig zu vertrauen.
Und dieser Streit bringt mich um Kron und Leben.
Die Halbheit bahnt den Weg mir zum Schafott.[14]

[. . . wavering between the craving for power
And the desire to protect the people,
I was called tyrant when I tightened the reins,
And weakling only when I relaxed them.
The human being in me was at loggerheads with the King;
The one counselled me to force back the stream,
The other courageously to trust it;
And this conflict is depriving me of crown and life.
Half-measures are only clearing the way to the scaffold.]

The other four poems dealt with the period between Mary Stuart's return to Scotland as a widow from France in 1561 and her flight to England seven years later. More particularly, they took as their theme Mary's marriage to Henry Stewart, Lord Darnley, in 1565 and all of its dire consequences—the death of David Rizzio, her secretary and musician, with her husband's complicity, Darnley's murder and her marriage to James Hepburn, fourth earl of Bothwell, who was popularly believed to be responsible for it, her imprisonment in Lochleven castle by Bothwell's enemies, and her escape and the subsequent defeat of her forces at Langside, which led to her exile from Scotland.[15] Fontane's telling of this story, which showed his growing mastery of the ballad form, was all the more effective for being episodic. His first poem, written in May 1846 and received by the Tunnel with enthusiasm, was called "The Dying Douglas"; it described Mary at the lowest point in her fortunes, watching from the castle of her allies the Hamiltons as the levies raised by her gallant young captain Willy Douglas were defeated at Langside and Douglas killed.[16] Fontane's handling of the scene in which Willy Douglas dies in Mary's arms is so affecting that one hesitates to point out that the poet was misled by his sources. Neither Willy Douglas nor his cousin George Douglas, also a supporter of Mary, died at Langside. Both went into English exile with Mary, George eventually making his way to France, and Willy remaining in Mary's service until her death and being mentioned in her last will at Fotheringhay.[17]

A month later, Fontane read a more ambitious work—this time on the Rizzio murder—in which the effect was heightened by subtle variations in meter and by shifting the focus of the developing drama, from the treacherous earl of Ruthven telling Darnley that Rizzio is his wife's lover to Rizzio's dream of approaching death, and from there to Darnley tearing the terrified secretary from the queen's side and hacking him to death with his claymore, and finally to Mary sitting by Rizzio's dead body.

> Es hält, die lange Nacht hindurch, Marias Totenwache,
> Zum ersten Mal durchzieht ihr Herz das heiße Wunsch nach Rache:
> Die Morgensonne sah den Schwur auf ihrer Lippe beben—
> Herr Darnley hat des Sängers Tod bezahlt mit seinem Leben.[18]

[The whole night long Mary kept the death watch,
And for the first time her heart was pierced by the hot desire for
    revenge.
The morning sun saw the oath trembling on her lips—
Darnley has paid with his life for the minstrel's death.]

Again, Fontane was a better poet than a historian, although the story
he told was one that the public over the centuries has preferred to
believe. But Rizzio was no *"blonden Edelknaben,"* as Fontane would
have us believe, but a man considered ugly by the standards of the
day, hunched and ill-favored, and Mary's intimacies with him were
confined to singing to his music and playing cards with him late at
night. Moreover, although Darnley knew of the plot against Rizzio,
he did not commit the murder, which was the work of a group of
Ruthven's followers, who stabbed the secretary more than fifty
times.[19]

A third poem, also written in 1846, was inspired by the legends
that clung to the person of Bothwell after his disappearance following
Mary's surrender to the confederate lords at Carberry Hill and her
imprisonment in Lochleven castle. In Fontane's ballad, Bothwell is
driven around the world like another flying Dutchman, the prey of
guilt and the fact that

    . . . Der Klabautermann
    Läßt keinen Mörder schlafen.

    [The kobold
    Lets no murderer sleep.]

He is reported to have been last seen wandering among the Finnish
lakes, but no one really knows what became of him in the end.[20] After
these grim verses, Fontane returned to Mary Stuart, seeing her this
time—in a poem called "Maria Stuarts Weihe"—as an infant and
describing her service of consecration, in the course of which the
blessing of the muse of history is rudely interrupted by the appearance
of three wraithlike spirits, the Lady Vanity, the Harlot Sensuality, and

a third guest, dressed all in red, who dedicates the child to blood and murder.[21]

When Fontane edited his poems for publication, he decided to make a cycle of romances out of those that dealt with Mary Stuart and to introduce them with an epigraph taken from the third act of Schiller's drama.

Ich habe menschlich, jugendlich gefehlt,
Die Macht verführte mich, ich hab' es nicht
Verheimlicht und verborgen, falschen Schein
Hab' ich verschmäht mit königlichen Freimut.
Das Ärgste weiß die Welt von mir, und ich
Kann sagen, ich bin besser als mein Ruf.[22]

[I have erred humanly and because of my youth.
Power misled me. I have not
Masked or disguised it; false appearance
I have scorned with royal candor.
The world knows the worst of me, and I
Can say that I am better than my calling.]

In place of "The Wandering Bothwell," however, he placed a poem written in 1851, "Mary and Bothwell," in which the queen is seen rewarding her husband's murderer with her love—

Dem Lande kleidet die Trauer,
Der Königin kleidet die Lust,
Kalt-heiße Wonneschauer
Durchrieseln ihre Brust—

[Mourning clothed the country,
Lust clothed the Queen,
Hot-cold shudders of bliss
Ran through her breast.]

after the consummation of which they sleep and dream, Mary of the downfall of her family and the execution of her grandson Charles, Bothwell of Mary's own end in the Tower.[23] The tone of this effort, which hardly accorded with the Schiller quotation, worried some members of the Tunnel, and in the meeting of 26 October 1851, at which it was read, Paul Heyse, among others, complained of its sensuality. Fontane cited Raumer in his defense,[24] but the dramatic unconditionality of his poem certainly strengthened what in Raumer were merely hypotheses and implications. Modern scholarship has shown that Mary was not, in fact, given to carnality and that, if her marriage to Darnley was the result of physical infatuation, her union with Bothwell was quite the reverse, being forced upon her by reasons of state and the exigencies of the moment.[25]

Well before this meeting, Fontane's interest in Scottish history had been sharpened and broadened by his discovery of Percy's *Reliques of Ancient English Poetry* and Scott's *Minstrelsy of the Scottish Border*, which he was later to describe, in a list of "best books" that he drew up in 1890,[26] as the ones that had exercised the greatest influence upon his life and writing. They became, with Shakespeare, his favorite reading, and it may perhaps be said of him, as of his hero Lewin in the novel *Vor dem Sturm*, that he learned English in order to be able to read them.[27] He never seems to have felt the need to search out other early Scottish poetry. The great poets of the fifteenth century, for example, Robert Henrysoun, whose *Testament of Cresseid* has been called the greatest poem in the Scottish language, William Dunbar, who wrote *The Lament for the Makaris,*

I that in heill was and gladnes,
Am trublit now with gret seiknes,
And feblit with infermite;
    Timor mortis conturbit me.

Our plesance heir is all vane glory,
This fals warld is bot transitory.
The flesche is brukle, the Fend is sle;
    Timor mortis conturbat me.

The stait of man dois change and vary,
Now sound, now seik, now blith, now sary,
Now dansand mery, now like to dee;
    Timor mortis conturbat me,

and Gawain Douglas, who translated the *Aeneid* into Scottish, and Mark Alexander Boyd, who wrote the lovely sonnet

Fra banc to banc, fra wod to wod. I rin
Ourhailit with my feble fantasie,
Lyk til a leif that fallis from a trie
Or til a reid ourblawin with the the wind

seem to have been unknown to him. This is a curious lapse, and one
that shows the limitations of Fontane's knowledge of Scotland. Even
Robert Burns, whose poems are included in his list of best books,
appears only occasionally in Fontane's writings about Scotland, and
he translated only two of his poems,

Scots, wha hae wi' Wallace bled,
Scots, wham Bruce has aften led,
Welcome to your gory bed
        Or to victory.

[Schotten, schwört und tretet her,
Wallace führt euch nimmermehr,
Aber *ich* zu Ruhm und Ehr,
Oder auch zum Tode.]

a tribute to Robert Bruce's victory at Bannockburn in 1314, which
serves as a kind of Scottish national anthem,[28] and "The Lovely Lass
o' Inverness," a lament for the battle of Culloden in 1745, which
ruined the Young Pretender's cause.

The lovely lass o' Inverness
    Nae joy nor pleasure can she see;
For e'en and morn she cries, "Alas!"
    And aye the saut tear blin's her e'e:
"Drumossie moor—Dromossie day—
    A waefu' day it was to me!
For there I lost my father dear,
    My father dear, and brethren three.[29]

[Die schöne Maid von Inverneß
Wie freudlos ihr der Tag vergeht,
Sie schafft und spinnt und webt, indes
Ihr dunkles Aug' in Tränen steht:

'Drumossie-Moor, Drumossie Tag,
O bittrer Tag, o blut'ge Moor,
Wo kalt und starr mein Vater lag,,
Und ich der Brüder drei verlor.][30]

Percy and Scott remained his great resource, determining, as he wrote later, his taste and direction, and providing him with a source of deep enjoyment for the rest of his life.[31]

II

During the year of revolution in Germany, Scotland did not disappear entirely from Fontane's thinking, and we have seen that in November 1848 he announced to his friend Lepel that he had decided to write a drama on the English revolution of the seventeenth century. The first half of this was to have dealt with the reign of Charles Stuart and the second with that of Oliver Cromwell, and the central figure was to have been Charles's loyal supporter, the earl of Strafford, who was impeached and executed, without the king's being able to save him, for his ruthless implementation of royal policy. This was stuff to re-joice "a republican heart," Fontane wrote, adding that he was already applying himself to "three thick novels of Scott" from which he hoped to learn enough about Independents and Covenanters to enable him to write about the anti-Stuart cause with assurance.[32]

This project proved to be more difficult than he had originally imagined, and, although he was still discussing it in his letters to Lepel in the summer of 1849,[33] he gradually abandoned it, perhaps in part because of the less than enthusiastic reception of the first act by the Tunnel in October.[34] He had, in truth, other pressing concerns, what with getting married in 1850 and then almost immediately losing his position as a correspondent for the *Deutsche Reform* and the *Literarische Cabinet*.[35] At this low point in his fortunes, as he cast about wildly for a means of livelihood, it is perhaps not surprising that he began to think of the possibility of working abroad, indeed, in Scotland. In August 1851, after months of frustration, he wrote to Lepel:

The ultimate reason why it goes badly with me lies in myself; what I lack is something positive upon which I can build and about which

I can if necessary—boast. I want to go to Edinburgh in order to have *something at least* entirely in my power and in order to feel more secure in English. A stay of six months ought to be sufficient for that. If I come back then, I shall be able to search for my salvation as a *Sprachmeister* with *good conscience* and therefore with energy.—The above is the minimum that I expect. In general, I hope for more: I am thinking both of the opportunity to earn money in Edinburgh (whether as teacher of German or collaborator in different reviews and magazines) and of making Scotland and my stay there into a milk-cow for myself after my return.[36]

The obstacles, he admitted, were the lack of money for the fare and incidental expenses and the understandable opposition of his bride to his prolonged absence. And these kept Fontane from Scotland for a long time. In October 1851, as we have seen, he swallowed his pride and began to work for the government press, and it was his decision to do so that in the end, unexpectedly, took him first to England as a Prussian press attaché, first in 1852, then again in 1855, for a stint of three years, and finally to Scotland. In August 1858, prior to his return to Berlin, he and Bernard von Lepel set off for Edinburgh, which, seven years earlier, at the nadir of his fortunes, had been the El Dorado of his hopes.

III

Fontane's wanderings in Scotland in 1858 became the basis of *Jenseit des Tweed*, his second book-length work of prose, which was published in 1860. It was a book that showed that, after three years of exhausting journalistic activity, reporting almost daily on subjects that were often of little interest to him, he had at last found a literary form that was congenial to him and a style that fitted it. *Jenseit des Tweed* is as lively and readable today as it was when it was written, not only because of the freshness and energy of its prose and its richness of anecdote but also because the reader is constantly aware of the author's friendly presence and of his willingness to admit that his own views need not be necessarily regarded as the correct ones.

There is a striking illustration of this last quality early in the book. During their stay in Edinburgh, Fontane and his companion paid a visit to Calton Hill to look at the monuments there. They found an uncompleted templelike structure, built to commemorate the gallantry of the Scottish regiments that fought in the battle of Waterloo and, close to it, three monuments, one of Robert Burns and the others to the memories of Dugald Stewart and Professor Playfair. Fontane admits that, although he had hitherto believed from his reading of Scottish poetry and history that he knew all of the Scots who might be celebrated in this way, he had a very indistinct notion of who Stewart and Playfair were. He added:

> The fact is that we in foreign parts know only the romantic half of Scotland and little or nothing of the reverse side. Reading poetry and history, we have remained emotionally stuck in Scotland's past, while the Scots themselves have felt that there was nothing more important for them to do but break with that past and raise up new and entirely different men of distinction.

When he was in Oban on the west coast, he added, he found a book in a guest house that was called *Worthies of Our People*. Leafing through it, Fontane found martyrs and reformers, discoverers and philanthropists, artists and poets and scholars, but none of the heroes about whom he loved to read and write, the rebellious Douglases and Hamiltons, the partisans and foes of Mary Stuart. "This appearance of two wholly opposed elements, which coincide only in the sense that each *in its own* way has contributed to national strength and a country's importance, can nowhere be as clearly observed as in Scotland, because the contrast seldom emerges so starkly as precisely here."[37]

Admission of this fact did not mean, however, that Fontane had any doubts about his own allegiance to the Scotland of Archibald "Bell the Cat" and the warring clans or that he had any intention of seeking a more balanced view. Upon their arrival in Edinburgh, at the beginning of their Scottish tour, Fontane and Lepel, after establishing themselves in Johnston's Hotel in Waterloo Place, walked to Princes Street and, standing by Scott's Monument, looked across the declivity that divides the city toward the Salisbury Crags, Canongate and the High Street of the Old Town, and the towering mass of the castle, with its guns and battlements. He wrote later:

Every honest Scot regards this point as the most beautiful in the world, a view that he will debate with the residents of Naples and Palermo and even more with those who, making pilgrimages to the south from sadder localities, see those beautiful places with the advantage of contrast and in the transforming, holiday mood.[38]

This is a statement that certainly calls for an authorial intervention. As a Scot myself, albeit one who was born in Glasgow, I feel that I should object to being excluded from the honest portion of my countrymen because I do not share Fontane's rather touristic enthusiasm, and I feel it necessary to point out that, while he was reflecting on the beauties of Auld Reekie, his back was turned to the New Town, the part of Edinburgh that housed its bankers and merchants and lawyers and engineers, and his eyes were fixed upon the past rather than upon the future. Modern Scotland had so little charm for Fontane that at the end of the Scottish tour, when he and Lepel arrived in Glasgow's Central Station and his companion evinced a desire to stop in the town, he pointed to some factory chimneys in the distance and, saying, "The smokestack is the symbol of Glasgow!" dragged him to the Edinburgh train.[39] There is something paradoxical about this response, for Fontane was never a reactionary in either a political or an aesthetic sense. In his last years he wrote: "My hatred against everything implicit in the present age increases steadily, and the possibility, yes, the probability that a fearful battle must come before the victory of new cannot prevent me from wishing for this victory of the new."[40] One must assume that his passion for Scottish history was an indulgence that defied common sense and remember that, for all he knew, this was his last chance, as it was his first, to indulge it.

Fontane's Scottish tour lasted just short of a month and carried him and Lepel in a circular route from Edinburgh to Stirling, Perth, Inverness, Oban, Loch Lomond, and back to Edinburgh, with side trips to Linlithgow and Flodden Field, Loch Katrine, the setting for Scott's *Lady of the Lake*, the battlefield of Culloden, and the islands of Staffa and Iona. More than a third of Fontane's book is devoted to Edinburgh and takes the form of a series of walks about the city and descriptions of the most notable historical sites, intermingled with historical anecdotes and observations on such things as the similarity of Edinburgh street life to that of south European cities and the part

played by ghost stories in the culture of northern peoples and Edinburgh's contribution to this genre, the history of the haunted houses
of the Old Town. Fontane's method forecasts that of the *Wanderungen*, and like that work his Scottish one is replete with memorable set
pieces that stick in the memory.

Thus, in his description of a walk from Holyrood Castle up Canongate, he talks about the still imposing houses of the Scottish nobility
that line it, remarking that most of them are in ill repair and resemble
the kind of grandfather clock that one finds offered at bargain prices
in junk shops. The exception is Moray House, which in comparison
looks like "the *Rokokopendüle* in a collector's room." As he begins
to describe it, he is reminded of something that happened there on 11
May 1650, when guests gathered to celebrate the wedding of the duke
of Moray's daughter with the eldest son of the duke of Argyll. Both
families were leaders of the Puritan cause in the civil war. At the
height of the festivities, the news came that the leader of the Stuart
forces, Montrose, had been captured and was being brought into the
city, and almost immediately it became known that he was at the
bottom of Canongate and that a mob was dragging him up toward the
castle, mocking and jeering at the once invincible commander. Fontane continued:

> As the column approached Moray House, which still stood in its
> wedding decorations, the Morays and the Argylls appeared on the
> balconies before their windows to feast their eyes on the misfortune
> of their stricken enemy. Argyll muttered curses. Calmly, almost
> gayly, Montrose looked up to the thick-beset balconies. The oaths
> died on old Argyll's lips, but his lady leaned far out over the bal-
> ustrade and spat down upon the hated foe.[41]

Fontane's romanticism was not always proof against his critical
intelligence. Despite his love of the Douglases, he was not blind to
the cultural state of the highland clans, and, during his trip down the
Caledonian Canal toward western Scotland, the sight of Fort Augustus
moved him to make a comparison with America. (Fontane's remarks
about America are always interesting: he once said that a lock of Mary
Stuart's hair was more interesting than all of Buffalo and Milwaukee
together.)[42] He noted that Fort Augustus was like one of the block-

houses built in America in the first half of the eighteenth century to repel attacks of the Chippewas and the Sioux, whom the highlanders of the same period resembled, being "equally poor, equally brutal and warlike, given to hunting and whisky with equal exclusivity, and filled with equal hatred against the Saxons, 'the white man.' "[43]

Similarly, despite his devotion to Mary Stuart, Fontane found it difficult to repress his admiration for her implacable Protestant opponent John Knox and described with approval the scene in which Mary asked furiously, "What have you to do with my marriage? What are you within this commonwealth?" to which the dour evangelist replied unanswerably, "A subject born within the same, madam."[44] Finally, in his description of the Old Tolbooth prison, which was the centerpiece of Scott's *Heart of Midlothian*, Fontane, despite his love of adventure stories, felt compelled to point out that the tales of hairbreadth escapes from this fastness differed in no significant particular from prison stories in other countries and literatures. "On the one hand, the listener at the door, the closets on the wall, the exchanged letters, on the other, the guard who has been made drunk, the women's clothes, the stuffed puppets, and above all the coffins, laundry baskets, and cases of books in which the hero of the story is carried off, perhaps by his own bailiffs." The fact was that the Old Tolbooth was a singularly porous prison, from which anyone with energy and wit could escape, particularly if he had a little money. "It seems to me that the only true characteristic of the place was the protection that it gave at different times to political refugess. Old Tolbooth became, contrary to knowledge and intention, a sanctuary."[45]

The interests that later made Fontane a famous *Schlachtenbummler* are on prominent display in *Jenseit des Tweed*, which includes an impressive reconstruction of the battle of Flodden in 1513 and a moving description of the field of Culloden on which the clans loyal to the Young Pretender were slaughtered in 1846. Flodden was the result of the vanity and ambition of James IV, who scorned the counsel of his wisest adviser, Archibald "Bell-the-Cat" Douglas, as well as of the duke of Angus, and the warnings of ghostly apparitions, to mobilize the flower of Scottish chivalry and invade England. Fontane's account of the battle is written with the authority and command of military affairs that later distinguished his histories of the wars of German unification. He prefaces his account with the observation:

On the morning of 9 September the battle began. Any kind of skillful
maneuver, any exploitation of advantages of terrain was left out of
play, because it would have seemed an unworthy play-acting. It was
as if both nations had come together, as in a mere boxing match, to
see who could strike the strongest blow.[46]

Fontane then charted the course of the contest from the initial attack
of the Scottish borderers on the left flank, shaking English troops
unused to the savagery of the Scottish charge, through the five hours
of hand-to-hand combat that followed until that ghastly lull in the
fighting, when the Scots, with victory apparently in their hands, looked
about them and realized that they were utterly destroyed, the
thousands of clansmen reduced to hundreds, all their leaders dead, and
the king hidden somewhere beneath a heap of corpses. It was, Fontane
writes, Scotland's real hour of death, from which she would not re-
cover and on which the only appropriate comment was Jean Elliot's
song:

> I've heard the lilting at our yowe-milking,
>   Lasses a-lilting before the dawn o' day;
> But now they are moaning on ilka green loaning:
>   "The Flowers of the Forest are a' wede away."[47]

> Ich hörte sie singen, wenn morgens sie gingen,
> Die Herde zu melken, die draußen steht;
> Nun hör' ich ihr Wehe, wo immer ich gehe—
> Die Blumen des Waldes sind abgemäht.[48]

In the case of Culloden, Fontane described not the battle but the
field on which it was fought, and his account is the more effective
because there was nothing much to see. Fontane wrote that no battlefield that he had ever seen had left such a strong impression upon
him, and it is clear that this was because of its utter desolation—a
space that seemed too small to have been the site of a decisive battle,
an untended graveyard, in which the Frazers and MacIntoshes and
MacPhersons and MacDonalds who fell in the battle were buried, a
heap of stones that had been meant to be made into a monument but
was not because the promoters ran away with the money, and nearby
a brook and a small tower marking the place where the northern clans

made their last desperate stand. And all around the gray heathland, useless for any purpose apparently except as a setting for lost causes and untimely death. A stricken field. Fontane completes his account with a macabre story that fits the mood of the place. In May 1823 the House of Lords was adjudicating a complicated process involving the disposal of the estate of Lord Glenmore, who was supposed to have died at Culloden, although there was no clear evidence of this. Since much depended on this question of proof, there was great excitement when an eyewitness was discovered, an Adam Graystone, a former army captain in the Enniskillen Dragoons, aged ninety-five years. The lord chief justice asked him if he had known Lord Glenmore and whether he could attest to his death, and the witness answered affirmatively in both cases. "When and where did he die?" asked the lord chief justice. "In 1746, at Culloden," answered Graystone. "How do you know that?" asked the lord chief justice. "Because I stabbed him myself," the witness replied.[49]

During his Scottish journey, Fontane often found himself thinking about his own country, perhaps because, after three years in the British Isles, he was eagerly awaiting the time for his return to it. Early on in his tour, as Lepel and he set out from Edinburgh to go to Stirling, they discovered that, instead of doing so by rail, they could go to Leith, Edinburgh's port, and from the docks in neighboring Granton take a steamer that would bear them up the Forth of Firth to their destination. They decided to do this and sailed up the stream past villages, towns, and castles with names famous in Scottish story. Fontane wrote:

> In lively conversation with a young Scot who looked about him with shining eye, we heard the names Morton and Moray, Keith and Dundas, Abercrombie and Elgin [which] embraced more than five centuries of history, from the day of Bannockburn, when the name Bruce made itself famous, to the day at Aboukir when Sir Ralph Abercrombie triumphed and fell.

But it was not so much Scotland's past glories that occupied Fontane's thoughts on this voyage as the history of his own country. It occurred to him that the Forth was like the Havel, and he thought of "the almost insular piece of land around which the Havel draws its blue ribbon . . . the healthy core from which Prussia grew, that eagle land, whose left wing rests on the Rhine and whose right wing plunges into the Njemen,'' the land around Fehrbellin, the foundation of Hohenzollern greatness, the home of all the families from the Quitzows onward who believed more in character than in talent and lived along the Havel's shores, of the manors of the Zietens and the Knesebecks and the Humboldts, and of the places in which Winckelmann and Schadow and Schinkel lived, the last of whom turned a garrison town into a city of beauty.[50]

Such thoughts were not new to Fontane. He had already, before leaving Edinburgh, made a trip by train and ferry to Kinross and then by boat to the castle of Linlithgow, where Mary Queen of Scots had been imprisoned by her rebellious lords after the battle of Carberry Hill, and from which, with the help of Willy Douglas, she had won an illusionary freedom that ended in the defeat of her followers at Langside and her exile and death in England.[51] The sight, across the water, of the ruins of this Douglas castle reminded him of a day in the past in which he had sat in a rowboat on the lake before Schloß Rheinsberg, the castle of Frederick the Great when he was crown prince, and this memory, like his thoughts while sailing up the Forth of Firth, had consequences. Three years after his Scottish tour, Fontane wrote in the introduction to a work that would mark the opening of an important new stage in his career as a writer: " 'It is only when abroad that we discover what we possess at home.' I have experienced that myself, and the first idea of these 'Wanderings through the Mark' came to me during my prowlings about in foreign parts. The idea became a wish, and the wish became a resolve.''[52]

IV

In the years that followed Fontane's return to Prussia, his passion for Scotland diminished. There were no more poems on Scottish themes, and Caledonian references in his works were intermittent and, when they came, sometimes a bit odd. In the first volume of his work *The War against France*, which appeared in 1873, he describes the social round at Ems in late June 1870, after the arrival of King William of Prussia in that fashionable resort, and mentions among the notables "a Scottish lady, the fifty-third translator of *Faust*, who followed Prince G. at every step." Charlotte Jolles has pointed out that no such Scottish translator is known, although Fontane may have been thinking of Anna Swanwick, an Englishwoman who brought out an English edition of the first part of Goethe's work in 1850.[53] It is more likely that Fontane thought a Scottish touch would add an exotic charm to his description of a society that was about to be shocked by rumors of war.

Again, in 1874, after seeing a performance of *Henry IV*, Part I, in the *Königliches Schauspielhaus* in Berlin, he complained in his review that in the battle scenes the Douglases were wearing McGregor stockings.[54] This was a historical lapse on Fontane's part that almost suggests that he was prone to "Scotchiness" of the kind that equates Scotland with whisky, the haggis, and the regalia of the modern pipe band. A few years back, I interviewed Willy Wolf, the head of the Scottish National Party, who cheerfully admitted that his party, while pledged to devolution, a heightened form of autonomy, was really working for independence, and that he had just visited the headquarters of the United Nations and noted that Scotland's flag would stand between those of Saudi Arabia and Senegal. This struck me as a splendid idea, and I asked him whether, as he led the first Scottish delegation into the UN Assembly, he would wear the kilt. "Aye," he answered. "In what tartan?" I asked. "Ma own," he replied. "I didn't know that there was a Wolf tartan," I said. "I made it up maself!" he said proudly, adding jocosely, "All yon stuff about clan tartans is the purest blethers! They were a' made up by sartors on Princes Street in the first part of the nineteenth century." He was quite correct in this view,[55] and certainly the clans did not wear identifiable tartans in Mary Stuart's day, let alone that of Henry IV. But Fontane can perhaps be forgiven for preferring to think of them in the more colorful Highland dress of his own age.

In the novels, which Fontane began to write in the 1870s, there are few references to Scotland, the conspicuous exception being *Cécile*, published in 1887. An early example of Fontane's deft and moving portraits of women, this novel tells the story of a former mistress of a ruling prince who is now married to a retired soldier, Colonel von St. Arnaud, who is considerably older than she. In a vacation resort at Thale in the Harz, she meets a young engineer named Gordon and is attracted to him by his cosmopolitan interests and the charm of his conversation. During a discussion at the dinner table in the hotel, the talk turns to trout, and she asks him what, in his opinion, were the best that he had ever eaten. In Germany, he answers, the *Felchen* of the Bodensee, which should be eaten with a Markgräfler wine, and in Italy the *Maränen* of the Lago di Bolsena. But the very best came from his family home in Scotland, the lake trout of Loch Kinross. He continues:

> Mary Stuart was imprisoned there in an old Douglas castle in the middle of the loch, and if anything comforted her during these days of imprisonment, aside from the love of Willy Douglas, an incidentally illegitimate and therefore doubly seductive son of the house, it must have been the lake trout.

Later, during an excursion in the countryside, Gordon lends his attractive fellow guest a tartan plaid, and the sight of her in it reminds him of a portrait he had once seen, in Hampton Court or Edinburgh Castle, of Queen Mary, and it occurs to him that the old colonel is not unlike Bothwell in appearance. Thereafter, all of the characters in the drama play out their predestined roles. Saint Arnaud kills Gordon in a duel, and Cécile dies of her own hand.[56]

If *Cécile* is an exception, it must be added that all of Fontane's novels were influenced, if not by Scotland, at least by one of Scotland's greatest sons, Sir Walter Scott. Of Fontane's admiration of Scott, as a person and as a writer, there was never any doubt. In his great essay on Willibald Alexis, another writer who had influence on his own work,[57] he wrote:

> [Scott] had the complete stamp of genius, and really not in the one thing or the other but in everything. Ever young until the moment when misfortune and sickness overthrew him; ever with equal strength and vitality. He was surrounded by sunshine. . . . His whole life was one of unending kindness; he carried a cornucopia that was inexhaustible because his love, his rich gifts, and the happiness that accompanies goodness and gaiety kept replenishing it. . . . Without guile or envy, loyal and reverent, his heart for Scotland and his works for the world, he passed through this life like a great benefactor, leaving blessings in his wake.[58]

Scott's benefactions to Fontane were, first, the inspiration to turn his talent to the writing of novels and, second, technical advice about how to go about it. *Waverley* was the force that inspired *Vor dem Sturm*,[59] and *Waverley*'s subtitle, *'Tis Sixty Years Since*, supplied the principle that underlay the composition of that book and, later, of *Schach von Wuthenow*. Fontane defined this in an article on Gustav Freytag's *Die Ahnen* in 1875, writing: ''The novel should be a portrait of the age to which we belong, or at least a reflection of a life on whose borders we ourselves still stand or of which our parents have told us.''[60] Restricting a novel's historical depth to sixty years gave the author sufficient distance from his material to provide perspective, while at the same time allowing him to take advantage of the memoirs of actors in that earlier time and even to correspond with them. Thus, in the 1860s, Fontane had frequent contact with Fräulein von Crayn, now seventy-five years old, who was, or would become, the model for Fräulein von Carayon in *Schach von Wuthenow*, and he also knew the family of the dead Schach who would be the hero of that book.[61]

When he wrote his historical novels, Fontane was conscious also of Scott's rule with respect to the appearance in novels of the great figures of history, the Cromwells and the Napoleons. Balzac, a great admirer of Scott, once wrote that he allowed such personages to make an appearance only when the action demanded it and then only briefly and, more important, only after the reader had made the acquaintance of dozens of minor figures and learned something of their attitudes toward the great man. When he finally appeared, the reader saw him through the eyes of these secondary figures. Balzac added: ''Scott never chose great events as subjects of his pen, but he always carefully developed the causes that led to them, by depicting the spirit and morals of the age, and presenting a whole social *milieu* instead of moving in the rarefied atmosphere of great political events.''[62]

This was Fontane's operating principle also. The focus in *Vor dem Sturm* was on the countryside and village, and on the reaction of ordinary people to events, rather than upon the centers where the political decisions were made. There were no great personages in *Vor dem Sturm*, and, if King Frederick William III appears in *Schach von Wuthenow*, it is only in reaction to the problem caused by the novel's main characters, and we see him through their eyes. As we shall see in a later chapter, Otto von Bismarck is talked about a lot in Fontane's later novels, but he is never on stage.

As a novelist, Fontane was one of the great realists of the nineteenth century, and we shall have occasion later to comment on how skillfully he learned to portray the social ills and paradoxes of his time. He always believed, and often said, that the task of the novel was to portray "a life, a society, a circle of human beings in such a way that it is an undistorted reflection of the life we lead."[63] It was not by chance, then, that he remained a lifelong admirer of Walter Scott. In September 1868 he wrote to his wife from Erdmannsdorf that he had been reading *The Heart of Midlothian*:

> In separate passages not much more than a superior kind of thriller, but the whole is of such colossal beauty that I—not to mention my streaming eyes, for I wept buckets—kept jumping up and pacing the room as I made speeches of admiration to the dead man. Through the whole of the book, leaving a hundred other excellent things aside, there runs a talent for letting people say the natural and always the right thing, which, if we leave Goethe and Shakespeare out of contention, nobody else has. I find this the greatest.[64]

It was a gift that he tried to emulate, with a not inconsiderable success.

3

Wanderings

Boswell tells us that on an April afternoon in 1778 he was returning from church with Dr. Samuel Johnson, and they were accosted in Butcher-row by a Mr. Edwards, "a decent-looking elderly man in grey clothes and a wig of many curls." Edwards reminded Johnson that they had both been up at Pembroke College in Oxford in 1729, although they had not seen each other since then. He walked along with them to Johnson's home in Bolt-court, where they sat in the library talking on various subjects, until Edwards suddenly said, "You are a philosopher, Dr. Johnson. I have tried too in my time to be a philosopher; but, I don't know how, cheerfulness was always breaking in."[1]

The story is not as irrelevant as it may seem. When the first of Fontane's *Wanderings*, which had received a warm reception from readers when they appeared in newspapers, were about to be gathered together and printed in book form, and Fontane was thinking of a second volume, he began to worry about whether his approach to his subject matter had not been too frivolous and had failed to do it justice. Should he not, he asked his publisher Wilhelm Hertz, give up the "comfortable wanderer's tone" and adopt a narrative style that distanced itself from the writer, whose appearances in the story were apt in any case, if they were excessive, to annoy the reader? Should he not place more emphasis upon the history of the Mark rather than upon the more trivial things that he came upon in his travels through it?[2]

He did make some adjustments, and he was certainly more faithful to the historical muse than Mr. Edwards was to the philosophical one. It is impossible not to be impressed by the prodigies of research that he accomplished in family and parish records, in old chronicles and forgotten local records, and in interviews with descendants of ancient families before he sat down to write the articles that in the end filled the four stout volumes that the *Wanderings* became. But, in the writing, cheerfulness was always breaking in. "That I have not given up *plaudern*" he wrote to Hertz, "and will not do so, goes without saying."[3]

The essential good humor of Fontane's prose is in sharp contrast to the heaviness and aridity that are the usual characteristics of regional history. Fontane gave his readers an entirely new kind of travel writing that told the history of his homeland, its ancient families and its ordinary people, its economy, and its fauna and flora in rich and accurate detail, but it was the way in which he spoke to them—in a tone that was easy, friendly, amusing, at one moment faintly ironical, at another deeply committed, and always as entertaining as it was instructive—that made the difference. If Fontane had obeyed his momentary whim and removed himself from what he wrote, it is highly unlikely that the *Wanderings* would be much read today.

But as important as the personal voice was something else, the gift of seeing things in their variety and their uniqueness. His purpose, he once said in a memorable phrase, was the animation of locality (*Belebung des Oertlichen*), the discovery of what was special about a particular place and what gave it its specific energy and life. He wrote to a friend, "Even in the sand of the Mark the springs of life have flowed and still flow everywhere, and every square foot of ground has its story, and is telling it too—only one has to be willing to listen to these often quiet voices."[4] Fontane always had that willingness, as well as the ability to see the poetry that lay in those stories. And all this he passed on so that others could see it too, and "as is true along the Rhine, and in Switzerland and Scotland and many places, so in the future any inhabitant of the Mark, when he hears a *märkisch* place or family name, will at once associate a *definite picture* with that name. At present that is not at all the case or, if so, only in a prosaic ugly way."[5]

That there was a certain conflict between Fontane's didactic purpose and his scholarly one is perhaps true, but there is no doubt that he accomplished his purpose. For what was Brandenburg before him? A long-disregarded land, of which Wolf Jobst Siedler has written that "it had to become Prussia before it exercised any fascination, for good or ill, upon anyone. But Prussia was the king, the army and the bureaucracy and, of course, the idea that held everything together. The territory itself was quite poor and unproductive, not only aesthetically, but economically too: nothing but turnips, barley, and rye."[6] It was never a land that attracted tourists; there were in fact no accommodations for them. That being so, "would it ever have occurred to anyone in Munich to travel to the Rheinsberger See simply because it was there that the young Frederick had actualized his Watteau-like dreams with trips by gondola to the sound of flute music?"[7]

The Mark had to be brought out of history before it became a concept, something that was interesting and attractive. That was Fontane's achievement: to give it back its individuality, to make it again what it was before it became Prussia, to restore it to popular recognition and feeling.

I

In the spring of 1962, when I went for the first time as visiting professor to the Free University of Berlin, I found in Elwer und Meurer's bookstore on the Hauptstraße near the Innsbrucker Platz a splendid one-volume edition of Fontane's *Wanderungen durch die Mark Brandenburg*, abbreviated and illustrated by Martin Hürlimann with the assistance of Dr. Walther Meier and Horst Hank-Jentsch.[8] I had at that time a very limited acquaintance with the work, for the focus of my reading and writing since the end of the war had been diplomatic and military-political history, but my discovery turned out to be the ideal means of repairing the deficiency. The text included almost fifty of the most characteristic and admired sections of the *Wanderings* (or so I was told, for I was in no position to make such a judgment myself), which ranged from the splendid pieces on the Katte tragedy and the Rheinsberg of Crown Prince Frederick and his brother Prince Henry to essays on trips to the Spreewald and the Müggelsee, on Karl Friedrich Schinkel and his *Denkmal* to Queen Luise in Granson, on the Cistercians and their work, on Paretz and the Pfaueninsel, and on Fontane's birthplace, Neuruppin. The photographs that illustrated the text showed a land of somber, sparse beauty, with straight roads, sometimes lined with trees, crossing flat, empty landscapes toward the occasional lonely windmill, with lakes whose still waters were made dark and mysterious by the pine forests that surrounded them, with small towns with parts of their medieval walls and gates still standing and massive brick churches: a land of basic loyalties and hard work and discipline and memories of great days—those of Fehrbellin and Großbeeren, for example—when these virtues proved themselves.

It was not an easy book to read, for much of it was unknown territory to me. I started with the chapters that dealt with figures with whom I had some acquaintance—those on Frederick and Ziethen and Schinkel and the Humboldts—and then, operating at a venture, made sallies into the chapters on the Oderbruch and the Spreewald and Quilitz and Kloster Lehnin. I might have foundered on more than one occasion had it not been for Fontane's evident enthusiasm. In the end I read with mounting pleasure and a desire for more, so that by the time I had finished Hürlimann's abbreviation I had—surely a daring venture for a Scot—subscribed to the Nymphenburg edition of the complete works, which provided everything that he had left out.

One result of this binge, which is what it was, was that I soon wanted to see what I had been reading about. Politics made this difficult, for most of the places that Fontane had searched out and described lay in the German Democratic Republic, which was not easily accessible to me. But there were exceptions. Fontane had written notable chapters on Kleist's grave, on Schloß Tegel, and on the Pfaueninsel, and these all lay within the boundaries of West Berlin. When my work at the university permitted, I mounted small expeditions to them.

Fontane's account of his visit to Kleist's grave, which appears in his volume *Fünf Schlößer*, a kind of continuation of the *Wanderings*, shows why we should be grateful that he decided against excluding

himself from his texts. He describes how, as he made his way along
the wooded path that led to the grave site, he fell in with a party of
four, a married couple from a Berlin suburb, their daughter Anna, and
a young man who was presumably her suitor. The daughter discoursed
sentimentally on Kleist's poverty, which she thought was the cause
of the poet's untimely end, while her father, in a rather muddled way,
seemed to feel that the nobility was at fault, all being poor but arrogant, which led to this kind of *Kladderadatsch* and *Schlappe*. Thank
heaven, he added, one didn't have to put up with that sort of thing
any more, thanks to Bismarck. The mother, obviously offended by the
intrusion of politics into their rural excursion, pointed out that there
was a sick woman involved, with whom Kleist was deeply in love.
"I, Gott bewahre," her husband murmured. By this time they had
reached the little bit of park on the bank of the Kleiner Wannsee,
where Kleist's monument stood, and Anna read the inscription on the
stone aloud,

> Er lebte, sang und litt in trüber, schwerer Zeit,
> Er suchte hier den Tod und fand Unsterblichkeit,
>
> [He lived, sang and suffered in a dreary, hard time.
> Here he sought death and found Immortality.]

while the others listened in quietly, perhaps in the embarrassed silence
that often affects people when they hear poetry.

As they began to retrace their footsteps, the young man felt em-
boldened by the occasion to speak of Kleist's poetry, particularly of
Käthchen von Heilbronn, whose heroine he described as a *"holdse-
liges Geschöpf."* This expression appeared to strike the object of his
affections as indelicate, and she reproached him sharply for using it
(following the principle, Fontane guessed, of beginning the education
of a mate as soon as possible) and was staunchly supported by her
mother. (*"Ja, Herr Behm. Anna hat recht."*) At this point Fontane
lifted his hat and made his adieux, noting as he looked back a moment
later that opinions about him appeared to be mixed among his late
companions, with only the mother in his favor. He stopped for a moment to look to the west and to admire the beauty of the wood and
water in the evening sun and the roofs of villas in the distance. Every-

thing he saw was full of life and richness and happiness. And he thought of the poet's grave, lonely despite the hordes of visitors who came to it, and the little heap of earth on the gravestone, in which someone had planted a bunch of wildflowers.[9]

This little drama aroused the liveliest expectations in me. In what cast of characters, I wondered, would I be allowed to play the part of the gentle ironist? Alas! When I reached the grave site, after making my way from Wannsee Village to the Bismarckstraße and then ducking through the opening to the lake, it was quite empty and, indeed, had the faintly unkempt look of a place that had long ceased to attract any visitors. Anna would not like it now, I thought. The monument of Fontane's time had been replaced by a new one, whose inscription read:

Nun, o Unsterblichkeit, bist du ganz mein.[10]

This would give her not nearly the scope for expressive reading as the old one had done, and she would, in any case, have to contend with the never-ending sound of cars on the Bismarckstraße and, even heavier, on the bridge that carried the traffic coming from Neu Glienecke over the junction between the two lakes and on to Greater Berlin.

"I just can't imagine it!" Anna had said on the way to Kleist's grave. But it was not really difficult, in Fontane's time, to imagine the poet and his friend coming to this still remote, and beautiful spot to die. It was much harder now, with two large boat clubs impeding the view, and the atmosphere charged with cheerful muscular, noisy activity. Had Kleist had the gift of foresight, he would not have tarried here and might, as he left, have echoed Anna's father, *"I, Gott bewahre!"*

My first visit to the Humboldt *Schloß* in Tegel had a happier result. Not that I did not have fears, as I traveled toward it, that I would find it also overrun by modern progress, for the way by U-Bahn passed the towering palisades of Siemenstadt and, before we reached Tegel village, we had to pass the sprawling Borsig Works in Reinickendorf. But at Tegel U-Bahn station the world of heavy industry was behind me, and there were glimpses of water and woods.

Setting my face in their direction, I was soon in Tegel Forest and, in a few minutes, at the *Schloß* itself.

It was smaller than I had expected. To Americans the word *castle* conveys an impression of grandeur and romance, and one expects something with lots of towers and the occasional golden dome. *Schloß* Tegel had been built as a country house in the time of Joachim II and was used, according to Fontane, as a hunting lodge by the Great Elector. A simple building in the classical mode, with two stories and four squat towers at the corners, it was acquired by the Humboldt family in 1765 and left pretty much as it was, except for some interior remodeling by Schinkel to accommodate the needs of Wilhelm von Humboldt, who lived in it after his retirement from public service and used it to house his collection of classical antiquities.

The charm of Tegel lies in the unity of spirit that exists between the house and the woods that surround it, mostly fir and linden, and the little graveyard at the bottom of the park, which is the final resting place of the brothers Wilhelm and Alexander von Humboldt and their closest relations. This is overlooked by a thirty-foot-tall granite column, from whose Ionic capital a marble statue of Hope looks down upon the graves. At the end of his chapter on Tegel, Fontane wrote,

> I dare not leave untouched and unnamed the one thing that makes this castle and this cemetery unique among all the seats of the nobility of the Mark. The *märkische Schlößer*, if not excessively strong fortresses of the Old Lutheran confession, have seen faith and lack of faith alternate between their walls: firm religiosity and lax freethinking have taken turns there. Only Schloß Tegel has accommodated a third element in its walls, that spirit which, equally distant from orthodoxy as from frivolity, nurtured itself slowly in classical antiquity and, smiling at the strife and feuding of both extremes, enjoyed the here and now and has hopes for the mysterious beyond.[11]

The garden invited one to linger, and I delayed my departure, sitting under a tree for a while and reading. The book, which I had shoved in my pocket that morning without design, could hardly have been more appropriate. It was an odd volume of *Ansichten vom Niedderrhein*, the account of a trip through Brabant, Flanders, Holland,

England, and France in 1790 by Georg Förster and Alexander von Humboldt, both wanderers like Fontane, although on a somewhat larger scale, and one now lying in his grave a few yards from me. Goethe had said after reading Forster's book that he wished he could travel with such a good and well-informed guide. It was a remark that often came to my mind as I read Fontane.

A few weeks later I returned to Tegel, this time with my friend and colleague Wolfgang Baumgart, a professor of theater science at the Free University, as invited guests on the occasion of the two hundredth anniversary of Wilhelm von Humboldt's birth. I was excited at the opportunity of seeing the interior and the contents of the house, which Fontane describes in some detail; but there was a great crush, and this was not easy. After a glimpse of Humboldt's study, we were swept up Schinkel's remarkable staircase (remarkable for what he was able to accomplish in so restricted a space) to the upper floor, where we paid our respects to our hostess, Frau von Hentze. The fact that the classical statuary in the room was greatly outnumbered by the guests made it impossible to identify and study the former, so we got a drink and joined Caroline von Sydow and a Bertrand von Humboldt and his wife and were soon engaged in lively conversation, since Herr von Humboldt was a man of pronounced views. His wife, who seemed very nervous, was standing with her back to a large and not particularly prepossessing plaster copy of an antique statue of Hermes. As our conversation became more animated, she suddenly gave a little shriek and, her husband asking her, a bit fiercely, what was wrong, shamefacedly brought her right hand from behind her back and revealed that it was holding Hermes' big toe. Her husband did not seem to take this tragically, and the rest of us used the incident to excuse ourselves and go off to the *Friedhof*, which was decked with flowers. But over the years I thought intermittently of the rape of the toe, and I was happy to find, when I next visited Schloß Tegel in May 1992, that it had been cemented back into place.

The Pfaueninsel, the subject of one of the most charming sections in the Havelland volume of the *Wanderings*, is a small island (a little short of a mile long and three-quarters of a mile at its greatest width) that lies in the Havel between the Grosser Wannsee and the opening to the Jungfernsee and is overlooked by the blockhouse and church of Nikolskoe. Over the centuries it was unremarked and unnamed[12] until Friedrich Wilhelm II, a dedicated huntsman, was drawn to it by the snipe and the ducks that lived in the reeds that girdled it and was then attracted by the unspoiled beauties of the island itself. He began to have himself rowed over from the Marmorpalais on the Heiligensee with the lords and ladies of his court and with musicians and cooks and sommeliers and to have elaborate picnics under tents pitched on the meadows. These were so successful that the king's mistress, Countess Lichtenau, the "beautiful Wilhelmine," decreed that a pleasure dome should be built on the southwest corner of the island, and other buildings were erected and a park laid out. King Frederick William III was no less attracted to the Pfaueninsel, as it was now called, and, in the latter part of his reign, Peter Joseph Linné, the director of the Royal Gardens, transformed the island, laying down meandering walks through the heathland and forest that offered sudden enchanting vistas over the Havel and striking settings for such Schinkel creations as his late Gothic *Kavalierhaus*, modeled upon a house in Danzig.[13] Pheasants were introduced, and a large rose garden designed and planted, and a building for palms and cactuses and other unusual plants erected, and a menagerie with all sorts of exotic animals laid out in a zoological garden designed by Linné.

"Pfaueninsel!" Fontane writes.

Like a fairy tale a picture from my childhood days rises before me: a *Schloß*, palms and kangaroos; parrots shriek; peacocks sit on high perches or spread their feathers; birdhouses, fountains, shadowed meadows; winding paths that lead everywhere and nowhere; a mysterious island, an oasis, a carpet of flowers in the middle of the Mark.[14]

It was only natural that I should want to visit the Pfaueninsel, although, to tell the truth, I did not expect that the parrots and the kangaroos would have survived Hitler and the war and was not much interested in them in any case. What had lured me to the Pfaueninsel was Fontane's account of the appearance there of the famous French tragedienne Rachel.

Born in Switzerland of Jewish descent as Élisabeth Félix, and making her living when she was a girl as a street singer, Rachel had her first triumph in Corneille's *Horace* in 1838. Her subsequent performances in the tragedies of Corneille and Racine, and also in the title role of *Adrienne Lecouvreur* by Scribe and Legouvé, were responsible for the revival of the Comédie Française. Fontane saw her in Racine's *Phèdre* in 1850 or 1851 and, though he disliked the play (or pretended to do so in deference to his wife's opinion), calling it five acts of nymphomania that was more appropriate to the Charité than to the theater, he never forgot her appearance on the stage. "Even the moment of her entrance," he wrote, "before she had uttered a word, was worth six German evenings in the theater."[15] It is not surprising that his account of her visit to the Pfaueninsel, even if it is that of a historian rather than an eyewitness, is one of the most spirited set pieces in the *Wanderungen*.[16]

As he tells the story, after the accession of Frederick William IV in 1840, the Pfaueninsel ceased to be the summer residence of the court, but nevertheless the king liked on occasion to come over from Sans Souci and have tea in the rose garden at sunset. On 13 July 1852 (not on the fifteenth, as Fontane wrote), when Czar Nicholas I of Russia was his guest, he planned such an outing, and Rachel having just arrived in Berlin, to repeat a series of guest performances begun in 1850 (when Fontane probably saw her), she was invited too. When she arrived in Potsdam and learned that she was not to perform in the Neue Palais or the Stadttheater but alfresco, she was understandably annoyed, declaring that she was no *Bänkelsängerin;* and she refused to go on until the court councillor Louis Schneider (a Tunnel comrade of Fontane) had explained to her that the Czar would be present and might, if he were pleased, restore to her the right to perform in St. Petersburg, which he had withdrawn in 1848 after she had appeared on a Paris stage dressed as the goddess of freedom and singing "La Marseillaise." Rachel was always mindful of the demands of her career, and she gave way now. Standing on the grass before Countess Lichtenau's *Lustschloß* with the court and the czar's suite in a half circle before her, in an improvised costume and with her brother holding a flickering light in a glass globe to fight off the darkness, she performed the greatest speeches of her repertory—not from the last two scenes of *Athalie*, as Fontane supposed, but from *Phèdre, Virginie,* and *Adrienne Lecouvreur*. The effect was prodigious, and height-

ened by the absence of the usual trappings of the stage. The two
monarchs were deeply moved; the expected invitation came from the
Czar (''J'espère de vous voir à Petersbourg.'' ''Mille remerciments
... Mais, Votre Majesté ...'' ''Je vous invite, moi''), and the whole
party returned across the dark waters to Potsdam. But the evening was
long remembered, and, in the place where Rachel had enjoyed her
triumph, a statuette of her by Johann Bernhard Afinger was erected,
bearing her name and the date 13 July 1852.

It was this scene that was in my mind when I made my first trip
to the Pfaueninsel. The menagerie had, as I had expected, disappeared,
but I toured the island and saw Schinkel's *Kavalierhaus* and was taken
in hand by an attendant who gave me an interesting and amusing
lecture on how to lay out an *Uferweg* and on the proper care of meadows, which were, apparently, not to be walked upon (so much for
Frederick William II's picnics). But of Rachel's statuette I could find
no trace until someone told me that it no longer stood in its old place
but had long ago, because of the ravages of wind and water, been
removed to the entrance hall of the *Schlößchen*. And indeed I found
it there, but it was a disappointment, for the new location appeared
inappropriate and seemed to impose upon the great actress a sad dim-
inution of her grace and majesty.

That was in 1976. Nineteen years later, having heard that a copy
had been returned to its original place, I traveled once more with a
friend from Zehlendorf out along the Potsdamer Chaussee and the
Königstraße to the Nikolskoe road and then, through the dark trees to
the Pfaueninsel ferry. It was late in the afternoon, and the school-
children who had spent the day on the island had already started to
pass us in the opposite direction. The light was beginning to fail as
we approached the castle, and the peacocks were exchanging their
harsh cries, but we had no ears for them. What was important was
that Rachel was once more standing in the place where she had performed long ago before the king of Prussia and the Czar, dressed in
the diadem of Theseus's unhappy queen, and caught up in all of the
ecstasy of her tragic power.

Ce n'est plus une ardeure dans mes veines cachée:
C'est Vénus toute entière à sa proie attachée.

II

In 1899, Fontane wrote a poem called "Changes in the Mark" in which he told how the ancient inhabitants of Mark Brandenburg—the Semnoni, Burgundians, Vandals, Langobards, and Hermunduri, who had spent the centuries since their passing in Valhalla—were seized after Bismarck's dismissal by a longing to visit their old home again and to see once more the Spree and the Havel, the Notte and the Nuthe, and the robbers' lair near Neu Ruppin. At their request, Father Odin granted a vacation to a representative of each of the five peoples, and they set off. But once they had achieved their goal, landing at Bentschen in the New Mark and traveling over Landsberg and Zielenzig to Schwiebus and Reppin, and eventually to Berlin, they cut short their leave and returned to Valhalla as quickly as possible.

> Ihr Rücktritt ist ein verzweifeltes Fliehn.
> "Wie war es?" fragt teilnahmsvoll Odin.
> Und der Hermundure stottert beklommen,
> "Gott, ist *die* Gegend 'runtergekommen."

> [Their return was a desperate flight.
> "What was it like?" Odin asked sympathetically.
> And the Hermundure stuttered uneasily,
> "God, has *that* neighborhood gone to pieces!"][17]

These lines were often in my mind in June 1990, when with two friends[18] I spent some days in the Oderland, the Grafschaft Ruppin, and the Havelland, which I had hitherto known only from the pages of the *Wanderings* but which were now, thanks to the fall of the Wall, open to my exploration. There were times, as we traveled on cobbled roads lined with linden trees through fields full of rape and a beautiful heatherlike purple flower that we never succeeded in identifying, when we could imagine ourselves back in Fontane's Mark. This was our feeling when one afternoon we encountered a gaily caparisoned horse and wagon carrying a wedding party to some happy destination and, later, in Müncheberg, when we discovered, on top of a tower set in the town wall, a stork, sitting in its nest and feeding its young. But these were rare occasions. In the open countryside, the blighting hand of the communist regime was everywhere obvious. The depressing effects of the transition from peasant culture to collectivized farming could be seen in the monotonous fields planted with fodder and the tubers called *Teltower Rübchen*, which Goethe, according to report, considered a delicacy, broken intermittently by the dilapidated buildings of a *Landwirtschaftliche Produktions-Genossenschaft*, which usually belied its name by being totally inactive. In the towns, the streets were for the most part empty (a circumstance that was perhaps in part induced by the pending currency reform, for wherever there was a bank it usually had a queue in front of it of citizens anxious to open accounts so that they could derive some meager profit from the new fiscal system). Even in the larger towns, like Neuruppin, the shops had a forlorn air (nothing was stirring in the Lion pharmacy where Fontane was born, and no one was buying anything in the bookstore nearby), and there seemed to be few functioning restaurants, and those that existed not anxious for custom, for the help was surly and the proprietors seemed to be nursing some secret resentment. In smaller places, like Buckow in the so-called *märkische* Switzerland, *Wurschtlbuden* and stalls dispensing ices were points of light against a gray background. Wherever encountered, school buildings were of a uniform official ugliness, relieved somewhat by their exotic names (the Albert Schweitzer School, for example, and the Salvador Allende School), which may have bewildered their students. When there was a railroad station, it did not seem to be heavily used, and the yards and sidings were filled with rusting rolling stock.

Fontane was always interested in the Vineta myth and stories of lost cities that had disappeared in water and forest, and he could easily be induced to gaze into the depths of sun-covered lakes in the hope of catching a gleam of an ancient tower or balustrade or to strain his ears in the woods to catch the echo of the song and the laughter of long-dead voices. It is with no intimation of disbelief that he wrote in *"Der Blumenthal"* about the High Barnim that "anyone who passes over here at noon hears from the gorge and the lake a ringing and tolling, and who comes this way at night, when the moon is in its first quarter, has no need to complain of stillness, for strange voices, calls and laughter go by his side."[19] But many of the places that he himself wrote about have disappeared as effectively as if they had been swallowed up like Gerstäcker's sunken village, nor are they likely to have the privilege, as it did, of reappearing on earth at fixed intervals. We set off one morning from the Seelow Heights, where there is a monument to the thirty thousand Red Army troops who died in the battle of the Oderbruch between January and May 1945 (and where some glum-looking Soviet troops were being led through the museum by instructors) and crossed the Oderbruch in the direction of Küstrin. It was there that the Katte tragedy was played out and, as Fontane tells the story, the young Crown Prince Frederick was forced to watch the execution of his friend, calling out to him from the window of the castle, "Mon cher Katte, je vous demande mille pardons," to which Katte replied, "Point de pardon, mon prince; je meurs avec mille plaisirs pour vous."[20] We knew, of course, that the old fortress city was now a part of Poland and could hardly, since it had been flattened in the furious fighting of 1945, bear much resemblance to the town of Frederick's time. Still, with vivid memories of Fontane's account, we drove to the border crossing on the Oder, in a kind of Vineta mood of our own, hoping to catch a glimpse or a sound of the place we couldn't reach. Alas! there was no traffic at the crossing, which may, indeed, have been closed, and not even a traffic sign or direction post that might have been photographed and taken home as proof that something of Küstrin survived.

Nor was this a unique case. In the Havelland we sought out Paretz, where Frederick William III and his wife Luise spent the happiest years of their married life, living modestly in their *Schloß Still-im-Land*, mingling with the common people, and joining their dancing during the harvest festival.[21] Fontane himself, visiting the *Schloß*, found that little had been changed since the royal couple had lived there and that, while the rooms were replete with sad memories, in the park around the house all was light and life, which prompted him to write, "Individuals die, the whole remains."[22] He was, of course, incapable of imagining what a totalitarian regime driven by ideological zeal and ill-conceived notions about the requirements of planned economy could do to a small treasure like Paretz. When we drove into the town, it was clear to us that it had, to all intents and purposes, been destroyed. In the place where the *Schloß* had once stood there was now an Institute for Animal Husbandry; the lake had been drained; the park had been put into cultivation, mostly fodder; the woods, the "temple," where Queen Luise often rested after her walks, and all of the other memorials to her were gone, and the town had become a dreary hole in which one could not imagine that a harvest festival had ever taken place. In exasperation, we fled to Uetz, which the *märkische* poet Schmidt von Werneuchen had called "the most beautiful place in the whole Havelland," eliciting from Fontane the comment, "whether the most beautiful or not, certainly the stillest."[23] The attempted escape proved bootless, for Ütz was even worse, a nest of shabby and mostly empty houses that Schmidt von Werneuchen would certainly not have recognized.

Still, not everything had fallen to the ravages of the communist regime. The beautiful wrought-iron memorial to Queen Luise, for whom Fontane's veneration was almost unlimited,[24] was still standing in the marketplace in Granson as we passed through the town, although, if we are to believe the story in Strittmatter's novel *Ole Bienkopp*, it was saved from the ideological designs of the party secretary of the Gransee only by the fact that it had been designed by Schinkel.[25] In Rheinsberg, the rather incoherent castle (made so by the pair of round stunted towers that fit awkwardly on either end and are, as Fontane wrote dryly, "more characteristic than beautiful")[26] was standing jauntily in its place, apparently unaffected by the fact that it had been downgraded from a prince's residence to a clinic for diabetes. In the sunlight, now shimmering through a light rain, the castle and the park, with its classical statues, and the lake comprised a portrait that was more charming than anything we had seen since we had crossed the border. The effect was enhanced by a chorus of young people singing folk songs, a circumstance that deeply affected a West German television team that was present, whose leader said to me, as they trooped off singing *"Das Wandern ist des Müller's Lust,"* "That is the real German *Innerlichkeit*! That wouldn't be possible in the West!" And, finally, when we went on to the Stechlin, I had no difficulty in recognizing it from Fontane's own description in his novel *Der Stechlin*—lonely, mysterious, the light on the lake's surface changing in curious ways and with resultant isolated turbulences. I felt glad that no red cock burst from its depths to announce a catastrophe somewhere in the world but I was reassured only momentarily. A quiet, well-spoken man on the lakeside pointed across the water and told me that the German Democratic Republic's first nuclear reactor had been built there and that the lake's water, which was used as a coolant, was already one degree warmer than it had been before.[27]

Fontane often wrote in the *Wanderings* of the Cistercians, that remarkable order of White Monks, founded in France in the eleventh century, who were strictly ascetic and dedicated to a life of poverty and who made farming and the reclamation of land their special vocation. In their early days, Fontane tells us, they did their work by preference in lowlands, swamps, and other unhealthy regions, "so that the brothers would always have death before their eyes."[28] In the second half of the twelfth century, the first Cistercian monks appeared in the Mark, called in by Albrecht the Bear to help colonize the lands formerly under the control of the Wends. By the year 1300, they had built twenty-one cloisters, eleven for men and ten for women, as centers for the proliferation of the faith and education in the useful arts, a task accomplished in the most difficult of circumstances and with the sacrifice of many lives.[29]

The most important of these were Kloster Lehnin and Kloster Chorin, which Fontane visited in 1863 with his friends Bernhard von Lepel and the architect Richard Lucae, when both cloisters had long been in ruins. Chorin, a monks' cloister in the Uckermark, had apparently been the center of a flourishing economy with many workshops and farms, but, as Fontane noted with some irritation, it seems to have had a singularly quiet existence, and no legends grew up around it, and even its ruins were not very interesting.[30] Lehnin, on the other hand, the oldest and richest of the cloisters, and, in its time, with its reception halls, and dormitories and guest quarters and administrative buildings and schools and workshops and storerooms and tanneries, a Gothic city in petto, interested him much more. Its first abbot, Sibold, had been murdered by the Wends, and his successors had led adventurous and sometimes violent lives. And now, when all the glory was gone, and the Gothic parts of the church were turned to rubble and only the Romanesque pillars had survived, nature had turned the ruins into a thing of beauty, and legend had invested them with a mysterious charm. By night, if you held your ear to the ground, you could hear the monks singing far below, and if you were lucky you could see, flitting between the broken pillars, the White Lady, searching for the monk she loved.[31] This was the sort of thing that fascinated Fontane, and it is not surprising that he worked a midnight meeting at Lehnin into his first novel, *Vor dem Sturm*.[32]

We found no sign of the White Lady when we came to Lehnin, and there was no quiet place to put one's ear to the ground, for the place was filled with visitors being led about by *dozenten*. Indeed, Lehnin and Chorin were the first places during our travels where we actually found crowds of people and solid evidence of growth rather than decay. The restoration of the cloister complex in Chorin was begun under state auspices in 1957, and the church, a sturdy example of *Backstein-Gothik*, is now the center of a summer music festival and other activities that bring visitors year-round. In Lehnin, the restored church, a pillared basilica with three aisles and very little ornament, is once more the center of bustling activity, for where the White Monks once strove to carry the faith and a knowledge of husbandry to the rude peoples on the frontier, the Luise-Henriette Foundation administers a network of hospital and school services. During our visit all the buildings seemed full and busy.[33]

This should have cheered us up a bit, after our disappointments at Paretz and Uetz, but we returned from Lehnin to Berlin by way of Werder, and our gloom returned. Werder was a substantial town, with some good-looking houses, but dark and unfriendly. "Where are the restaurants?" we asked. "Where are the pubs?" Wolf Jobst Siedler has written:

> In Werder there were five locals on the water side by side, segregated socially for rowboats, canoes, wherries and yachts, and then naturally the garden restaurants for excursionists, who came from Potsdam for the blooming of the fruit trees or from Berlin by steamer along the Havel, the Spree and the Hohenzollern Canal. Of all of these there remained a single HO-Restaurant.[34]

How did the inhabitants stand it? What did they do for amusement? As we drove through town in the direction of the ferry at Kaputh, which Fontane for some reason called "the Chicago of the Schwielowsee,"[35] we passed a Kino Fontane. It seemed hardly enough.

III

In late September 1994, I was back in the Mark, having driven from Hamburg to Schwerin and then through Mecklenburg and Brandenburg to Berlin. During the next days, with three friends,[36] I once more explored parts of Fontane country. It was clear that much had changed in the intervening four years. The young Red Army soldiers whom we had seen on the Seelow Heights in 1990 were gone, and one afternoon as we drove through wooded country there loomed at us out of the trees a gigantic complex of menacing buildings behind a wall crowned with barbed wire, abandoned and already deep in decay, which was one of the barracks in which they and their comrades had been kept, for it was not possible to imagine that anyone had really lived there. Again, the former atmosphere of discouragement seemed to have lifted, and everywhere there was a new vigor that was being expressed in building. On all sides—from Schwerin in Mecklenburg, where half of the city, left by the authorities for forty-five years in the state to which the war had brought it, was now under total reconstruction, to Hankels Ablage on the Wendische Spree, where an Institute for High-Energy Physics was building a new wing in the space where the guest house had stood that Fontane considered his "line of retreat in times of nervous collapse"[37] and where Botho and Lene in his novel *Irrungen Wirrungen* became aware of the imminent end of their love affair—[38] one heard the sound of hammering and the shrieks of power saws and drills.

We found also—an important change since our last expedition— that we no longer had to carry our own food and drink, for everywhere we went there were unpretentious but decent restaurants. This was true in Fehrbellin, where there was a comfortable lunchroom at the base of the column that celebrates the victory, in Zinna, near Jüterbog, where the Cistercians built their first cloister in this part of the world and where we had a very good Saturday *Mittagessen* in a comfortable restaurant packed with local families, and—perhaps not surprisingly— in Ribbeck, where there is a very ugly *Gasthaus* decorated with Liebermann's portrait of Fontane and a large reproduction of the poem

Herr von Ribbeck auf Ribbeck in Havelland,
Ein Birnbaum in seinem Garten stand,[39]

where food and—naturally—pear brandy is available in abundance. Nor is the traveler entirely dependent upon such establishments for sustenance, for the spirit of private enterprise appears to be catching on, and along one otherwise lonely road we found an informal fruit and vegetable market, without stalls, to be sure, but nonetheless busy despite the fact that the produce was arrayed unsystematically on the roadside.

As this work of reconstruction goes forward, it will doubtless become harder to see the Mark as Fontane saw it. In Buch near Berlin, for instance, to which he was drawn by his fascination with the tragic story of Sophie von Voss, the mistress of Frederick William II and the inspiration for the central figure in his novel *Cécile*,[40] the rural setting of the church in which Sophie was buried has been completely destroyed by the incursion of clinics, hospitals, and apartment buildings in the modern style. Today Fontane would probably be most at home in the open countryside, like that of the so-called Dossebruch between Nauen and Seelenhorst in the Duchy of Ruppin. This was land reclaimed from the swamps during the reign of Frederick II, and Fontane has provided us with a splendid account of an inspection trip by the king in 1779, during which he met a Captain von Rathenow and there was the following exchange:

"Who are you?"
"I am Captain von Rathenow of Carwesee."
"My God, lieber Rathenow! Are you still alive? I thought you were long dead. How goes it with you? Are you in good health?"
"Oh yes, Your Majesty."
"But, my God! How fat you've become!"[41]

The country where this meeting took place is not built up, and Fontane would have no trouble in recognizing it.

This would certainly be true also of the Spree Forest, where we spent a pleasant afternoon. Fontane was always interested in the history of the Wends, who controlled most of the Mark until the time of Albrecht the Bear and were then pushed back to the east and south, to places like this corner of the Spree valley. In Fontane's time, the natives here still wore traditional costumes on ceremonial occasions, and spoke their own language. Fontane heard a funeral service in Lübbenau, in which the sermon was in Wendisch, whereas all the announcements were in German. This tendency to reduce the scope of the old tongue has probably increased. If so, it would probably be the only change that Fontane noted. Lübbenau is still, as it was in his time, the center of a rich trade in *Gurken*, horseradish, pumpkins, and celery, which one can buy at stalls in the richly animated market square, and it is from here also that one buys a seat in one of the long, flat boats (*Kähne*) propelled from the rear by men with long poles which they use like gondoliers, to explore the network of rivulets and arms of the Spree that lie between Lübbenau and Lehde.

Fontane came to the Spreewald in August 1859, with Wilhelm Lübke, Otto Roquette, and several other friends, under the leadership of School Councillor Karl Bormann. A *Kahn* had been reserved for them, with comfortable backrests and baskets filled with liquid refreshments, and their steersman, a stalwart man of fifty named Christian Birkig, was waiting. Fontane later wrote:

> We embarked and the trip began. Even the first half mile was a prize exhibit of landscape and was surpassed by nothing that followed in the way in which it revealed most clearly the characteristic nature of the Spree Forest, its netlike and island character. This is, to be sure, everywhere present, but it frequently hides itself, and only someone who flew in an air balloon over the much intersected terrain would see at his feet in all its clarity how the threads of the stream are twisted everywhere in a mesh similar to that between Lübbenau and Lehde.
>
> It is Sunday . . . and work is at rest. But on weekdays the road that we are silently traveling is lively early and late, and everything that otherwise would go its way on corduroy road or highway travels up and down this watery thoroughfare. Even the rich herds of this locality stir up no dust but are driven on to boats and carried from stall to stall or meadow to meadow. The daily traffic moves along this endless river net and is only momentarily interrupted when a bride goes to church in a *Kahn* decorated with flowers and with music ahead of her, or when, silently and alone, and followed by ten or twenty *Kähne* of mourners, a dark-draped boat glides down the stream.[42]

We encountered neither wedding nor funeral, but I had no doubt that we might have, for nothing seemed to have changed since Fontane's time, except for the fact that our *Kahn* held a dozen people besides our party of four and that—another sign perhaps of the growth of capitalist ingenuity in the Mark—on two occasions, as we passed under arching bridges, we were photographed by enterprising youths who then, using long poles, reached tickets down to us which we could use to claim the prints in Lübbenau if we were interested. Otherwise we floated down to Lehde happy in the thought that we were repeating Fontane's experience, and in this "pocket-size city of lagoons, this Venice as it might have been fifteen hundred years ago, when the first fisher families came out of the swamps seeking protection,"[43] we dined more than adequately at the sign of the Happy Pike. Fontane and his friends had had their meal in a similar *Lokal*, a great blockhouse in the *wendisch* style, and had eaten pike, since no Spreewald meal was genuine without it, and because

> Der Leber ist von einem Hecht und nicht von einer Schleie.
> Der Fisch will trinken, gebt ihm was, daß er vor Durst nicht
>   schreie.

> [The liver comes from a pike and not from a tench.
> The fish likes to drink. Give him something so that he doesn't
>   complain of thirst.][44]

Fontane is always interested in fish, and in his chapter on the Oderbruch in the premodern period, he tells us of its astonishing riches in this respect, for the Oder was all but clogged with fish of every variety: Zander, Fluß- and Kaulbarsche, Aale, Hechte, Karpfen, Bleie, Aland, Zärten, Barben, Schleie, Neunaugen, Welse, and Quappen, the last-named so numerous that they were cut in small strips, dried, and used as wicks for lamps. There were so many fish that at times near Quilitz five hundred tons were caught in a single day. No wonder that the carp, which was the king of all the fish that preyed on others, became lazy or sated, so that in the years 1693, 1701, and 1715 near Wriezen one could catch it even by hand.[45] The balance of nature had presumably been restored by Fontane's time, and the carp he ate in the Spree had regained its agility and taste.

IV

At the end of the fourth volume of the *Wanderings*, Fontane announced that he was taking farewell of his readers. The whole enterprise, he said, had begun by drawing up before the *Dorfkrug* or clambering over the churchyard wall to read the inscription on a gravestone or to listen to a ghost story. It had become more serious at times since then, but not invariably, and he had to admit, he wrote, that anyone who gave a book the title he had used, and then filled it up with descriptions of the country and genre scenes and the testimony of coachmen and cottagers and sextons and the like, had no right to expect to be considered as one of the worthies of historical science, particularly since he has taken so much pleasure in gossip and entertainment.

And yet, at the end of his enterprise as at its beginning, Fontane was in a state of some ambivalence. Should he not, he asked himself, have placed more emphasis upon the history of the Mark than he had done? As he went on to thank all those members of the nobility, and all the schoolteachers and his "favorites, the country pastors and Vicars of Wakefield," who had supplied him with so much of his information, and as he thought of all the labors involved in recording what they had to say, he could not prevent himself from inserting a modest footnote to record his contribution to the art of history. He wrote:

> Whatever is historical in what is enclosed here can be divided into the generally known, the little known, and the not known at all. It goes without saying that the professional must pass over the first group, which is the most extensive in size and that he can pass over the second (in which, by the way, a few rarities are to be found). But the third group, to which, for example, all the notes from church records belong, has claims also on the attention of professional historians. To say as much and to supply details is not at all the same as making pretentious historical claims for the whole.[46]

After what Fontane had accomplished in the *Wanderings*, this was a gross underestimation of what the historians owed to him, even when they might not acknowledge it. The rarities were more numerous than Fontane thought.

4

War

The dean of military historians in the English-speaking world at the beginning of the twentieth century was Sir Charles Oman. He once wrote an essay called "A Plea for Military History," in which he remarked that the civilian historian who dabbled in military affairs had always been an exceptional phenomenon, because, as he went on to explain, "Both the medieval monastic chroniclers and the modern liberal historiographers had often no closer notion of the meaning of war than that it involves various horrors and is attended by a lamentable loss of life. Both classes strove to disguise their personal ignorance or dislike of military affairs by deprecating their importance and significance in history," which had the effect of discouraging scholarly study of war and leaving the field to professional soldiers.[1]

Theodor Fontane's military writings have not escaped the kind of criticism implied by Oman's words. In their own time his histories of the three wars of German unification were subject for the most part to the condescension of the soldiers, who assumed, without much reflection, that mere civilians were incompetent to understand the mysteries of their calling, an attitude that Fontane understood and accepted with good humor. But in more recent times, some critics have taken a line not dissimilar to that of the monastic chroniclers and liberal historians, arguing that war was not a subject suitable for a writer of Fontane's talents and that the time he devoted to it was wasted.

Thus, in an otherwise perceptive study, Herbert Roch referred to a letter of Theodor Storm about a visit that Fontane had made to him during the Danish War and cited Storm as saying, "Despite his editorial responsibilities for the *Kreuzzeitung*, [Fontane] is a nice person with whom one can get along—and a poet." Roch added,

> Anyone who did not know [Fontane] more closely, would never in any circumstances [after his three war books] have thought of him as a poet. These are the most voluminous and unpoetical books that he left behind him, weighty tomes without any weight. Mere writing for hire. A publisher made him an offer to describe the Prussian campaigns with all the trimmings for a wider public. And he accepted. Unfortunately, one might say today. But for him these three thousand pages in lexicon format, which nobody reads any more and hardly anyone knows, belonged to the detours he had to take in order to reach his own vocation.

Choosing a standard that military historians in any age would find difficult to meet, Roch went on to say that Fontane's "chronicles" had neither the pregnancy of Thucydides' *Pelopennesian War* nor the drive of Schiller's *History of the Thirty Years War*, and accused him of superficiality in describing the background and causes of the three conflicts and little more than journalistic talent in using the miscellaneous materials with which he sought to enliven his battle descriptions. He added that only the Danish book had a second edition, and that the others fell dead from the presses.[2]

In point of fact, Fontane's war books have not been quite as neglected as Roch would have us believe. Over the years they have always found discerning readers, and interest in them has grown in recent times. Extensive selections from them are now available in the Nymphenburg edition of Fontane's collected works;[3] a handsome new illustrated edition of *The War against France* was published by the

Manesse press in Switzerland in 1985;[4] and plans are currently being
made in the United States to publish all three of the war books in
translation. Leaving that aside, however, we must concede that Roch's
principal point has some weight. There is no doubt that the writing
of the war books did, for an appreciable time, postpone the dawn of
Fontane's career as a novelist, and that being so, we owe it to those
who feel as strongly about this as Roch does to try to explain why
Fontane chose to write the war books, what special talents he brought
to the task, and what the war books had, and still have, to offer to
readers whose minds are somewhat more open than is true in his case.

I

In August 1866 Fontane wrote to the publisher Wilhelm Hertz, with
whom he had contracted to write a novel (the future *Vor dem Sturm*,
published in 1876), to explain why, having already postponed it once
in order to write about the war in Schleswig-Holstein, he was now
giving a second war book, a history of the Austro-Prussian War, pri-
ority over it.

> I want to write the war book, first because it will enable me to bring
> the Schleswig Holstein book to a proper conclusion, second because
> I take joy in and have a certain talent for such works, and third
> because I shall derive a considerable pecuniary advantage from it.[5]

Fontane was not exaggerating when he talked about his talent for
writing about military affairs. For one thing, he possessed a command
of what can be called the vocabulary of war, a familiarity with military
terminology and usage that sometimes baffled laymen, who were apt
not to know the difference between a brigade and a battalion or a
howitzer and a 24-pound gun. From his father's lectures on Napoleon's campaigns and his own childhood reading—and, of course,
from his own military service—he knew about such things as the ways
in which armies are organized and the functions of the different
branches of service and how they were supposed to support each other
and what that involved; he understood tactical forms and movements
and all of the other things that make armies effective fighting organ-

izations; and he appreciated the mystique of command and its responsibilities and the ways in which it is exercised and the chains of communication that carry its impulses to the smallest of an army's component parts. Without having read Clausewitz—at least, there is no reference to that great theorist in his books or letters—he was aware also that armies at war move in the most uncertain of media, that the simplest things in life become difficult in war, which is the province of what Clausewitz called *friction*, that companies and battalions and regiments, being made up of individuals, are subject to the faults of omission or commission of each of these, which may result in fatal delay or error, that rain and fog and fatigue conspire against perfection in the execution of orders, and that the difference between victory and defeat may be due less to the talents of an army's commander than to accident or chance.[6]

Knowledge of these things gave Fontane confidence as he wrote about technical matters or described, and made judgments about, complicated operations. But his knowledge was reinforced by industry and method. Despite the fact that his accounts of the Danish, Austrian, and French wars were written very shortly after the events that they described, they are far from being mere exercises in journalism, and they have survived not merely because of their stylistic grace but because of their author's search for every kind of material that would throw light upon the opposing strategies, the operations that gave them expression, and the physical and human context of the struggle. In his book *The Schleswig Holstein War*, his account of the attacks on the trenches at Düppel depends for its specificity and color upon letters and reports from frontline soldiers on both sides, just as his description of life in bivouac areas and at Prince Friedrich Karl's headquarters in Gravenstein are derived in part from reports in the German and foreign press. In the immediate aftermath of the 1866 war, Fontane was zealous in collecting frontline testimony and at the same time wrote dozens of letters to commanders who could elucidate operational problems for him, like Colonel (later General) Franz von Zychlinski, commander of the twenty-seventh Infantry Regiment at Münchengrätz and Königgrätz, who became a firm friend.[7] The bibliography to *The German War of 1866* included the Prussian and Austrian General Staff histories of the war and the official staff reports of the Saxon, Bavarian, and Badenese armies; almost two dozen corps, brigade, regimen-

tal, and battalion histories; professional critiques of the operations by
the well-known specialists Willisen, Dragomirow, and A. C. Cooke,
as well as Captain Hozier's reports from the Bohemian theater of war
as they appeared in the *Times* of London; numerous personal memoirs
and *Tagebücher* and accounts of single engagements; such professional journals as the *Militair-Wochenblatt* of Berlin and the *Oester-
reichische Militairische Zeitschrift*; and sixteen German and Austrian
newspapers. The bibliography appended to *The War against France*
is even more impressive, including not only all of the then available
official and semiofficial diplomatic and military works—white papers,
war histories based on General Staff papers, operational histories of
the separate armies and corps, and the like—but memoirs, diaries, and
articles by soldiers, journalists, and private citizens in Germany,
France, and England, and the files of twelve German newspapers. And
this did not include personal testimony that Fontane received and miscellaneous information and opinion that he gathered from sampling
the foreign press.

He was not content, however, to do his work in libraries. "Making
books out of books," he wrote to his wife in April 1871, "is not my
affair."[8] He always felt it necessary to follow the principle that had
guided him in the *Wanderings* and to see the terrain about which he
intended to write. In the case of the Schleswig-Holstein war, he took
advantage of the armistice of May 1864 to travel with a colleague
from the staff of the *Kreuzzeitung* over the theater of war from the
Eider to Flensburg and from there to the trenches of Düppel, which
had been stormed by the Prussians a month earlier. Later in the year,
after the final cessation of hostilities in July, he returned to the war
zone, studied the terrain in which the Alsen operation had been
launched, and traveled through Jutland, following the route of the
Austrian II Corps and the Prussian Guards in their advance on Fredericia. Two years later, he followed the same procedure in the case of
the Austrian war, going as soon as possible after the end of hostilities
to view the scenes of the firefights at Podol, Münchengrätz, and Gitschin and the battlefield of Königgrätz and then turning westward to
the area of operations of the Main Army and visiting the field of
Langensalza.

Fontane wrote a number of articles about his wanderings in Bohemia, which were published in Rudolf Decker's *Berliner Fremden*

und Anzeigeblatt in September and October 1866.[9] In one of these, an account of the firefight at Podol on the Iser on 28 June 1866, between the *avant garde* of the Prussian First Army and the brigade commanded by General von Poschacher, he wrote about how study of the terrain is often vital to the understanding of operations. In the second phase of the battle, when the Austrian commander Clam Gallas sent two additional brigades forward to support Poschacher, the lead companies suffered such heavy losses that he gave up the attempt to hold the river crossing and ordered a general retirement, suffering a loss of 33 officers and 1,015 men (among them 500 prisoners) to a Prussian loss of 12 officers and 118 men.[10] Fontane could not understand this result until he noted that the main route of retreat was flanked by a railway line at some distance to the west.

> It seemed to me as good as certain that the fight was in the end decided by the advance on the flank (the railroad bed). Only in this way can one explain the five hundred prisoners. A mere frontal attack would have made it easy at any time for the enemy (which in addition brought elite troops into the fighting here) to have effected his retreat without a loss of prisoners.[11]

These visits to the battle sites in Bohemia, and those he made in 1871 to the scenes of major Franco-Prussian engagements at Amiens, St.-Quentin, Gravelotte, St.-Privat, and Sedan, were important not only for the flashes of illumination that they provided but also because they gave an authenticity to his battle accounts that could be attained in no other way. Moreover, they helped Fontane remain unshaken in the face of military critics who held that civilians did not understand enough about war to write about it. Commenting late in life upon this professional prejudice, Fontane pointed out that, provided the civilian historian had done his work carefully, there was no reason why he should not be as proficient as the military specialist, except perhaps on technical points, while on other matters he might be the more reliable commentator because he possessed ''greater freedom and was less inhibited about bringing in extra-military factors, like the imponderables.'' He added:

> In the last analysis, the writing of military history is not at all different from the writing of history in general and is subject to the

same laws. How does it go? You are confronted with a lot of material, and it is a question, given what you have, of making choices,
for or against, yes or no. In addition, the depiction of the military-
historical is to a very essential degree a matter for literary and not
mere military criticism.[12]

This is perhaps too easily said. Fontane's habit of shifting the
perspective from which he viewed events and enabling his readers
periodically to see the course of the fighting from the other side of
the hill was, indeed, a literary device, and a successful one. Thanks
to it, his readers were protected from the impression that the events
he was describing had had to end as they did. By destroying the
assumption of inevitability, by restoring to history the options that it
once had, Fontane gave a tension and excitement to his battle accounts
that was not usual in this kind of writing.

But the military historian is required not merely to describe but,
like any other historian, to explain, and explanation involves making
judgments, in his case, of such difficult questions as the strategy and
tactics, the command decisions, the fighting qualities of the two sides.
This is not an easy task, and in undertaking it he has to resist the
tendency to find all of the victor's actions commendable or, alternatively, to seek to give the impression of objectivity by over-
emphasizing the disadvantages that his opponent had to contend with
or attributing his defeat to chance factors. It is an admirable feature
of Fontane's battle accounts that he was aware of this problem and
strove to deal with it. He was evenhanded but hardheaded in his judgments, generous but just to the beaten foe, and, in matters where
professional judgment was divided, careful to let his readers know the
reasons for the disagreement. In his account of the Danish supreme
commander's decision to evacuate the Danewerk without fighting for
it—a decision widely criticized by those who were influenced by the
virtually unanimous opinion of the international press that this defensive line was invulnerable—Fontane not only made a reasoned defense of General de Meza's action but also declared that by making
it he had saved his whole army.[13] In his treatment of the action of the
Austrian cavalry at Stresetitz in the last phase of the battle of Königgrätz, the last great cavalry action in history, he did not hesitate to
write of "the misfortune and the bravery of these outstanding regi-

ments,'' which kept the Austrian line of retreat open for so long, but this did not prevent him from explaining the tactical and other skills of the Prussian horse that guaranteed their victory.[14]

When one remembers the emotionalism of the popular mind in Germany at the end of the Austrian war and during the whole of the conflict with France, one cannot but be impressed by another quality of Fontane's war books, their freedom from ideological generalization and moralistic attitudinizing. This is especially true of the history of the war in France, which justified everything that Hans Scholz has said about Fontane's ''cool detachment'' and the absence in his writing of any trace ''of rancor, of mean triumph, of chauvinism and boasting.''[15] Fontane wrote at a time when Gustav Freytag was claiming that the victory over France revealed ''the power of divine providence in the apportionment of rewards and punishments,'' when Heinrich von Treitschke was describing it as a triumph of German *Kultur* over French arrogance and superficiality, and when Richard Wagner was writing a patriotic farce called *A Capitulation*, which made light of the rigors of the siege of Paris and joked about the suffering and starvation of the French populace.[16] One would look in vain for anything of the sort in *The War against France*.

This was true in part because Fontane was never, even momentarily, affected by the war fever that clouded the critical judgment of other writers. He was far from taking a romantic view of war and, after describing a particularly bloody firefight during the Schleswig-Holstein War, wrote that war had developed, or degenerated, into ''a science of killing.''[17] The murderous efficiency of the Prussian breechloader (*Zündnadelgewehr*) made him think more of its victims than of the victories it brought. He was not, therefore, inclined to succumb to the popular mood. In ''the patriotic excitement,'' he wrote to his Tunnel colleague Karl Zöllner at the outset of the French war, there was ''an endless amount of nonsense,''[18] and in a more elaborate description of his reaction to the rush of events, he wrote to his wife:

> The whole situation works upon me like a colossal vision, a Wild Hunt that rushes over me; one stands and stares and is not sure what to make of it all. A *Völkerwandlung* organized by railroads, yet always *masses*, inside of which one whirls like an atom, not standing aside and in control but surrendered to the great movement without

any will of one's own. It is like being swept away, when someone
shouts "Fire!" in the theater, to an exit that is perhaps not there,
squeezed without pity, shoved, choked, a victim of dark impulses
and forces. Many people like that, because it is an "excitement";—I
am too artistically organized to be comfortable in such circumstances.[19]

In a postscript, Fontane alluded to the news that had arrived the day
before of the victory of the V Corps and the Silesian Regiments 46
and 47 at Weienburg and added:

My heart beat higher at this news, and yet I couldn't free myself
from a feeling of sorrow. What is all that for? For nothing! Merely
so that Lude Napoleon can be firm in his seat or that the Frenchman
can go on imagining that he is the prize specimen of creation—for
such a chimera, the death of thousands![20]

Even in 1866, the poet Fontane had shown that he was skeptical about
the meaning of victory in war, writing after Königgrätz,

Ja, Sieg! Er hat die Herzen uns erhoben,
Es gab uns viel—er hat auch viel genommen;
Ein Tag de Ruhmes, aber schwer erkauft.
'nen Schleier über Not und Tod und Wunden.[21]

[Aye, victory! It has exalted our hearts,
Given us much and taken much away,
A day of glory bought at heavy cost,
A veil cast over misery, death, and wounds.]

At the beginning of 1871, celebrating the triumphs of the past year,
he suggested that it might be well to bring them to an end.

Das alte Jahr, in Kampf und Mut und Streben,
Hat's uns gefeit, gewappnet und gestählt.
Das neues Jahr, o woll' auch das noch geben,
Das Eine noch, das uns allein noch fehlt:

"Laß jenen Ölzweig zu uns niederschweben,
Auf den ein jedes Herz jetzt hofft und zählt,

Zu allem, was das alte Jahr beschieden,
Du neues Jahr, o gib uns Frieden, Frieden![22]

[The old year, in combat and courage and aspiration,
Has made us invulnerable, has armed and steeled us.
The new year, oh, may it also give us that,
The one thing that we still lack:

Let that olive branch bend down to us,
Which every heart now hopes for and counts on,
In addition to all that the old year blessed us with,
O thou new year, now give us peace, yes, peace.]

II

In the history of European diplomacy, the Schleswig-Holstein question
was generally recognized as being one of peculiar complexity: the
British foreign secretary Palmerston once said that only three men
ever fully mastered it, and that one of these (Queen Victoria's consort,
the late Prince Albert) was dead, a second (a Foreign Office clerk)
had gone mad, and the third (he himself) had forgotten it. The two
duchies were personal possessions of the king of Denmark but not
part of Denmark proper, an arrangement that was given a dangerous
potential by the additional circumstances that, although they had been
declared permanently inseparable by ancient writ, Holstein, almost
completely German in population, was a member of the Germanic
Confederation, Schleswig, which wanted to be, had a sizable Danish
minority, and there was a strong nationalist (*Eider-Dane*) movement
in Denmark that wished to absorb Schleswig into the kingdom. It was
this combination of forces that had induced the people of Schleswig
and Holstein to take advantage of the revolutionary situation in 1848–
1850 to seek to win their independence from Denmark by force of
arms, a movement aided by the Germanic Confederation and, rather
feebly, by Austrian and Prussian forces but defeated in the end by the
efficiency and élan of the Danish army and the diplomatic pressure of
Russia and Great Britain, which took the lead in persuading the European Concert, in 1852, to restore the *status quo ante bellum*. This
did not, however, stop the agitation of the *Eider-Danes*, and on 18

November 1863, after a change in dynasty in Copenhagen, the new king Christian IX signed a new constitution incorporating Schleswig into the kingdom. This led to Austrian and Prussian intervention and war against Denmark.

When Theodor Fontane wrote his account of the war, he began it with a long section on the history of the Schleswig-Holstein question since earliest times. This was done with authority and style: Fontane had long interested himself in the duchies' affairs, and it will be remembered that in 1850, at a low point in his fortunes, he had actually set off to fight for their freedom. But he must have known, or suspected, as he began to write, that the early history of this confusing story had become largely irrelevant from the moment that the Austrians and Prussians intervened. For they did so not on behalf of the freedom of the duchies but rather to force the Danes to return to the basis of the 1852 settlement. And when the Danes refused to do so, even when they were defeated, Prussia and Austria simply took over the duchies as trustees, administering them jointly. This was not an arrangement that was destined to be amicable, and long before Fontane had finished his book relations between the two German powers had deteriorated sharply, largely because Prussia, more and more openly, was working for the outright annexation of the duchies, a result that the Austrians were bound to oppose by war, as they did in 1866.

None of this was clearly seen, of course, two years earlier, when the war began, and Fontane did not allow it to prejudice his account of the military operations. Instead, he stopped his discussion of the politics of Schleswig-Holstein when Christian IX signed the new Danish constitution of 1863 and turned his attention exclusively to the military mobilization it called into being and the war that followed.

His analysis of the two opposing forces was shrewd and argued, in an interesting way, that the outcome of the war was largely determined by the superiority of the German military system over the Danish one. Both the Austrian and Prussian armies were made up by long-term conscripts, backed in time of war by reserves composed of former soldiers who took part in periodic training exercises. The troops were well trained and armed and, in the case of the Austrians, blooded in the campaigns of Radetzky and the war of 1859. The Austrian commander was General Ludwig von der Gablenz, who had won the *Ritterkreuz* of the Maria Theresa Order at Kaschau in Hungary in 1849 and distinguished himself at Magenta in 1859. His opposite number in the Prussian army, Prince Friedrich Karl, had less field experience and in difficult situations—at Düppel in 1864 and on the Bistritz in 1866—had a tendency to discouragement and indecision, but these moods did not last long, and in general he was a thruster. Both the Austrian cavalry and artillery were considered to be outstanding. The Prussians, on the other hand, were outfitted with new infantry weapons and field guns that had not yet been tested in battle. Their infantry was young and spirited.

The Danish commander, Christian Julius de Meza, was the descendant of a Portuguese Jewish family that had come to Denmark in the eighteenth century. An artillerist, he had entered the service in 1807, at the time of the British bombardment of Copenhagen, had fought with distinction in the campaigns of 1848–1850 and distinguished himself in the battle of Idstedt in 1850. He had spent long years teaching in command and staff schools and was, perhaps, more of an intellectual than the average Austrian and Prussian staff officer. But it was thanks to his work that the artillery was the strongest arm in the Danish army, apart from its outstanding engineering corps. Less good was the infantry, and this, in Fontane's view, was due to Denmark's reliance on a militia system that did not provide for proper training. He wrote:

> The doubling of the twenty-two battalions, which was ordered at the outset of the war, led to the use of men who were in part too old and in part too young, who had either not learned to use their weapons or who had forgotten how to do so. In the same way, the officer corps was supplemented by so-called reserve officers who were wanting in intellectual and even more in military education. The arming of the infantry was excellent in respect to weapons and clothing, but the real soldierly spirit was often lacking. The individual soldier, in and for himself excellent material, lacked physical and moral adaptability and self-reliance in action.[23]

This weakness, in Fontane's view, determined the course of the war from the beginning.

The allied armies crossed the Eider into Schleswig on 1 February. To the west, the Austrians moved from Rendsburg up the railroad line to Ober-Selk, meeting heavy opposition from well-deployed troops and suffering not inconsiderable losses. At the end of the day, however, Colonel Leon Count Gondrecourt's "Iron Brigade" had seized the heights of Ober-Selk and Königsberg and overlooked a considerable stretch of the supposedly impregnable system of trenches and bastions called the Danewerk. The key to this, however, was the fortress complex of Missunde, which dominated the Schlei. Here the Prussians had taken position after crossing the Eider and moving swiftly and unopposed northward from Eckernforde, and it appeared that a major battle would develop here. The Prussians, however, doubting that their artillery could force a capitulation, elected to pin down the bulk of the Danish force at Missunde, while sending a detachment downstream to effect a crossing of the Schlei at Arnis. Threatened on both flanks, the Danish General De Meza, as already noted, decided to pull out of Missunde and to evacuate the whole of the Danewerk.

Within a week of the opening of hostilities, therefore, the allies had done the apparently impossible, and the way was open to the north. Hot in pursuit of the retreating Danes, the Austrians caught them at Oeversee and, after a hard-fought battle, occupied Flensburg and were poised for a crossing into Jutland. To the east, the Prussians took the town of Schleswig without opposition and then moved toward the massive fortification complex of Düppel. A prime objective of the contending forces during the war of 1848–1850, Düppel had proved impregnable to German assault in May and June 1848 and was stormed by Saxon and Bavarian troops in 1849 successfully only after they had suffered dreadful losses. Nicknamed *"der Blutloch,"* Düppel was reinforced by the Danes after the end of hostilities and was now girdled by an elaborate complex of interconnected and supporting trenches, the so-called *Düppeler Schanzen*, ten in number, so arranged that troops attacking one of them received enfilading fire from others. The whole complex connected the waters of the Alsen Sound and the Wenningbund, which protected its flanks, and its powerful buttresses and redoubts derived additional protection from the Danish fleet, which included the redoubtable *Monitor*-type ironclad, *"Rolf Krake,"* which fascinated Fontane and led to some of the liveliest writing in his book.[24]

The Prussians took their positions before Düppel on 9 February and were still there two months later, a circumstance that led some bored war correspondents to complain that the Austrians were doing all the fighting in the war. One need only read Fontane's meticulous description of the Düppel position, however, to understand that precipitate action might have been fatal. As it was, much time was spent on studying the terrain, trying the effects of various kinds of bombardment on the trench system, sending raiding missions to test the alertness and spirit of the defenders, investigating the possibility of an elaborate flanking operation by invading the island of Alsen, and waiting for the arrival of heavier artillery, since the guns available made little impression on the Danish defenses.

Meanwhile, the Prussian troops settled in good-humoredly and made the best of the situation. In one of his best, and most revealing, chapters, Fontane described life in the rear areas, at Gravenstein, where Prince Friedrich Karl's headquarters was located and in the nearby villages and camps that served as bivouac areas for the troops. Gravenstein, where Friedrich Karl lived in the castle with a staff of six hundred and sought to determine the best way to get around the great obstacle before him, was a magnet for all sorts of people besides combatants. In its few cafés and guest houses were to be seen tourists, *Schlachtenbummler*, reporters for the leading German and Austrian papers and for the *Times* of London and the French and Scandinavian press, diplomats and military attachés from foreign powers, army suppliers and weapons salesmen, speculators and gamblers, and—the center of much attention—the exotic Enemotto Kamadiro and Fiune Taki, Japanese naval officers, who had come from The Hague to learn something about European ways of war.[25] In the villages and camps where the troops were stationed, the atmosphere was lively and carefree, as if war were a kind of holiday. When on patrol the young Prussian troops developed an elaborate barter system with their Danish opposite numbers, in which the object of their greatest desire was the Danish water bottle, which was large, solid, and covered with tightly sewn leather. In their hours of recreation they played furious games of a kind of handball that they called *Sauball* and *Bullenjagen*. For the rest—and this betokens a certain innocence that was soon to disappear—they made up comic war games. They had discovered that the

Danes were not very good shots, and they strove to induce them to give proofs of this. In one village, they found a large number of Mardi Gras dolls (*Fastnachtpuppen*) some of almost human size. These they dressed up in bits of uniform and gave them mock guns and stationed them behind hummocks or walls close to the Danish outworks, hoping to attract fire. A favorite pastime was to fashion mock artillery pieces, out of barrels or stovepipes and wheeled plows, placing these on roof-tops and going through the ritual of loading and firing, simulating the sound of the discharge. When I was young, I once saw a Harold Lloyd film in which the hero and two friends are being pursued by a band of South American revolutionaries. They take refuge behind a wall, where they find a stovepipe and a drum. Lloyd points the former over the wall and, when one of his friends smites the drum, heaves a co-conut in the general direction of the enemy and then blows cigar smoke through the pipe.[26] I thought this was charming at the time, but I never dreamed that I would one day discover, from reading Theodor Fontane's history of the Schleswig-Holstein war, that Prussian troops had done much the same.

All of these diversions halted at the end of March. The weather, generally bad, had become worse, making impossible the execution of the plan for an invasion of Alsen. Friedrich Karl finally decided there was no alternative to a frontal assault on Düppel and, after some probing attacks that revealed faults of determination and mutual support in the defense, sent his army forward. Starting on 17 April, the *Schanzen* were attacked by forty-six companies in storm columns, and before the next day was over they were in Prussian hands.

The doubts that had circulated about the fighting qualities of the Prussian army did not survive this victory, which the historian Droysen called "one of the events that mark an epoch in a nation's history." The young infantrymen who charged the trenches showed an élan, a courage, and an initiative that swept everything before them. Speaking of the capture of the first trench, Fontane wrote:

> Soon after our companies had settled in *Schanze* I, "Rolf Krake" appeared, stationed itself in front of the trench and bombarded it with grenades. Lieutenant Schmolzer of the artillery, however, had brought the only usable gun that was left in the trench into position against the Wenningbrod and met "Rolf Krake" with well-aimed

fire. He loosed off 14 rounds, of which several were seen to be hits. At any rate, "Rolf Krake" did not take up the fight and removed itself from the vicinity.[27]

As the attack proceeded, there were many instances of individual bravery and self-sacrifice, and Fontane wove them skillfully into his narrative: Major General Raven, fatally wounded at the head of his troops, calling to them, "A general has to bleed for his king too. Forward, comrades!"—the first Prussian general to die before the enemy since Scharnhorst;[28] the sapper Klinke, who met his death while blowing a breach in Schanze II by throwing himself and the bag of gunpowder against the palisades;[29] and the drummer Probst, who seized the colors from a dying comrade's hand and led his company forward.

> Tambour, schlag an!
> Es gilt einem Mann,
> Der stürmt mit Hurrah die Schanzen hinauf,
> Und pflanzt die Fahne des Königs darauf.[30]

In this first significant victory since Waterloo, which signaled to Europe that Prussia was once more a military power of major consequence, it was perhaps natural that individual deeds of valor should almost immediately assume a legendary character.

The capture of Düppel broke the Danish will to resist, and subsequent allied actions—the crossing to Alsen[31] and the bombardment and seizure of Fredericia[32]—were operations against a beaten and retreating army As Fontane had argued at the outset, the operational result in 1864 was merely the expression of the superiority of the German military system over that of its opponent.

III

The war that broke out between Austria and Prussia in 1866 exceeded in all of its dimensions—area of the theater of war, number of troops engaged, casualties, political consequences—those of the Danish conflict, and this involved new problems for Fontane. Instead of describing a war of fixed positions and frontal assaults, he had now to concern himself with strategies of movement and envelopment and with tactical operations that required the most sophisticated coordination between the different arms of the service. The result was a book that had far less of the homely and intimate detail of the Danish one but was more interesting in its handling of operations and its judgment of command decisions.

When it became apparent in the late spring of 1866 that war between the two great German powers was imminent, the Austrian command had two options. After concentrating the bulk of its forces at Olmütz in Moravia, it could either send it northward into Silesia to reclaim the province lost to Prussia in the first of Frederick's wars; or, alternatively, it could mount a swift penetration of the mountain passes in northern Bohemia, sending its armies by way of Dresden directly against Berlin.

The Prussian chief of staff, Helmuth von Moltke, had to guard against both possibilities, which meant that he had to deploy his forces along an arc that extended from Torgau north of Dresden, where the so-called Elbe Army was stationed, over Görlitz and Hirschberg north of the Erzgebirge, the assembly area for Prince Friedrich Karl's I Army, to the Neisse River, where the II Army of the Prussian crown prince provided a screen in front of Breslau. The Prussian dispositions were the subject of considerable criticism at the time from people who pointed to dangerous gaps in the line and who talked about the primary importance of concentration. But, of course, as Fontane pointed out, Moltke could not concentrate until he knew for sure in which direction the Austrians intended to move, and that he did not know until mid-June, when the tangled Schleswig-Holstein dispute reached its ultimate incarnation, when the Germanic Confederation, taking Austria's side, called for a mobilization of federal troops against Prussia. At that point, Prussia declared the Bund dissolved, declared war on Hannover, the Electorate of Hesse, and the kingdom of Saxony, and, on 17 June, ordered its troops to advance toward Dresden.

These events galvanized the Austrians into action. Their commander, Feldzeugmeister August Ludwig von Benedek, was suddenly aware that, unless he broke out of Olmütz in Moravia, the assembly point of his Northern Army, and linked up with the Saxons, and possibly the Bavarian army, he was in danger of being outnumbered. On

18 June, he ordered an immediate advance of his forces—180,000 strong—to the fortress of Nikolsburg on the upper Elbe, with the evident intention of joining I Army Corps, commanded by General Eduard Count von Clam Gallas, and the First Light Cavalry Division, which were already stationed at Gitschin south of the Iser River, and then destroying the Prussian armies separately. This decision clarified the situation for Moltke, who nevertheless waited until the direction of the enemy march was confirmed beyond any reasonable doubt before ordering the commanders of I and II Armies to march through the mountain passes into Bohemia, seeking a junction with the Elbe Army in the vicinity of Gitschin.

What happened from then on, Fontane made clear, did so less because of the strategic vision of the two commanders than of other circumstances. Benedek's hope of defeating the Prussians before they had united was crushed in the end by ''the great tactical superiority [of the Prussian army], in which the *Zündnadelgewehr* played a not inessential role'' and, on the other hand, by ''obstacles that have been characterized as 'the Austrian system.' '' Elaborating on this, Fontane wrote:

> The Austrian army command was in no way deficient in intellectual qualities, but rather in moral ones, and what was well-planned, daring, and well thought-out was not ruined by any violation of so-called fundamentals, but suffered shipwreck precisely on ''the system,'' on secret-mongering and officiousness, on rivalry and false scruples, on mistrust and selfishness.[33]

The key to the tactical weakness of the Austrian infantry lay in their reliance—which was not unaffected by a personal predilection of Emperor Francis Joseph—on the bayonet. The new drill regulations of 1862 prescribed shock tactics as the key in the offensive, and little emphasis was placed either on the firefight or on skirmishing. Both the war in Italy and that in Denmark seemed to validate this doctrine, and it was little noticed that in neither conflict had the Austrians been opposed by an antagonist proficient in delivering massed fire. But the Prussians, in the *Zündnadelgewehr*, possessed a breechloading rifle that was capable of firing five rounds a minute with 43 percent accuracy against formations at seven hundred paces; and its success in the Danish War, which was little heeded by the other powers, confirmed the Prussian army in its preference for a tactical doctrine that emphasized the offensive with advance in open order and aimed fire.

The devastating effects of this are apparent in Fontane's accounts of the first encounters of the war—the Austro-Saxon operations against the Prussian I Army between the Iser River and Gitschin, and the Austrian attempts to prevent the Prussian penetration of the mountain passes at Nachod, Skalitz, Schweinschädl, Soor, and Trautenau. Over and over again, the Austrian losses were significantly higher than the Prussian: at Nachod, for example, 7,372 to 1,210;[34] at Skalitz, 5,577 to 1,412.[35] Even at Trautenau, where the Austrian X Corps, led by the former Austrian commander in Denmark, Lieutenant Field Marshal Ludwig von der Gablenz, shocked Bonin's I Corps and drove it back in confusion to the bivouac area it had left the day before, Austrian losses exceeded those of the Prussians by three to one.[36] One can understand the plaintive cry in the letter of an Austrian *Landser* at Königinhof, "Dear Peppi: I guess I won't see you any more, for the Prussians are shooting everyone dead."[37]

This grave disadvantage might have been offset by energetic leadership in the first stages of the war. But Benedek had made his reputation in Italy, where he had spent virtually all of his military career, and he lacked assurance in the theater to which he had been assigned. His doubts were reinforced by the fact that his chief of staff, Major General Gideon von Krismanic, former head of the Topographic Bureau, was a pedantic and basically timorous adviser, who did not believe in taking risks, and by the additional circumstance that the current chief of staff in Vienna, Lieutenant Field Marshal Alfred Freiherr von Henikstein, a perpetual naysayer who had no faith in victory, had also attached himself to his headquarters. This situation militated against decisiveness and was responsible for other errors, notably the long delay in moving north from Olmütz and the decision to leave what turned out to be an inadequate screen against the Prussian II Army when Benedek started his advance from Nikolsburg to Gitschin. Fontane was inclined to believe that Benedek himself was responsible for the failure of the Iser campaign, pointing out that he was apparently incapable of making up his mind whether the Iser line, or for that matter Gitschin, should be held or not, sending orders to his frontline commanders that changed from day to day.[38]

These faults at the top were compounded by sins of negligence, inattention to detail, and irresponsibility farther down the chain of command. In November 1866, Fontane passed through the mountainous terrain between Podol and Gitschin, following the line of the Austrian retreat from the Iser earlier in the year. In the vicinity of the Musky-Berg in particular, he was struck by the number of potential defensive barriers that had been left unreinforced by the Austrians, and he wrote, "A little prudence, a little good will, a little determination would have sufficed to turn this mass of rock into an invulnerable fortress. But it was Austria's destiny that it was over and over again destitute of one or the other of these qualities (and often of all three)."[39]

It was a combination of these weaknesses that led to the loss of the battle that decided the war. Until three o'clock in the afternoon of 3 July, Benedek was confident of victory. On his left, his Saxon allies were holding a strong position at Problus and preventing any advance by Herwarth von Bittenfeld's Elbe Army. In the center, the Prussian I Army had been for hours under bombardment in the woody terrain along the Bistritz River, unable to make progress and nearing the end of its endurance. Had Benedek committed his reserves here, the victory might have been his. But he kept delaying, on the advice of aides, and meanwhile paid too little attention to his right flank, toward which the Prussian II Army was slowly but surely advancing. This latter mistake was shared by those of his command who were stationed there.

The key to the defenses on the right flank was the village of Chlum, situated on the ridge of the chain of hills that overlooked Benedek's headquarters at Lipa. Chlum was held by the brigade of Major General von Appiano, who had, however, shortly after one o'clock, ordered elements of his force who were under fire to retire from Chlum to a place below and out of sight of the ridge. Fontane writes:

> The momentary protection which their changed position gave them was dearly paid for later. The officers had a presentiment of that. They said to themselves that the heights that they gave up voluntarily would shortly have to be stormed again. But the strict order left them no choice. . . . The defense of the village was entrusted to

the commander of the Regiment Sachsen-Meiningen, Colonel Sla-veczi, apparently no very fortunate choice. He was short-sighted and seemed to have only the vaguest conception of a Prussian II Army or of the possibility of its making an appearance and to the end answered reports that came to him suggesting this with the stereo-typed phrase, "You are a calamity-monger [*Schwarzseher*]."[40]

Against this slack defense forward elements of the crown prince's II Army achieved complete surprise. At about three o'clock, the first battalion of the First Regiment of Foot of the Guards burst out of the fog and into Chlum, killing or capturing all of its defenders. Coun-terattacks proved powerless to dislodge them, and they were soon, in any case, reinforced. For Benedek, the battle was now as good as over. His hope of smashing Friedrich Karl's army on the Bistritz had been vitiated, his headquarters at Lipa had become untenable, and his whole army was in danger of encirclement.

Theodor Fontane's history of the Austro-Prussian War—of which the storming of Chlum forms the climax—is distinguished by the clar-ity and detail of its battle scenes, not only those touched upon here but also those—the last bitter fighting as the Austrians fell back to-ward Königgratz, and the Prussian operations against the Hannoveri-ans at Langenzalza and against the army corps of the German Con-federation on the Main—that have had to be left out. Fontane's concentration on this aspect of the war prevented him from writing the kind of relaxed passages that one finds in his book on the Danish War in which he discussed the history of the area being fought over, or recounted local legends (like that of "the hostile brothers" of Mis-sunde), or reflected on the process of war itself and the reaction of people to it.

In one notable instance, however, he did write a somber counter-part to the happy account of camp life in the book on the Schleswig-Holstein War. This was his chapter "Gitschin on 30 June," which described the appearance of that historic city, once the home of the imperial *Feldherr* of the Thirty Years War, Wallenstein, on the day after the battle that had expelled the Austrians from the town and forced them to fall back to the west In this powerful piece of writing Fontane expressed something of his own growing disenchantment with war. He wrote:

All of Gitschin was a lazaret. Everywhere there was want, of food, of bandages, of surgical help. . . . Wounded Austrians and Prussians, wearing the Schleswig Cross or the Düppel Medal, now, in common misery, revived their old comradeship in arms and supported and comforted each other. . . . The churches offered a particularly gripping and picturesque impression. High procession lanterns, carved in the baroque manner and painted red, between them banners from the Thirty Years War, dusty, tattered, hung from or stood against the walls. On the steps of the altar, however, crouched Hungarian hussars, some wrapped in blue and gold cloaks, some in white; the bright morning light fell upon eagle feathers and *kucsma*. Italians from the Regiment Sigismund lay around in the aisles and niches, one with a rose between pale lips. Bohemians from the 18th Jaeger battalion cowered in the pews and looked pleadingly at the picture of Mary, begging for help—or release. At the side, on the bare tiles and leaning against the pillared wall, sat a Bohemian woman, and close by her a mutilated soldier from the Regiment Gyulai. The woman had fallen asleep from exhaustion. The mutilated one didn't move. He had laid his arm around his protectress and drawn he her head to his breast. . . . On the evening of the 30th, two thousand wounded lay in Gitschin. A similar large number were put up in the hamlets and villages in the immediate vicinity of the battlefield.[41]

IV

Fontane's history of the war against France is probably the best of his war books. Certainly it is the best written, the one with the greatest epic sweep, and the one that is the most modest in the name of Germany. Perhaps this was because, when he wrote it, he was reacting against the public mood at the end of the war with France. After having been content to ascribe Prussia's victory over Austria to "mass education, sense of honor, love of fatherland, *Zündnadel*, tactics, and higher command,"[42] he was appalled by the jingoism and social Darwinism that was prevalent in Germany in 1871 and the assumption, later castigated by Nietzsche, that the war had been a victory for German culture.[43] He never for a moment believed that the French were inferior to the Germans in any fundamental sense, however much they may have suffered in battle from the technological advantages enjoyed by their opponent. In his book about his own misadventures in France after the war—his capture at Domrémy while doing research for his war book and his subsequent imprisonment—he annoyed a good many Prussian patriots, including his own soldier son George, by pointing out that the French were really very much like the Germans and by praising their fortitude, their resilience and their humor.[44]

The glorification by the press of Prussian military exploits in France also alarmed him, for he sensed that it was potentially dangerous and might give the military an inflated conception of their own worth and lead to an excessive degree of military influence in public affairs in the postwar period. In his account of his trip through northern France and Alsace Lorraine in 1871, he gave an unflattering portrait of the young Prussian lieutenants who were moving into the occupied territory and spoke of the dubious blessings of being ruled by "climbers, adventurers, and persons who were restless and ambitious."[45] While he was in detention at Moulins, he had, for want of other reading matter, read fifty pages of Rabou's *La grande Armée*, an unrelieved paean to Napoleon's genius and the army that followed him. He did so with growing discontent and, laying it aside, said to himself, "Such books you write yourself. If they are just like this, they're worthless. The mere glorification of the military, without moral content and elevated aim, is nauseating."[46]

Fontane approached the formidable task of writing a history of the Franco-Prussian conflict, therefore, with a strong sense of the dangers that the public mood posed for anyone seeking to be objective, but with the resolve, nevertheless, to write a book that would be as complete and as free from prejudice as possible. The result, four stout half volumes that totaled some nineteen hundred pages and, after beginning with a bravura description of the atmosphere in Ems in July 1870, described the Prussian invasion of France and the victory of Moltke's strategy at Sedan, the *guerre à outrance* fought by the new French Republic, the battles for Orléans, the siege of Paris, and the desperate but unavailing campaigns of Chanzy, Faidherbe, and Bourbaki—was impressive enough to meet the most exacting standard.

The comprehensiveness of the work is less important than the understanding that Fontane brought both to the hardihood and the sacrifices required of the soldier in the ranks, which he sometimes points up by a studied juxtaposition of the kind of sentimental dog-

gerel that the war produced and the casualties that it demanded, and
to the frailties of judgment to which commanders are prone in the
heat of battle. Without in any way depreciating the superior staff work,
the coordination of arms, and the dedicated leadership that were responsible for Prussian victories in the field, he constantly reminds his
readers that the foe was a worthy one. His account of the bloody fight
at St.-Privat ends with the words:

> The French army—and this cannot be said often enough—was ex-
> cellent. Never had the Empire, either the first or the second, placed
> anything better in the field. The enemy was defeated by a power
> that was superior to him in numbers, in self-confidence, and above
> all in leadership. The armies themselves were equal.[47]

The same balance characterized his analysis of the tactics of the
opposing forces and the errors of command that determined the issue.
Fontane showed no hesitation about putting his finger on crucial fail-
ures of judgment, but he was always quick to add that war was a
realm in which mistakes were easily made. Thus, his assessment of
Bazaine's conduct of the battle of Vionville concluded that the French
commander should have been better informed about the size and the
march route of the army corps opposing him, but then continues:

> Precise knowledge of the enemy, when it is a matter of whole square
> miles covered with troops, is under the most favorable circumstances
> imaginable always a highly difficult task. In the pressure of time
> and events, however, acquiring any of that kind of exact knowledge
> becomes almost an impossibility. The reports are inadequate or con-
> tradict each other, and at best you are at the mercy of guess work.
> Bazaine's guesses, however, were justified.[48]

One of the most attractive features of *The War against France*
and one that distinguished it from other accounts of the war that were
published in Fontane's lifetime was the unusual role that he gave
foreign observers and commentators.[49] The number and variety of
quotations from British and French politicians and especially from
English and French newspapers not only stand as testimony to the
breadth of Fontane's miscellaneous reading but also add to the overall

objectivity of the book's tone and to its color. By such excerpts Fontane was often able to heighten the verisimilitude of his account and to provide circumstantial descriptions of the *étappe* and of such things as the war's effect on civilian life and the practical results of the decrees of national emergency that were issued by the French government after Sedan. In this connection, his brilliant use of historical flashbacks to illuminate regional differences and the attention he paid to careful geographical description deserve high praise, as does the care he devoted to character studies in the drama he was describing.

The War against France was, in short, a book in which the most critical of historians might have taken pride, and Fontane was well pleased with it. He quickly discovered, however, that others were less so and that these included not only the majority of contemporary military writers but also the king-emperor whose triumph the book celebrated. Fontane had believed that after his hard work he had a right to expect some kind of recognition from his government. But when the Prussian minister of the interior asked the emperor rather obliquely whether he wished to reward the writer in any way, Wilhelm replied in the negative, Fontane wrote sardonically to his friend Mathilde von Rohr:

> I have worked day and night for twelve years on these war books; they celebrate, not in great words but in felt ones, our people, our army and our king and emperor. In 1864 I traveled through a Denmark that had been fanaticized against us; in 1866 I was in a Bohemia that was filled with roving bands and with cholera; and I escaped with my life in France only by a miracle. Unfrightened, because my work required the risk, I went back to the place of danger. Then my work began. And there it stands, if nothing else, the product of great industry, and representing with respect to its *subject matter* a unique thing in respect to which one has a right to expect the interest of the emperor, the hero of this great epic. . . . And it is precisely this hero and emperor, who, when he is asked "whether he has a reason to wish the author of this comprehensive work well or to be gracious to him," answers the question by saying No.[50]

It was a disappointment all the more galling because of the ingratitude that it revealed in those who caused it. Fontane swallowed it as philosophically as he could. *"Eh bien,"* he wrote. "It's got to be so. But really it has done more for my embitterment than for my moral improvement."[51] He consoled himself by reflecting that the writing of the war books had in itself been rewarding—he said later that it was the writing of *The War against France* that made him a writer[52]—and turned his attention to the work for which he is now chiefly remembered.

5

Bismarck

Otto von Bismarck and Theodor Fontane were contemporaries in an almost exact sense. Bismarck, the son of an ancient noble family with estates in Pomerania and Brandenburg, was born on 1 April 1815 in Schönhausen, Brandenburg, and died at Friedrichsruh, not far from Hamburg, on 31 July 1898. Fontane, the son of an apothecary, was born in Neuruppin, Brandenburg, on 30 December 1819 and died on 24 September 1898 in Berlin. They were both, therefore, true witnesses of the century, their conscious lives extending from the age of romanticism through the convulsions of 1848 and the thoroughgoing reconstruction of the European balance of power in the 1860s to the age of imperialism and materialism and its attendant political, social, and psychological changes.

Although there is no record of their ever having met and exchanged ideas—we can hardly count Fontane's formal introduction to the former chancellor by the chief editor of the *Norddeutsche Allgemeine Zeitung* on 2 February 1891[1]—there are some curious correspondences between their lives. Each was marked by a strong sense of individuality and the desire, as Bismarck put it when he terminated his career as a fledgling civil servant in 1839, "to make the kind of music I like or none at all,"[2] although Fontane did not have the financial means to realize that goal until 1876, when he finally severed his connection with the government service. Both entered upon the public stage during the revolutionary troubles of 1847–1849, although on opposite sides of the barricades. The *Landjunker* Bismarck, who threatened to arm his peasants and march upon Berlin to defend the king against the revolution, laid the foundation of his later political career by his eloquent and reactionary speeches in the United Landtag of 1847 and as a deputy of the extreme right in the new Landtag of 1849; Fontane played a more modest role as a radical journalist seeking to defend the revolution by means of his pen. In the years that followed, there was, at least on the surface, a convergence of their political positions. When Otto von Manteuffel headed a reactionary regime in Prussia during the Crimean War, Bismarck was ambassador to the federal diet in Frankfurt am Main, where he strongly opposed, and eventually defeated, Austria's attempt to persuade the German states to join it in intervening in the war on the side of France and Great Britain. At the same time, Fontane was a government press representative in London, where he sought to allay British indignation over the results of the neutrality policy that Bismarck had promoted, and largely designed. After his return from England at the end of the 1850s, Fontane worked for the *Kreuzzeitung*, the newspaper of the extreme right and the staunch supporter of Bismarck's policies during the conflict with Prussian liberalism that followed his assumption of the minister presidency in September 1862. And, in the subsequent period, while Bismarck was the chief architect of the unification process, Fontane was not only an admirer and supporter of his diplomacy but also, as we have seen, the historian of the wars that resulted from it.

The lives of the two men impinged directly upon each other on only one occasion, and that was when Fontane was collecting materials for his history of the war against France. In October 1870 his passion for history overcoming common sense, he crossed from the Prussian war zone into French territory because he wanted to see the birthplace of Joan of Arc and was captured by *francs-tireurs* and im-

prisoned on charges of espionage.[3] In this dangerous pass (whenever
in later life Fontane discussed his predicament with Prussian soldiers,
they always told him "If *we* had captured you, you would have been
shot!"),[4] it was Bismarck who came to his assistance. In an official
note, he asked the United States minister to France, Elihu B. Washburne, to intervene with the French government in behalf of "Dr.
Fontane, a Prussian subject and well-known historian," who had been
arrested while on "a scientific trip" and was being held at Besançon
at the risk of his life. Such measures against "a harmless scholar,"
Bismarck added, were unjustified, and he requested that Washburne
make it clear to the French government that, if Fontane were not
released, Prussia would retaliate by subjecting French subjects who
were caught in similar circumstances to the same treatment.[5] Washburne acted in this sense, and Fontane was released.

Whether Bismarck even remembered the incident in the days
when Fontane had become a well-known novelist, we do not know;
nor is there any evidence that he had ever read any of Fontane's
novels. This is not because the chancellor had no interest in, or time
for, literature. Compared with the politicians of our day, who rarely
give any indication of reading anything but public opinion polls, Bismarck was remarkably well read. In his speeches he quoted frequently
from Schiller, Goethe, and Shakespeare, and less so from Horace,
Gellert, Uhland, Scheffel, and the Irish poet Thomas Moore. His favorite poet was Schiller. Goethe he considered to have been a bureaucrat, more interested in court preferments than in literature, and
his poetry, especially the second part of *Faust*, often unintelligible.
He was particularly fond of the lyric poets of his youth, and his friend
the Baroness vom Spitzemberg has written that each of his residences
was provided with the works of Chamisso, Uhland, Rückert, and
Heine, and that on his desk, among his state papers, one or more of
these could always be found. He knew and had read the historians
Taine and Mommsen and Ranke, and was on friendly terms with the
last of these, and he was remarkably knowledgeable about foreign
writers, admiring George Eliot and considering Turgenev the greatest
writer of the modern age. But although, among contemporary works,
he had read Spielhagen's *Problematische Naturen*, Freytag's *Soll und
Haben* and the *platt-deutsch* novels of Fritz Reuter,[6] and although he
may have known Fontane's verse, or at least those poems that Fontane

dedicated to him, as well as his war books, which Fontane sent to him,[7] he had never, as far as we know, read any of Fontane's novels, which is a shame, for it would have been interesting to know what his reaction was to his own not infrequent appearances in them.

I

One literary distinction that the two men had in common was the ability to write letters that brought pleasure not only to their recipients but also—after their posthumous publication—to thousands of other readers as well. When Thomas Mann, in a famous essay, wrote in 1910, "No writer of the past or the present awakens in me the sympathy and gratitude, the unconditional and instinctive delight, the immediate amusement and warmth and satisfaction that I feel in every verse, in every line of one of [Fontane's] letters, in every snatch of his dialogue,"[8] he was not only speaking for many of his own contemporaries who were discovering the charms of Fontane's letters to his family and friends, but was also unconsciously echoing the enthusiasm of earlier readers of the letters of Fontane's great contemporary. In 1869, when a number of Bismarck's personal and political letters appeared for the first time in Hesekiel's *Buch vom Grafen Bismarck*, the novelist and playwright Paul Heyse wrote, "If this gentleman, instead of busying himself with politics, would enter into the field of novel-writing, he would be considered as an earnest competitor for the favor of the public."[9] And Fontane himself wrote to Georg Friedländer in 1890, "Bismarck had no greater admirer than I; my wife never read me one of his speeches or letters or sayings without my feeling a real enchantment."[10]

It is interesting to compare these two masters of the epistolary art. Of Fontane's letters, it is those of his old age that have the greatest appeal to the general reader, a fact that led Thomas Mann to the eccentric view that the letters of Fontane's early and middle years are inconsiderable, and that he had to grow old in order to become himself.[11] Bismarck's letters, laden with political concerns in his later years, became progressively less attractive to the nonspecialist. The chancellor, who from his youth onward had enjoyed letting himself go in letters to friends and colleagues, was conscious of this development, and lamented that politics was the bane of letter writing and that the big trout in his pools ate up all of the more attractive little fish.[12] But the letters of his youth and early maturity often startle and move us by the brilliance of their language and their range of mood and feeling. This is true, for example, of the exuberance of his letters to his Göttingen friend Scharlach, like the one in which he describes his decision to devote himself to a life in the country and to become

> a well-fed *Landwehr* officer with a moustache, who curses and swears a justifiable hatred of Frenchmen and Jews until the earth trembles, and beats his dogs and servants in the most brutal fashion, even if he is tyrannized by his wife. I will wear leather trousers and allow myself to be ridiculed at the Wool Market in Stettin, and when anyone calls me Herr Baron I'll stroke my moustache in good humor and sell two dollars cheaper. On the King's birthday I'll get drunk and shout "Vivat!" and in general get excited a lot and my every third word will be "On my honor!" and "A superb horse!" In short, I shall be happy in my family's rural circle, *car tel est mon plaisir*.[13]

And few readers can fail to be moved by the tenderness and passion of his letters to his betrothed, Johanna von Puttkamer, with their not infrequent shift into the didactic or the romantic mode or—most astonishing, because unexpected in a man who came to live for politics—by his ability to convey the appearance and the feel of landscape, the impression of light and shadow in the woods, the way the sun and the spume played on the bosom of the sea, the quiet of the park in Schönhausen on a long summer afternoon, an art which the author of the *Wanderings* never mastered, perhaps because he was always more interested in people than in nature.

Bismarck's letters as a young diplomat are marked by a precision of language that reflects both a cheerful self-confidence and a sense of amusement at the doubts of his elders, as in a famous letter to Leopold von Gerlach after a trip to Paris:

> You criticize me for having been in Babylon, but you surely cannot demand of a diplomat hungry for knowledge the kind of political chastity that sits so well on a soldier like Lützow or on an independent country gentleman. In my opinion, I must learn to know the elements in which I have to move, and I must do so by my own

observation as far as opportunities present themselves to me. Don't
fear for my political health as I do so. I have much of the nature of
a duck, from whose feathers the water drains, and in my case it is
a pretty long way from the outer skin to the heart.[14]

As for the letters of the years after he had become the king's chief
adviser, they have the power to reveal, sometimes by what appears to
be a chance remark or a laconic reference, the dangers and responsibilities of his calling—"One really learns in this trade that one can
be as clever as the clever ones of this world and yet at any time find
oneself in a moment like a child in the dark"—or, with shattering
immediacy, its sacrifices, as in the letter to his friend Albrecht von
Roon in December 1872, in which he wrote, "Sitting in the saddle,
the king hardly realizes that I am a good horse that he has ridden to
pieces; the lazy ones hold up better."[15] And surely it would be difficult to find, among the letters of the chancellor's contemporaries, a
more eloquent definition of the ethos of statecraft, couched in language as simple and forthright, than his reply to a letter criticizing
him for ruthlessness in his conduct toward his antagonists.

> Would to God that I did not have other sins upon my soul besides
> those the world knows of. As a statesman I am not ruthless *enough*
> but rather cowardly in my feelings; and this is so because it isn't
> always easy in the questions that come to me to win that clarity in
> whose soil grows confidence in God. Anyone who reproaches me
> for being a politician without conscience does me an injustice and
> should sometime try out his own conscience on *this* battlefield.[16]

Fontane's letters had none of the demonic quality that often characterized Bismarck's. If the latter bring intimations from the world of
politics and the never-ending acrobatics of the balance-of-power system, Fontane's deal with the private sphere, with life in the big city
or in the seaside or mountain resorts where the German middle classes
spent the summer months. Their focus is on the routines and problems
and petty dramas of domestic life, on the ways in which professional
preferment and social status impinge upon the relations between individuals and groups, on the discoveries and disappointments that are
made along the way, and, of course, on the press, the theater, and the

world of literature of which he was himself a part. Fontane's role is
that of the interested but detached observer, amused but always a bit
appalled by the examples of human impercipience and folly that come
to his attention, but eager to be helpful by passing on the fruits of his
own experience in the hope that they may be helpful. The moral ear-
nestness of Bismarck's letter to the critic of his treatment of his antagonists is hard to come by in Fontane. Taken as a whole, his letters
may be described as an example of gossip in the grand style and,
appropriately enough, his style is easy and relaxed and generally conversational in tone. But Thomas Mann has noted an unmistakable
affiliation to the ballad in phraseology and diction and has made the
point that, despite first appearances, the prose of the letters is carefully
chosen and controlled, and that even the most casual of them has an
inner form and discipline.[17]

This in itself makes it a pleasure to browse in Fontane's letters,
quite apart from the treasures that fall in one's lap as one does so. Of
these last there are many that might be listed under various headings.
For example, genius:

> Genius I define thus: *disturbed balance of powers.* Dahse is a gen-
> uine genius, that is, a marvel and a numbskull at the same time.
> This mastery of one specific power at the expense of others makes
> the normal genius. There is to be sure still the abnormal genius,
> whom we should perhaps call real demigods, natures of such uni-
> versal superiority that admiration follows them everywhere, and they
> would have discovered perpetual motion or climbed down from the
> moon on a rope if they were not busy writing ''Hamlet'' or crossing
> the Alps with elephants.[18]

Or his growing misanthropy:

> I am not inimical to people but shy of them and that comes from
> my displeasure with my literary colleagues . . . who seem to be re-
> cruited from rascals. Of course this complaint is an old one, and
> every dying generation has spoken this way, but even so, just as it
> is true that nations change, so do professions. The French, once so
> well-behaved, are now insolent, and the same distinction can be
> applied to the young generation of writers. All modesty is gone from

the world, and in some quarters the atmosphere is such that one might think one was in the gold mines of California.[19]

Or the difficulty of making vacation plans:

If you book for 8 days, you can be sure of being able to stay comfortably in the place in question for 8 weeks or even 18. If, on the other hand, you book for 18 weeks something gets in the way after 18 hours: you get sick, or someone else gets sick, or a prince wants to take you to Italy, or a publisher or a newspaper editor writes that for a report on this or that inaugural or memorial ceremony (location Petersburg or Stockholm) he will pay you, with free travel costs, 1000 Mark. . . . Fate hates it when people plan something in advance.[20]

Or popular songs:

Faucher said to me on an unforgettable day when we went on a pub crawl through half a dozen London taverns and coffee shops, "Yes, there's something odd about the fame of poets. You know, there's that song from the last century: *Und wenn der Große Friedrich kommt Und klopft nur auf die Hosen, Reiß aus die ganze Reichsarmee, Panduren und Franzosen*. Now, what do you think? What kind of a face would old Gleim have made if someone had said to him then, "Yes, *lieber Kanonikus*, when your famous *Grenadier Songs* are forgotten, that *Gassenhauer* will still live!"[21]

Or small gratifications:

The famous niece's wedding—which, I should add, will take place here in Berlin—comes on the 14th, *Polterabend* on the 12th. Everybody is out of sorts and angry at each other. The father of the bride, however, is firm in his belief that the whole affair can be brought into shape with a little bag of *prallinés* and a bouquet of flowers, so that the "genuinely poetic" will come into its own. He may not be wholly wrong. If they can find three reserve lieutenants and there is dancing, everything in the end will dissolve into delight and later generations will speak of the wonderful day, when there was mock turtle soup that nevertheless was "genuine."[22]

Every lover of Fontane has his own favorite list of such gems. In my own, Fontane's description of his first acquaintance with *Parzifal*, in a performance at Bayreuth that he decided at the last moment to forgo, ranks very high.

It is now nine o'clock, and when I think that *Parzifal* will not be over, at the very earliest, for another hour, then I don't know how I would have stood these aeons inside the theater. I heard the overture and, as I left, had a glimpse of the first scene. Then I strolled slowly back to the hotel (quite a distance) and did some reading; and then I went into town and had coffee in the teahouse near the big bridge (across from the garrison) and then for a second time at the much talked-about Sammet's, because I had to have something to do. Then back to the hotel, where I wrote two letters. These I took to the post office and then went for a walk for half an hour. Then I read, back at the hotel again, for a whole hour and then had my supper and tea in my room—*Parzifal*, despite all this, is far from being over. The 1500 who were there today will have to be marvelously healthy people or in three days time—for it's raining and is dead cold—750 of them will have catarrh, diarrhoea, stomach flu, and rheumatism. The impassioned man can withstand anything; for my part, I am almost sad that while traveling, and perhaps at other times too, I have always been a weakling.[23]

There is, of course, much more to be found in the letters than trivia of this sort. They are the best source for information about Fontane's marriage and his family, about his financial problems before he became a successful author, about his many friends from the early days of the Tunnel until those in which he was a leading supporter of modernism in the German theater, about his changing views on German society and culture, his disenchantment with the Prussian aristocracy and his deepening awareness of the frailties of the German bourgeoisie. About politics, as we shall see, they have less to say, but about the greatest man of politics of his age a great deal. In a curious way, Bismarck is the dominating figure in Fontane's letters, with whom he is always in contention, forever seeking to define his historical stature and significance for German life and, above all, to clarify and justify his own feelings about him.

II

Fontane was not allowed to confine his thoughts about the great man to the privacy of his diaries. After 1870, Bismarck's stature was such that his birthdays, and the anniversaries of his greatest achievements, were the subject of official commemoration. When this happened, it was not uncommon for Fontane, as the country's most distinguished writer of ballads, to be called on to crown the occasion with verse.

It cannot be said that the poet took great pleasure in this or that his efforts to meet his obligations are among his best poetry. Fontane was always a virtuoso when it came to writing birthday odes and other *vers d'occasion* for his friends, but he was not comfortable when asked to provide something of the same sort for a public or official ceremony, which, he felt, not only invited the stereotypical but made it all but inevitable. Too much was always expected of the poet in such circumstances. It was one thing for him, in pursuit of his private career, to write a ballad about Marshal Keith or the old Derffling, for his readers had no private commitment to such subjects and, if he did his job right, were likely to be surprised and charmed. But in the case of the chancellor, the same people who always "knew everything better than Bismarck"[24] also knew exactly what kind of poems should be written in his honor and were loud in their disapproval when their standards were not met. Fontane was always reluctant to accept responsibility for such productions, and his doubts before the fact were generally justified.

The two odes written for Bismarck's seventieth birthday in April 1885 suffer from this unease. "Jung-Bismarck," which was published in Paul Lindau's *Nord und Süd*, was apparently intended to accompany a picture of Bismarck in his nineteenth year. It begins with a stanza of such startling triteness that few readers can have felt much inducement to read further:

In Lockenfülle das blonde Haar,
Allzeit im Sattel und neunzehn Jahr,
Im Fluge weltein und nie züruck—
Wer ist dem Reiter nach dem Glück?
    Jung-Bismarck.

[His blond hair in thick locks,
Always in the saddle, nineteen years old,
Rushing ahead and never back,
Who is it that rides after fortune?
        Young Bismarck.]

For those who might want to continue, the poet inquires after the
nature of the Fortune that the youth is pursuing and then—after providing glimpses of Germania at the fountain holding out the full and
empty jars and the coronation at Versailles—concludes with the crash-
ing commonplace that it consists in living and dying for the fatherland.[25]

Fontane himself seems to have felt the inadequacy of this and
composed another poem for the occasion called "Zeus in Mission."
In this, regrettably, he took refuge in discursiveness and jocularity,
telling a story of how the Almighty God looks down upon Germany
in the latter half of the year 1862 and finds it torn and divided and
wasting its energies on worthless causes. To shake it out of this moral
confusion, he commissions Zeus, the father of the Olympian gods, to
go to earth and restore law and order and overthrow all of Germany's
enemies. This Zeus accomplishes, apparently by the simple device of
shaking his brows so that they sound like thunder.

Und war's nicht Donner, waren es Kanonen.
Missunde, Düppel. Hurra, weiter, weiter:
Nußschalen schwimmen auf dem Alsensunde.
Hin über Lippa stürmen die Geschwader,
Ein Knäul von Freund und Feind. Da seht ihn selbst,
Der mit dem Helm ist's und dem Schwefelkragen.
Und Spichern, Wörth und Sedan. Weiter, weiter,
Und durchs Triumphtor triumphierend führt er
All Deutschland in das knirschende Paris.[26]

[But it wasn't thunder, it was cannon.
Missunde, Düppel. Hurrah! Farther, farther!
Boats like nut shells on the Alsen sound.
Up over Lipa storm the squadrons,
A tangle of friend and foe. Look! There he is himself.
The one with the helmet and the sulfur collar.

And Spicheren, Wörth and Sedan! Farther, farther!
And through the gate of triumph triumphantly he leads
All Germany into teeth-gnashing Paris.]

This was no improvement over the earlier poem. The portrayal of Bismarck in the uniform of the Halberstadt Kürassiers, which he had worn during the battle of Königgrätz in 1866, was probably Fontane's way of escaping the necessity of defining his attitude to the Bismarck of more recent years, who, as we shall see, no longer seemed as heroic to him as he once had. But, in any case, as Reuter has written, neither the form of the poem nor the reversion at the end to a kind of patriotic verse that was no longer fashionable was appropriate to the occasion.[27]

The memorial poem ''Where Bismarck Should Lie,' '' written after Bismarck's death at the end of July 1898, with its simple message that the chancellor should be buried in the woods that he loved, is an improvement on the birthday odes, although weakened by its mythological trappings and the appearance of Widukind as deus ex machina.[28] In view of all this, one is almost forced to the conclusion that the best of all of the Bismarck poems is one that Fontane wrote in 1892 and called ''Ja, das möcht' ich noch erleben.'' It is about the repetitions in life and the fact that, despite them, there is always something that one would still like to experience.

Hin stirbt alles, ganz geringe
Wird der Wert der ird'schen Dinge;
Doch wie tief herabgestimmt
Auch das Wünschen Abschied nimmt,
Immer klingt es noch daneben:
Ja, das möcht' ich noch erleben.

[Everything dies away. Insignificant
Is the value of earthly things.
And yet, although my capacity for wishing
Diminishes in deep depression,
There is always an accompanying thought:
Yes! I would still like to find out about that.]

And chief among those desiderata, he admits in the poem's first lines, are those political surprises that he has enjoyed through the years.

Eigentlich ist mir alles gleich,
Der eine wird arm. der andre wird reich,
Aber mit Bismarck—was wird das noch geben?
Das mit Bismarck, das möcht' ich noch erleben.[29]

[Everything is really all the same to me.
One person becomes poor; the other rich.
But with Bismarck—what's going to come out of that?
That business about Bismarck—I'd still like to find out about
    that.]

This, of course, is a poem not about Bismarck but about Fontane.

III

At Eastertide in 1871 Fontane set off to northern France and Alsace
to complete the trip that had been interrupted by his apprehension by
francs-tireurs the previous October. In the train from Strassburg to
Saverne (which had just been renamed Zabern), he fell into conversation with an elderly man in a pepper-and-salt suit who seemed to
him at first from his appearance and accent to be a Swabian land-
owner. The versatility of his conversation and the penetration of his
remarks about art and literature hinted, however, at something more
than that, and Fontane could not resist introducing himself, whereupon
he learned that his fellow traveler was Friedrich Theodor Vischer,
author of *Kritische Gänge* and *Aesthetik, oder Wissensschaft des Schö-
nen* and professor at Zurich and Tübingen.

   In the two days that followed, the two men canvassed many subjects and, naturally, did not neglect the tremendous changes taking
place in France and Germany. Vischer said that he hated all particularism, especially that of the Guelfs, and had an unconditional passion
for the year 1870 and the building up of the German Reich. It was
only the architect who displeased him. "It pains me that it should be
precisely Bismarck who succeeded. I wrote recently that Germany,
after the German Michel had wooed her in vain with his songs, fell
finally to the boldness of a Prussian Junker. He grabbed and had her.''

"Let us assume," [Fontane] said laughing, "that it will turn out with Germany as it did with the Sabine women. They were thoroughly happy—and Romans were born."[30]

In the years after 1871, Bismarck was widely regarded as the man without whom the *Reichsgründung* would have been inconceivable, the hero of the hour whose name was on everyone's lips. He was also, because little known or understood, a figure of mystery, an incalculable force in politics, and hence a source, to the old ruling class, the professions, and the propertied, of speculation, controversy, suspicion, even apprehension. Fontane's conversation with Friedrich Theodor Vischer was certainly not the first or the last that he had that illustrated the way in which the chancellor's name divided the spirits, and as his mind turned to what became his Berlin novels, he conceived the idea of introducing Bismarck into them, not in the flesh, as an actual person, reacting with the other characters in the story, but as someone who, though never seen, always there. Much later, he wrote to Maximilian Harden, "In nearly everything that I have written since 1870, 'the Sulphur-Yellow [*der Schwefelgelbe*]' goes around and, although the conversation touches him only fleetingly, the talk is always of him as of Charles or Otto the Great."[31]

As a literary device, this had great advantages. It was an effective and economical way of giving the novels contemporaneity and verisimilitude and of demonstrating, as part of their general setting, an important psychological characteristic of the years after the founding of the Reich, namely, the strong influence of the chancellor's personality and policies upon Germans of all classes, leading many of them to try to imitate what they admired in him. Both Van der Straaten in *L'Adultera* and Treibel in *Frau Jenny Treibel* have marked Bismarck traits, which they cultivate. Moreover, what the characters in the novels have to say about Bismarck and his policies proved to be an excellent means of defining their personalities and interests and prejudices, thus advancing the story while allowing the author to remain relatively detached.

The first example of this is *L'Adultera*, which is set in the mid-1870s, at the height of the postwar speculative boom, the Prussian government's attack on Roman Catholicism, and the war scare with France. In this first, and not entirely successful, of his Berlin novels,

Fontane's concern was with the element of play (*Spiel*), in the double sense of gambling and unserious behavior, and the problem of originality and integrity in a society that preferred copies or types. He used the topos Bismarck to place these themes before his readers. At a dinner party in the Van der Straaten home, the host, a businessman who has profited richly from the boom times of the first postwar years, offers to make a wager with his brother-in-law, who is a member of the Prussian General Staff corps, that there will be a war, presumably with France, within two months. His brother-in-law replies calmly that this is highly unlikely and that the only problem his colleagues are studying at the moment is the likely theater of a purely hypothetical war between Great Britain and Russia. One of the other guests, a police councilor, supports the *Generalstäbler* by bringing Bismarck's name into play. The chancellor, he says, is too good a judge of risks to think of war in current circumstances. Having risked everything on three different occasions, in 1864, 1866, and 1870, and won each time, he would hardly be likely to play the *six-le-va*.

This is hotly contested by a retired counselor of legation, Baron Duquede, who mounts a remarkable attack upon the chancellor as a highly overrated man whose tremendous success is driving him toward new risks and encouraging a dangerous hero cult in the country.

> Yes, my friend, we have the hero cult. . . . statues and monuments are already there, and the temple will come. And his likeness will be in this temple, with the goddess Fortune at his feet. But it won't be called the Temple of Fortune, but the Temple of Luck. . . . Everything is gambling and luck, with no trace of enlightenment, of thought, or above all of great creative ideas.

He accuses Bismarck of professing, under the guise of conservatism, a revolutionary radicalism and of being "a Ghengis Khan" who operates with ideas that he has looted from others. "I warn you against being deceived," the baron cries, "and above all against over-estimation of this false knight, this crusader of luck, in whom the stupid mob believes because he has driven the Jesuits out of the land. And how does it stand with that? We are rid of the evil ones, but the Evil One remains."[32]

Duquede is encouraged by his host who, although a Bismarck admirer himself, has too much of the Berliner's delight in pulling down the great to come to the chancellor's defense. But the discussion shifts to other subjects, leaving the themes of gambling and imitation in the air, to play their part out in the plot.

In the novel *Cécile*, the same device is used to give a temporal setting to the story and to the nature of the society in which the heroine, the former mistress of a royal personage, is now forced to live, a *fronde* of the resentful naysayers in a world that has left them behind. Here, once more at a dinner party, a *Geheimrat* Hedemeyer, a former official in the Ministry of Culture who, despite strenuous efforts to ingratiate himself with the new minister Adalbert Falk by his pamphlets against the Catholic Church, has not managed to regain his position, vents his spite upon Bismarck. The chancellor, he declares, with an incoherent rage that arouses the delight of his reactionary tablemates, is "a Dalai-Lama" who requires veneration of all his ideas (like his religious policy, which, he insists, has no consistency and will result in the victory of Rome). He is also "an Omnipotenz" who is intent on stamping out all freedom of opinion, as is shown by his recent dismissal and persecution of the ambassador in Paris, Count Harry Arnim, who disagreed with his policy toward France.[33]

The Arnim case is raised again in *Irrungen, Wirrungen*, in a scene of great comic force, in which the protagonist, Baron Botho von Rienäcker, a lieutenant in the Kaiser Cürassiers stationed in Berlin, is faced with the necessity of having lunch at the famous restaurant Hiller with his uncle from the provinces, a man of decidedly conservative views. He invites a friend named Wedel, a lieutenant of the Dragoon Guards, to join them, hoping in this way to prevent the conversation from taking an undesirable turn. The plan does not work. A chance remark of Botho's is interpreted by his uncle as being a slur against his former Rittmeister, Edwin von Manteuffel, later chief of the Military Cabinet and an opponent of Bismarck, and this is enough to elicit from him an apoplectic assault upon the chancellor as a "pen-pusher [*Federfuchser*]." "But pen-pushers" he says, "didn't make Prussia great. Was the victor at Fehrbellin a pen-pusher? Was the victor at Leuthen a pen-pusher? Was Blücher a pen-pusher or Yorck? Here sits the Prussian pen. I can't stand this cult!"

When Both gets him quieted down, his uncle addresses himself to Wedel and asks his opinion of Bismarck's treatment of Harry Arnim. Tactfully Wedel suggests that in matters of high politics, the weaker party is well advised not to try to cross the plans of the stronger. Unless, he adds, his motives are completely pure and his convictions noble, in which he has a duty to take a stand of his own. But this was not true in the case of Arnim. This answer impresses the uncle, and he says that it will impress his pastor at home, and that leads him to draw Botho into a discussion of problems there and to raise the very question Botho had hoped to avoid, the family expectation that he will make up his mind to marry the rich cousin who is waiting for his proposal. He puts the matter so urgently that Botho realizes that his idyllic affair with Lene, a girl from the people, must now come to an end.[34]

Most of the people in Fontane's novels who talk about Bismarck are critical of him (the exception is Instettin in *Effi Briest*, who works for him and admires him), and his figure seems to invite historical comparison with tyrants and violent men. Baron Duquede thinks of him as a Ghenghis Khan, *Geheimrat* Hedemeyer as a Dalai Lama; the old general in *Die Poggenpuhls*, taken to the theater to see a performance of Ernst von Wildenbruch's *Die Quitzows*, thinks immediately of Bismarck as he watches the story of the great rebel chief Dietrich von Quitzow unfold, and he says so during the pause to his nephew, not without attracting the attention of other patrons. "Remarkable! Just like Bismarck! And in addition, as fate would have it, born next door to each other. I think you could shoot from Schönhausen to Quitzövel with an air rifle, and a rural post man could get there in a morning. Wonderful region, the country there; the land of the Langobards. Yes, where it sits, there it sits. What do you think, Leo?"[35]

Bismarck has a final incarnation in Fontane's last novel, *Der Stechlin*, in a conversation between old Dubslav Stechlin and Count Barby that takes place after the death of Emperor Frederick III. Barby argues that, but for his fatal illness, the emperor would have been successful in inaugurating a liberal era in Germany. Dubslav expresses the strongest doubt, arguing that the Junkers would have prevented this.

It seems to me as if our blessed Quitzows have risen once more from the grave. And when that happens, when our people think about things that they have not thought about for four hundred years, then something can happen. People always say, ''Impossible!'' Bah, what is impossible? Nothing is impossible. Who would have said before the 18th of March that the 18th of March was possible, possible in this true and unadulterated philistine nest Berlin? Everything has its turn one time or another, and that should not be forgotten. And the army! *Nun ja*. Who will say anything against the army? But every successful general is always a danger. And, given the circumstances, others too. Think of the old Sachsenwalder, our civilian Wallenstein. God knows what he would have done in the end.

"And you believe," interjected the Count, "that Emperor Frederick would have failed at this sharp Quitzow corner?"

"I think so."[36]

IV

How much of this, if any, represented Fontane's own thinking about Bismarck? Probably very little, since these were fictional figures whose opinions depended upon their roles in the novels. But what were Fontane's own views of the political issues that moved his characters so strongly? This is not easy to determine, because he has left us little to go on.

It is difficult, for example, to discover what Fontane thought about the chancellor's policies during the decade of the 1870s. About the *Kulturkampf*, which Bismarck himself, in a speech in the Prussian Chamber of Peers in March 1873, declared to be an example of ''the age-old struggle for power, as old as the human race itself, between kingship and the priestly caste,''[37] there is, apart from a fleeting reference to the new Prussian School Law,[38] nothing in the letters, and we learn no more about Fontane's views about this conflict and its effects than we do from the references to it in the novels. The same is true concerning Bismarck's efforts to destroy social democracy, which were to have profound effects upon German politics until the chancellor's dismissal in 1890. In June 1878, to be sure, in a letter to his wife, Fontane expressed doubts whether any campaign of the sort could succeed, pointing out:

Millions of workers are as clever, as educated and as honorable as the aristocracy and the middle class, often superior to them. . . . All of these people are completely equal to us and therefore it is impossible to prove that "they are insignificant" or that we have to deal with them with weapons in hand. They don't represent only disorder and insurrection; they represent *ideas*, which are in part justified and can't be beaten to death or dispelled from the world by imprisonment. They have to be fought by intellectual means and, as things stand, that is very difficult.[39]

This is a sensible view, but it is not one that Bismarck chose to accept. Why, then, did Fontane not come back to it as the antisocialist policy was elaborated? For the fact is that he didn't.

Perhaps part of the answer is that Fontane's interest in politics was always sporadic and never marked by consistency. He had, after all, other things to do, and during the 1870s his intellectual resources were absorbed by his labors on the last of the war books and his plans for his first novel. But it may also be that he never felt comfortable when his views opposed those of Bismarck, whom he regarded as a hero and as the historical figure of his age and hence entitled to a certain freedom from criticism. Commenting on a remark of Menzel's to the effect that someone "didn't have enough *Grütze* in her pot," Fontane once wrote that whether this was a permissible remark depended on Menzel's stature. If he was merely a good painter, then he shouldn't say it, but if he were "of the very first rank, an epoch-making Number 1, a nonpareil," then he *ought* to say it. "It's like our Reich chancellor, he went on. "If his name were Schnökel or Hasemann, then he would have to heed the president's bell, but if his name is Bismarck, he doesn't have to do so."[40]

Elaborating on this idea in March 1881, when Bismarck forced Count Botho von Eulenburg, the Prussian minister of the interior, out of office, Fontane wrote:

Bismarck is a despot, but he has a right to be one, and he *must* be one. If he were not, if he were an ideal parliamentarian, who allowed his course to be determined by the most stupid thing there is, by parliamentary majorities, then we wouldn't have a chancellor at all, and least of all a German Reich. It is true on the other hand, of course, that under such a despot only dependent natures and powers of the second and third rank can serve, and that any free man will do well at times to resign. In doing that, the free man does what is right for him, but the chancellor *also* does what is right for him when he doesn't allow that to cause confusion in his action or inaction.[41]

This is hardly a model of political ratiocination, and it doesn't say much for the depth of Fontane's faith in democratic institutions; but it does show that ten years after the unification of Germany Fontane was perfectly happy in leaving the direction of national politics in the hands of the man he considered to have been the founder of the Reich. "When he sneezes or says *Prosit*," he wrote a little later, "I find it more interesting that the spoken wisdom of six Progressives."[42]

At the same time, however, he was troubled by the fact that the chancellor's authority was being eroded not by his politics but by faults of character, and particularly by his tendency to suspect associates and coworkers. His once enormous popularity was receding, he wrote in April 1881, and people were beginning to say that he was "a great genius but a small man."[43] As Bismarck became more irascible in the treatment of his political opponents, Fontane began to revise his earlier view about the appropriateness of his despotic behavior. One had the feeling, he wrote in 1887, "that he believes he is permitted to do anything, like a god, and he operates on [Paul] Lindau's principle that a kick from the Duke of Ratibor is better than a kiss from Bleichröder."[44]

Even so, as Germany moved into the confusion and tragedy of the year of the three emperors, and it became clear to any detached observer that Bismarck's term of office was now nearing its end, Fontane almost instinctively rallied to his side. When a liberal newspaper speculated about the chancellor's diminished position under the new emperor Frederick III, he exploded with rage and wrote to his daughter: "After the greatest *political* achievement in a millennium (for Frederick's was smaller and Napoleon's more fleeting) to have to be told by a Jewish rascal, behind whom unfortunately many, many stand: He was only a 'servant' and can, if he is nice and polite, remain in his *servant's* position. Unheard of! Frightful! . . . Now they will all creep out of their swamps and holes and make their monkey business with him and tell him that it serves him right!"[45] The campaign that was conducted against Bismarck in court circles at the end of Frederick's short reign and more strenuously after the accession of William

II, he found demeaning, and he wrote to his friend Georg Friedländer that "at the last" he stood wholly on Bismarck's side and wished only that he would go to the Reichstag and confound his enemies by making "one of those speeches that in a flash run round the equator."[46] He remained, he wrote, *"trotz alledem und alledem,"* one of the chancellor's "most enthusiastic admirers."[47]

The differences between Bismarck and the young emperor soon proved to be unbridgeable, and the chancellor went into retirement on 29 March 1890, being followed to the railroad station by what seemed to be all of Berlin. His departure robbed Fontane of one of the keenest pleasures of his old age, reading (or having his wife read to him) the chancellor's speeches in the Reichstag.[48] At a more serious level, it deprived him of the element that gave his world significance, the "great man," as Jacob Burckhardt had once defined him, the one "without whom the world seems to us to be incomplete, because great achievements were possible within his time and context only through him and are otherwise unthinkable, [for] he is (essentially) interwoven with the (great) mainstream of cause and effect."[49] The loss made it seem necessary to Fontane to find an explanation for Bismarck's departure that would make it tolerable, and this led him to become ever more persuaded that the explanation was to be found "not in his political mistakes—which are in fact, as long as things are in flux, very difficult to determine—but in his failings of character. This giant had something petty in his nature, and because it was perceived it caused his fall."[50]

In the years that followed, Fontane never stopped wrestling with the problem and elaborating on Bismarck's characterological flaws. In 1891 he explained to his friend Friedländer that Bismarck's basic fault was a lack of noble-mindedness, which in the end took the "hateful form of the pettiest spitefulness" and would have destroyed him sooner if it had not been accompanied by his "infernal humor."[51] Later, to the same correspondent, he described Bismarck as a kind of Wallenstein, who made public professions of fealty to the emperor, but privately described the loyalty principle as *"Mumpitz."*[52] Still later, he saw the old Sachsenwalder in a series of contrasting roles that canceled each other out: *"Übermensch* and artful dodger," "state-founder and refuser to pay taxes on his stables," "hero and

cry-baby.''[53] The zeal that he showed in discovering ever new illus-
trations of his theme suggest that he was attempting to establish for
himself a position that was more detached than his early enthusiasm
for the chancellor. Thus, on Bismarck's birthday in 1895, he wrote
that such flaws ''fill me with mixed feelings and do not allow me to
experience a pure bright admiration. Something is missing in him, and
precisely that quality that lends greatness. The Jew Neumann across
from us has not put any flags out, and arm in arm with Neumann I
usher my century out the gate.''[54] Two years later, almost to the day,
he wrote, ''I am no *Bismarckianer*; the last and best in me turns away
from him; he does not have a noble nature.''[55]

That sounds unconditional enough to be convincing, and perhaps
it would be, if it were not accompanied in the same letter by a defense
of Bismarck against attempts by the emperor and his entourage to
diminish the old man's achievement. Bismarck had played too great
a role in Fontane's life to permit him to suffer detractors lightly, and
even the repetition of criticisms that he himself had made was enough
to make Fontane rush to his defense. On such occasions, his position
was both illogical and clear: ''Bismarck is being criticized around and
about (by me too); but he remains Bismarck, and that is exactly
enough.''[56]

Heinrich Mann once wrote: ''The person who appears and reap-
pears in Fontane's works and letters and poems is his contemporary
Bismarck. He sees him in his greatness and smallness; he knows more
about him than anyone since then can know.''[57] This is too overstated
to be taken seriously. We can judge Fontane's knowledge of Bismarck
only by what he wrote about him, and many aspects of the chancellor's life and work did not attract his consistent attention. It remains
a great pity, for example, that he does not seem to have reflected upon
what Bismarck's long tenure of office would mean for the next generation of Germans. It never occurred to him that they might be the
ones to pay for Bismarck's sins of commission and omission, for his
failure to train competent successors in the field of foreign affairs, for
example, and for his persistence in maintaining an anachronistic political system in which he had sought—in the case of liberalism with
success—to stifle every progressive tendency. Fontane was interested
in every facet of Bismarck's personality but hardly at all in the nature

of his political system. Because of that, his attempts to define the nature and limits of the chancellor's greatness were always unsatisfactory.

Which is not to say, of course, that the relationship between the two men is not fascinating in its own right.

6

Theater

Fontane's long and successful career as a theater critic came about
almost inadvertently. It was not something sought after and planned
for, but rather originated in his growing dissatisfaction with his position as a staff member of the *Kreuzzeitung*. He had long been exasperated by the way in which the editors of that publication constantly paraded their Christian principles while at the same time
refusing to take any responsibility for their employees' economic well-
being, particularly in time of sickness or old age. He became increasingly convinced that, if he were ever to be secure, he must become
so as a free writer, and in December 1869, taking advantage of his
wife's absence in London to make a decision that she would certainly
have opposed, he terminated his relationship with the paper.[1]

He was counting on a substantial income from the third volume
of the *Wanderings* and the war books, which would be supplemented,
he hoped, by the royalties from the novel he had long been planning
and was sure that he could write quickly. It soon became clear that

these hopes were exaggerated, and Fontane was fortunate when the *Vossische Zeitung*'s theater critic, the 84-year-old-Friedrich Wilhelm Gubitz, suddenly died, and the newspaper's editors asked him to take over his duties in the Royal Theater in the Gendarmenmarkt. He accepted with alacrity. It was a respected position, for ''the old Gubitz'' had been a man of great civic courage who had played an honorable part in Berlin politics since the days of the French occupation, and his articles on theater were widely popular. This could not help but benefit his successor, while at the same time alleviating his financial situation.[2]

Although some people may have been surprised by the appointment, no one was prepared to question Fontane's qualifications, He was by no means the *''Theater Fremdling''* that the actor Theodor Döring, making a play on the initials with which Fontane signed his reviews, called him in a moment of pique.[3] He had always been interested in the theater, and in 1848, as we have seen, he had begun to write a revolutionary drama based on the struggle between Charles I of England and Cromwell, giving it up only when technical difficulties proved too difficult for him to resolve. He was well-read in the German classics and particularly in Shakespeare, and while he was in England in the 1850s he had sent home articles on the English popular theater that included shrewd comparisons between English style and practice and prevailing modes in Germany.[4] He was familiar also with the history of the theater in Berlin, and in his novel *Schach von Wuthenow* he was to use a real theater scandal of the year 1806, the outrage caused by the performance of Zacharias Werner's play *Die Weihe der Kraft*, with A. W. Iffland playing the part of Luther[5]— the first time that the Reformer had ever been shown on the German stage—to illustrate the febrile atmosphere of Berlin on the eve of the battle of Jena.

In addition, Fontane believed in the importance of the critic's task and in his own ability to fulfill it. If the theater was a moral institute, as Schiller had said, then the critic's role was to see that its capabilities were not trifled away or corrupted in performance. He was, he thought, well prepared to do that. After a review of Gutzkow's *Uriel Acosta* in 1873, Fontane wrote to a correspondent who thought he had been too severe:

My justification for my *mètier* rests on something that heaven be-
stowed upon me in my cradle: sensibility with respect to artistic
things. In this quality of mine I have a firm belief. If this were not
true, I should have laid down my pen as a critic a long time ago. I
have an unconditional confidence in the rightness of my feeling.
That sounds a bit strong, but I have it and must admit it, however
the confession sounds. . . . At the same time, I know that I am
wholly free from veneration of names or the cult of literary heroes.
I believe in the rightness of my feelings, but the attempt afterwards
to explain them, so that a ''critique'' results, this attempt must fail
again and again.[6]

This is forthright to the point of immodesty. But if it shows that
Fontane entered upon his new position with a self-confidence that was
perhaps excessive, it also testifies to the inherent honesty in his stance
as a critic. He reviewed everything that came his way, and he told his
readers what he thought about it. He never sought to demonstrate that
his views were justified by a particular aesthetic theory or set of philosophical principles, always maintaining stoutly that he himself was
the theory and the principles. Whatever else it was, this was endearing.
Marcel Reich-Ranicki, himself a distinguished critic, has written:
''Those who bring themselves to make this declaration are much more
honorable than those among their colleagues who invoke a book of
rules that does not and can not exist.''[7]

Fontane's self-confidence, moreover, did not mean that he came
to his conclusions quickly. The contrary was the case. He was aware
that the theater was a world inhabited by people who were passion-
ately committed to their art and highly sensitive to criticism of any
kind, particularly when it came from people who were not members
of their profession. He was aware that this attitude was often carried
to ridiculous extremes, but he admired theater people and was reluctant to wound them by seeming to be unaware of the difficulty under
which they always labored, that of creating illusion in a world that
prided itself on its matter-of-factness. Writing a review was therefore
always a laborious exercise for him, performed behind closed doors
with strict injunctions against any kind of interruption. Visitors who
arrived while he was struggling to find the mot juste were never wel-

come, and were turned away at the entrance by the servant with the words "Sorry. The master has a review today."[8]

I

Before the writing of the review came the observation of the performance, which was made from Parkettplatz No. 23 in the Royal Theater on the Gendarmenplatz. Late in life, Fontane explained that this was no ordinary theater seat but a kind of annex built into the corner between the proscenium and parquet loges, sticking out into the aisle, so that the occupant's knees were always being bumped.

> Worst of all was the separateness. Anyone with a high opinion of himself could feel happy about being the object of attention, but to anyone who lacked this feeling it was unpleasant. For people who were vain, No. 23 was a curule chair; for the those who were not, it was a criminal's bench. For one should not think of a theater critic as a judge; all too often, he is a defendant. "There he sits again, that monster!" I have often read in their faces.[9]

The house itself recalled the whole tradition of Berlin theater from its beginnings during the reign of Frederick II, when Karl Theophil Doebbelin and his greater successor Iffland struggled to found a theater independent of control by the court. It stood where the original French Comedy House had stood in Frederick's time and, after it, the theater built by Langhans in 1802 and known for its presentation of the plays of Kotzebue. The Langhans theater burned to the ground in 1817, after a rehearsal of Schiller's *Die Räuber*, and four years later was replaced by the new house, which was one of the great triumphs of Karl Friedrich Schinkel. The gutting of the Langhans theater had left an awkward void between the two baroque churches that stood at the opposite ends of the Gendarmenmarkt. Schinkel solved the spatial problem by building his new theater in such a way that its wings reached out to these so-called French (Huguenot) and German churches and created a unity with them that is still striking to the visitor today. Gottfried Riemann has written: "Schinkel's genius gave the new theatre an incomparable form, with its broad flight of steps, imposing facade of Ionic columns, the two main and side pediments, and the structural grid system of lateral elevation. It was also the first architecturally significant theatre building to be built in Germany.''[10] As if reminding his contemporaries that first things come first, Crown Prince Frederick William (later King Frederick William IV) said of the *Schauspielhaus,* *"Ein vorzüglicher Bau. Und ist auch ein Theäterchen drin."* (A superb building. And there's also a little theater inside.)[11]

Whatever the quality of the theater in the days of Iffland and Ludwig Devrient and Karl Seydelmann, in Fontane's time there seems to have been a decided falling off in general excellence, so that the royal theater could not be compared with the Burgtheater in Vienna or the Théatre Française in Paris. The Danish critic Georg Brandes, who lived in Berlin from 1877 to 1883, said that it was the kind of ''melancholy peep-show'' that was to be found in any provincial capital. This was not because of a lack of talent among the leading charges, for in Luise Erhartt, Minona Frieb-Blumauer, and Clara Meier the royal theater had a trio of much loved actresses and in the character actor Theodor Döring a player whose Mephistopheles and Shylock left audiences deeply shaken. The fact that its performances were sometimes worse than those in the royal theater in Copenhagen Brandes attributed to its direction,

which wouldn't be tolerated for four weeks in a country where public opinion dared express itself against the crotchets of the monarch. In Germany no one opposes the expressed desire of Emperor William; reason is allowed to be taken captive by obedience. That is why a moth-eaten old courtier, a retired soldier who never smelt powder and at the same time hasn't the slightest glimmering of art, a Herr von Hülsen, whose wife writes feeble *Novellen* under the name Helene, received permission to form the national theater in his image—and there is not the slightest hope of his retirement until death or the emperor brings it on. It is known that no other theater director will replace him as long as the emperor is still alive, and one knows that his rule is one without inspiration. He has understood neither how to establish a repertory nor how to attract actors. Upon them and upon the spectators he has had, as far as understanding art goes, a demoralizing effect.[12]

These jaundiced views were not uninfluenced by Brandes's dislike of the conservative repertoire of the Royal Theater and the absence from it in the first years of the new Reich of plays from France or the Scandinavian countries or new productions of the drama of ancient Greece. To one of his temperament, the playhouse on the Gendarmenmarkt offered a stodgy and unexciting menu. He tended to overlook the fact that it was precisely what the new German bourgeoisie, the cultivated, liberal, patriotic readers of the *Vossische Zeitung* who patronized the Royal Theater, wanted. They expected the theater to provide them with entertainment, as long as it did not offend the rules of decency or morality, but, more important, they wanted to be edified by inspiring interpretations of life and human endeavor and examples of moral virtue, civic courage, and the beautiful and sublime.

The Royal Theater played to this taste with a repertory that was very extensive compared with that of modern theaters. Shakespeare was strongly represented not only by the tragedies but also the perennial favorites *Twelfth Night* and *Midsummer Night's Dream*, the late romance *The Winter's Tale*, and the histories, particularly *Henry IV*, Parts I and II, and *Richard III*, of which there were one hundred performances in Berlin between 1828 and 1887.[13] Shakespeare had, of course, been considered a German classic since the appearance of the Schlegel-Tieck translation at the beginning of the century, so there was no mystery about the regularity with which his dramas appeared on the playbill. Every leading player in the Berlin theater since Seydelmann's time had made his name with Shakespearean roles, and audiences were sophisticated enough to compare Döring's Shylock with that of Dessoir, or with the interpretations by players from other European theaters who, when invited to visit the Royal Theater, would often choose a Shakespearean role for one of their guest appearances, as the famous Italian actor Ernesto Rossi did with *Hamlet* in 1881.

Among the German classics, Schiller held pride of place, with *Kabale und Liebe*, the Wallenstein trilogy, *Maria Stuart*, *Die Raüber*, and—on patriotic occasions—*Wilhelm Tell*, the subject of Fontane's first review for the *Vossische Zeitung* on 18 August 1870 at the height of the war against France.[14] Lessing's *Minna von Barnhelm* and *Emilia Galotti* were played more often than his *Nathan der Weise*, and Goethe's *Egmont* more frequently than any of his other dramas; and Minna, Thekla, and Klärchen were among the favorite roles for visiting actresses throughout Fontane's tenure as critic.[15] Performances of Kleist's best play were rare, because the sight of the prince pleading for his life seemed vaguely unpatriotic and offended the sensibilities of male members of the audience, who had therefore to put up with the peasant humor of *Der zerbrochene Krug*. Grillparzer was represented chiefly by *Des Meeres und der Liebe Wellen* and *Medea*.

A large part of the repertory was given over to portraits of contemporary society in which the comic muse was more strongly represented than the tragic. Among these the plays of Charlotte Birch-Pfeiffer and Roderich Benedix were most successful in maintaining their popularity throughout the whole period. A member of the Munich court theater company at the age of thirteen, Charlotte Pfeiffer had toured Europe when she was in her twenties in such roles as Phédre, Medea, Lady Macbeth, and Mary Stuart. After her marriage in 1825, her husband, a Dr. Birch from Copenhagen, discovered that she had a remarkable talent for writing plays that were derivative of foreign models but exciting, sentimental, invincibly moral, always in the best of taste, and—not the least important—well constructed, so that all of the problems of the plot were resolved before the final curtain.[16] Six of her plays remained in the Royal Theater's repertory throughout the 1870s and 1880s, the most frequently played being *Die Waise von Lowood* (1856), based on the novel *Jane Eyre*, and *Die Grille* (1856), based on Georges Sand's *La Petite Fadette*.

Even more popular than Birch-Pfeiffer was Roderich Benedix, who went on the stage at the age of twenty and was director of the city theater in Frankfurt am Main from 1855 to 1859 and in Cologne and Leipzig from then until his death in 1873. Benedix wrote more than one hundred plays, most of them lighthearted comedies, which were as skillful in portraying German middle-class life in all its nuances as the plays of Scribe and Dumas were in doing the same for France. Plays like *Der Störenfried* and *Aschenbrödl* found their natural setting in the Royal Theater, where they were played to perfection by Harry Liedtke, much loved for his "uncle from America" roles and the veterans Döring and Frieb-Blomeyer.

It was not surprising, finally, given the ebullient nationalism of Germany in the 1870s and the distinction and high readability of historians like Ranke, Droysen, Mommsen, Burckhardt, and Treitschke, that much of the repertory of the Royal Theater should be given over to patriotic pieces and plays with historical settings. The victory over France inspired Karl Gutzkow's last play, *Der Gefangene von Metz* (1871), Paul Heyse's *Kolberg* (1871), about the war of liberation against Napoleon, and Karl Koberstein's *Um Nancy* (1873), about the defeat of Richelieu's intrigues against Lorraine during the Thirty Years War; and it probably explains the popularity of Hans Herrig's *Konradin* (1884), which dealt with the murder of Conrad of Hohenstaufen by the French in Naples in 1354. The history of the Hohenzollern dynasty and of the Prussian past also attracted more attention in the theater now than before 1870, and became the specialty not only of the prolific Gustav von Putlitz, the author of *Das Testament des Grossen Kurfürst*, which was written in 1859 but performed frequently in Fontane's time, and *Die Unterschrift des Königs*, but also of Ernst von Wildenbruch, whose play *Die Quitzows*, about the great robber barons whose reign of terror in Mark Brandenburg was suppressed by Frederick of Hohenzollern in the fifteenth entury, had a sensational success in 1888.

But the interest in historical plays was not limited by patriotic feeling. This was a period in which audiences trooped to see new plays about remote figures like the emperor Tiberius, about whom Julius Grosse wrote a tragedy in 1878. Gustav von Putlitz was perhaps best known for his Hohenzollern plays, but he also wrote one about English history, *Wilhelm von Oranien in Whitehall*, and another called *Don Juan de Austria*. Heinrich Laube, whose play about Schiller, *Die Karlsschüler* (1846), was still in the repertory in the 1870s and 1880s, had his greatest success with *Graf Essex* (1856) about the reign of Queen Elizabeth of England. And the playgoer who wished to enjoy dramatic action while at the same time adding to his knowledge of the past had many other choices, among them Albert Lindner's *Brutus und Collatinus* (1879), Ernst von Wildenbruch's *Die Carolinger* (1883), Richard Voss's *Der Mohr des Zaren* (1884), about the court of Peter I, Rudolf Gottschall's *Pitt und Fox* (1874), and two plays that always found enthusiastic audiences: Ernst Brachvogel's *Narziß*

(1857), about Madame de Pompadour and the French Revolution, and Karl Gutzkow's *Uriel Acosta* (1846), a tragedy about the struggle between free-thinkers and Orthodox Jews in the seventeenth century.

This was varied enough stuff for the most fastidious theatergoer, and challenging enough for the most dedicated reviewer.

II

One of the most fascinating aspects of Fontane's work as a critic was his relationship with his audience. From the very beginning of his work, he was acutely aware of the kind of people who were sitting around him, watching what he was watching. He knew their cultural values and pretensions, their petty prejudices and hypocrisies, the themes that pleased them and those that offended them or made them uncomfortable, and their tendency to read into the dramas they saw what they wanted to find there. He felt that it was his duty as a critic to correct them when he thought they were wrong, but he knew that he could not, without alienating them, do this too directly, by lecturing them or belittling their ideas. He therefore decided to accomplish his purpose by taking his audience into his confidence, by talking not at them, but with them, in the gossipy tone (*Plauderton*) for which he became famous, and by telling them stories that might amuse them and lead them indirectly to the point he was attempting to make. This gradually became the very heart of his reviewing technique and the key to his great popularity even with readers who did not share his basic ideas.

Many examples might be cited to illustrate this method. In 1881 he began a review of Gustav von Putlitz's *Die Idealisten* by recalling Albertus Magnus's great work *The World of Animals*, which has a chapter entitled "On Owls in Iceland," the contents of which comprise a single sentence: "There are no owls in Iceland." This raised the question, he continued, of whether there were any idealists in Putlitz's play, and this could be answered only by trying to define what an idealist was. Obviously, there were all sorts of idealists, particularly in Germany, and it might help to tell the story of one of them.

The idealist in question had in fact, as if to legitimize himself, written a philosophical book, and he offered it to a well-known publisher, who had been a friend of his since his youth and with whom
he was in fact on a *du*-basis. The publisher addressed himself to the
matter, and the following conversation followed between the two.
Publisher: "Well, dear Fritz, I will take your book, and I am happy
to say that I can offer you an honorarium of one hundred thaler."
Idealist: "My dear William, please don't think of that. That is a
matter of no importance to me. I was exclusively concerned with
[elaborating] a particular idea—." *Publisher*: "No, no. A hundred
thaler." And here the conversation broke off, and both friends took
seats in a horse-tram, since they were going the same way. A deep
silence reigned, and nothing was to be heard but the rustle of the
tickets or, now and then, a shrill tone as their corners were torn off.
The idealist chose this very moment of absolute silence, perhaps
under the impression of its solemnity, to resume the conversation
that had been ended ten minutes before. He leaned forward and said
quietly, "*Gold*, my dear William?" "No, *face value*," he answered.

In this story, he added, "We have our German idealist from top to
toe. Thank God he is dying out more and more, and only in this latest
Putlitz piece do we have a prime example." He didn't like him, or
the play about him, and his readers shouldn't either, for reasons he
proceeded to elaborate.[17]

Here, if you will, is an example of the kind of ingratiation of
which Fontane was such a master, intended to break down his audience's defenses and then to confront them with the unsettling thought
that a lot of what they themselves, and the German middle class in
general, smugly regarded as idealism was nothing more or less than
self-interest. He was to make the same point, of course, in his novel
Frau Jenny Treibel.

A different form of ingratiation was his use of what one critic has
called "extra-literary referentiality" to supply his readers with com-
parative data that would help them understand his critical judgments.[18]
He once wrote that to say of an actor, "The Bolingbroke of Herr X
lacked a courtly demeanor" was too imprecise to have much meaning
to the ordinary reader. "If, however, I write with conviction, 'His
Bolingbroke displayed the traits of a country councillor from New

Pomerania' or 'of a cavalry captain from the cuirassier regiment Emperor Nicholas of Russia,' then I present something concrete and with one stroke let the reader know how well or how poorly yesterday's guest presented Bolingbroke.''[19]

From the very beginning of his career as a critic, Fontane set himself the task of persuading his audience to think and not merely to go on repeating what they had been told they ought to think. He did this with an impressive degree of conviction, made all the more persuasive by the rhetorical construction of his argument. On 9 May 1874—to take a single example—there was a performance of *Iphigenie auf Tauris* in the Royal Theater, with Luise Erhartt in the title role and Gustav Karl Berndal, an enormosly versatile actor, particularly in classical roles,[20] as Thoas. Erhartt received fourteen curtain calls at the end of the performance, in what was clearly a triumph for the actress. Amid this enthusiasm, Fontane was a lonely dissenter. Although an admirer of Erhartt for her portrayals of Klärchen, Lady Milford, and Madame de Pompadour, roles which he said she understood, she had in his view no similar understanding of Iphigenie, and her interpretation was a failure from start to finish, too theatrical, too trivial, and showing no deep penetration into the spirit of the text. The performance as a whole was empty and melancholy, and the cast seemed to be oppressed by this atmosphere. Even Berndal, "who is always otherwise in form and does equal justice both to small roles and great ones, showed signs of endless boredom. I cannot blame him."

He didn't like to say all this, Fontane wrote. It hurt people's feelings, and, worse than that, it didn't do any good. *Iphigenie auf Tauris* was an acknowledged classic, and it would come back in the same form, and Erhartt would receive fourteen curtain calls again, and he would once again write what he was writing now and, for his pains, be attacked for being a hateful naysayer or defended with forced chivalry by a couple of honest men who would seek to rehabilitate him by quoting the well-known epitaph of Heine's *Atta Troll*,

Sehr schlecht tanzend, doch Gesinnung
Tragend in der zott'gen Hochbrust;
Manchmal auch gestunken habend;
Kein Talent, doch ein Charakter.

[Dancing very badly, but carrying
Conviction in its shaggy breast,
Many a time, stinking a bit,
No talent, but a character.]

People regard such *Iphigenie* evenings as a kind of religious service, Fontane wrote, and a deceased friend had seriously proposed that
modern Germans should be morally inspired, and ethically and aesthetically educated, on the basis of *Nathan der Weise*, *Faust*, and
Iphigenie. That would be all right with him, but if that was to happen
then the machinery that presented these works would have to change
radically. In a marvelous conclusion to his review Fontane wrote:

> What we experienced on Sunday evening is considerably inferior to
> an afternoon sermon, even from the standpoint of *entertainment*. I
> have the habit, now and then, at about six o'clock in the evening,
> of going into one of the old Gothic churches in our city, the name
> is not important. The assembled congregation generally consists of
> ten hospital nurses and twenty female orphans, behind whose blue-
> aproned front line sit six or seven castaways, like me, who come
> because they like it. Once, hidden behind a pillar, I saw a man
> crying, which shook me more than three acts of tragedy. First, usu-
> ally, there is singing, if you can call it that; then an apprentice cler-
> gyman steps up and delivers something that he has learned by heart.
> The gas lights burn only in a small circle around the pulpit. Every-
> thing else is in half darkness. The green curtains before the high
> Gothic windows move quietly in the draught, and the pillars grow
> ever higher and higher and lose themselves upwards as in a gray
> cloud. Meanwhile the word flows on peacefully. The women sleep,
> the children giggle; among all this comes a Bible saying or a quo-
> tation from Luther and falls into my heart, rousing me. Those are
> afternoon sermons. How far, far away from that was the *Iphigenie*
> worship on last Sunday evening."[21]

II

Fontane was always at his best when reviewing Shakespeare. His love
for the great Englishman had been deep and unwavering since his

London days, when he saw every Shakespearean performance that he could find and—apparently to deepen his own understanding—made a translation of *Hamlet*. It was thanks to this and to his feel, not only for the poet's astonishing ability to put into words the psychology of a mood or the motivation of an action, but even more for Shakespeare's theatricality which resulted from the way in which logic and necessity shaped and gave form to his dramas, that Fontane's Berlin audiences could always expect not merely an evaluation of the players' performances but also a critique of their success in revealing the true meaning of the play.

Thus, in a remarkable review of a performance of *Henry IV*, Part I, on 17 November 1877, he wrote that play had had "its traditional fate with us," having made the audience laugh for the first three acts and then boring them to death during the last two. The reason for this, Fontane suggested, was that the poetic side of chivalry had become unplayable for modern actors. They could hope to be successful only when they caricatured it or emphasized the bombastic aspects of war, for that allowed them a degree of condescension. The key to overcoming this difficulty, and the awkwardness of the play in general, was, Fontane argued, the part of Henry Percy, with his tremendous energy and color and his variation of mood from the chivalric to the commonsensical: "His is in a certain sense the most important role in the play. Through the tone it sets, it is, even more than that of the Prince, the means of mediation between the humorous-genre scenes and the historical ones and, if it is not in the best hands, it has the effect of causing the last two acts to become almost bare and empty."[22]

Similarly, in a review of the play's sequel, Fontane explained the apparent discontinuations between the two plays by pointing out that Falstaff cannot be expected always to be funny or to be funny in the same way. Time passes and makes subtle changes in character and mood and desire, and this has the effect of changing the relations between the characters. This is what had happens between the two parts of *Henry IV*; time exacts its toll. Anyone who wished simply to be amused by Part II would find what he wanted in Justice Shallow, Doll Tearsheet, and the Ancient Pistol, but an understanding of the play depended upon an appreciation of the deep changes in Falstaff.[23]

Fontane's standards of performance were always high, and particularly in Shakespeare he insisted that the players think deeply about the kind of people they were portraying. After a performance of *Macbeth* in December 1879, he complained that the second act, in which the king was murdered, was badly played by all participants, except the rain, which beat against the walls of the castle of Inverness in a wholly satisfactory fashion. But the others left much to be desired, and Macbeth and his wife, in particular, were too confused and uncertain in their movements and made too much noise striking attitudes. Fontane wrote:

> I did not know Macbeth and am, in any case, unfamiliar with the manners of murderers. But it couldn't have been this way. One must look at the nature of northern men, as they are, down to this day, not only in Scotland and Scandinavia, but also among us, in the area of Lower Saxony, in Altmark, Brunswick, Holstein, and above all in Westphalia, and ask oneself how these men go about their work. Presumably about *any* work. They are firmly self-reliant and depart from their statuesque calm only when it comes to deadly blows. They are inward natures, and they fight it through within themselves, even if it is a matter of murder. And if they allow their thoughts to take vocal shape first, as poetry requires, they do not cease to be quiet, set, stiff natures. But no trace of that in this *Macbeth* performance. Dessoir knew that one must play many roles almost without moving. I saw him for the last time as Buttler [in *Wallensteins Tod*]. A man deadly ill, and only one position and one tone. And yet what an effect! You cannot force that by a strong expenditure of means. Why all the noise? Inside "lives the creative power."[24]

The players did not always take kindly to these corrections, and Theodor Döring, who was proud of his interpretation of Malvolio in *Twelfth Night*, never forgave Fontane for his public criticism of it. Malvolio, Fontane wrote later, is perhaps best described as a character untouched by reflection, "a blockhead completely immersed in narrow-mindedness, imagination, and conceit." Döring had portrayed him as a self-important coxcomb, obsessed by a demonic vanity, which would have been perfectly acceptable had not the actor supplemented this with sly winks, reflective wrinklings of the brow, and smiles of cunning superiority, which weakened the characterization by destroying its purity. Döring played the role as if he were sitting with friends in a tavern, saying to them, "This is the way I play the part. What do you think?''—as if it were all a private joke and he was amusing himself at the expense of the poet and his play. Fontane wrote that this was

> witty and interesting and genuinely Döring-esque but, in a certain sense, the death of the role. For the essence of Malvolio consists precisely of the fact that he is absolutely incapable of such a stepping out of himself. All of those higher powers that enable people to make themselves the objects of reflection are totally lacking in him. He is stuck wholly in himself and, while possessing an inner evaluation of himself, has no self-irony.[25]

Fontane was no less rigorous in his reviews of performances of the German classics. Of one player in an 1884 performance of Schiller's *Maria Stuart* he wrote, "He stands there in stately insignificance and chews words, occasionally falling into a cozy singsong that reminds one more of *Dudelei* than Dudley.''[26] In general, he believed that Schiller was badly played in the Royal Theater—too few of the plays aside from *Die Räuber* and *Kabale und Liebe* were given the casts they deserved (here Fontane agreed with Brandes) so that the occasional outstanding Philip was offset by inadequate Posas and Don Carloses; there was too much of the kind of declamation that made interior monologues sound like a recitation at the *Singakademie*, and too much false pathos, of the *style larmoyante* that made it appear that Chopin's Funeral March was being played in the wings.[27] On the other hand, however, he remained fascinated by the plays themselves, which contained everything that the present-day theater seemed to be losing: idealism, romanticism, rhetoric.[28] Of all the plays, he wrote after a performance of *Wallensteins Lager* and *Die Piccolomini* in May 1878, he had come to believe that the latter represented the highest form of Schiller's art, uniting two artistic traditions that had been lost, the clarity, style, and lack of action of French classicism (for which he confessed an increasing longing in these degenerate days) and the historical sense and the sharp, rich characterization of the Shakespearean drama. Unfortunately, *Die Piccolomini* suffered, as did the whole of the *Wallenstein* trilogy, from the fact that we don't know what to make of the protagonist, and whether we are supposed to sympathize with him or detest him.[29]

This ambiguity did not exist in Schiller's other late works, and Fontane never faltered in his admiration for *Wilhelm Tell*, with its great Rütli, apple, and Küßnacht scenes, for *Maria Stuart* (in which he saw the famous Italian actress Adelaide Ristori play the role of the Scottish queen in November 1879),[30] and *Kabale und Liebe*, of which he wrote in March 1879 that it had lost none of its old enchantment, particularly the last scene in the second act (the Lady Milford scene), which he had seen twenty times at least and always been enraptured by it.[31] In contrast, the plays of Goethe seemed to arouse no great enthusiasm in Fontane, and after a rare performance of *Torquato Tasso* in October 1873 he wrote that the play was like an illustration of Talleyrand's quip that there were three kinds of human beings: black, white—and princes.

> Naturally that must read princesses here, to which there must necessarily be added another rubric as annex, in which the *Dichter* figure. Ah, how indifferent does this transfigured Weimar court seem to our modern way of thinking, even though we have not divested ourselves of our dutiful pietas! Other and greater things move the world, and interest shifts from the exceptional beings back to human beings themselves. Like "dissolving views," the figures of an epoch that belonged only to itself are disappearing.[32]

This forthright comment helps to explain Fontane's cordial openness of mind to plays with contemporary themes, whether they were genre pieces with strong local coloration, plays about psychological conflict, or pieces that were designed purely to amuse. He did, to be sure, have certain prejudices. He did not like plays about starving poets, or plays with professors who were quite unlike real professors as characters;[33] and on the positive side he had a preference for a solid piece by Birch-Pfeiffer or something by Benedix (of whom he wrote once, "I have the virtue and the weakness of being a Benedix enthusiast"),[34]—something like *Der Störenfried* "with a heroine who was an average North German girl, of middling figure and middling intelligence with a good heart and a good bosom, of whom, thank God, we have thousands of examples."[35] For the rest, he was open-minded, and, as long as the play was well written and showed imagination, he did not even demand that it hold to the line of realism. In a review of Ernst Wichert's comedy *Der Freund des Fürsten* in December 1879, he wrote:

> The real relations of life have long been banned from our stage, and one stamps oneself, not merely before the world but before oneself, as a philistine if one demands that sort of thing from a modern play. And I don't really demand it. I place myself much more wholly and without any condition in the position of the great public, and have no other wish and desire but one: to be well amused, to have something pleasant provided for me. I come riding in not as a critical Don Quixote with my lance at the ready, intent on the right moment to thrust. Oh, no. I much prefer—to stick with romantic-balladesque figures—to play the old King Harald, who allowed himself to be attacked by the happy elves and pulled from the saddle. But the elves, the elves! They must be there too, the little, gracious, over-spirited creatures, who disarm any criticism.[36]

III

The long series of patriotic plays and pageants that filled the theater in the years during and after the war against France soon exhausted Fontane's patience. He had admired Paul Heyse's *Kolberg*, which had its premiere on 22 August 1870, four days after the battle of Gravelotte, because it perfectly suited the mood of the day and was an appropriate tribute to the sacrifices made by ordinary Germans and their families, both now and during the fight against Napoleon, which was the Heyse's subject.[37] Four years later, when Rudolf Gottschall's *Herzog Bernhard von Weimar* was produced, which was set during the last phase of the Thirty Years War, he was heartily sick of the genre. Of Gottschall's play he wrote,

> The whole piece is a dramatized excursion of gymnasts and singers with the beer laid on and a program of speeches. First Number (Ceremonial Address): God created the Germans and rejoiced. Second Number: "They shall not have it [the Rhine]." Third: "O Straßburg." Fourth: "The German Maiden." (Declamation with the

kind cooperation of a blonde.) Fifth: Repetition of the Ceremonial
Address. With your kind attention: Return, 9:30 p.m. Train stops at
Finkenkrug Station.[38]

Fontane was tired not only of the way in which such plays were
produced, with all of the regalia and banners and trumpet blasts that
audiences were used to from *Wallensteins Lager*, but even more at
the lack of invention, the never-tiring threshing of the same straw,
and the insistence upon Germany's moral and spiritual superiority to
France that were their constant ingredients.

> What a difference between the deeds of our people and those of our
> writers! In that fearful hour, when the Guard, interrupting its attack
> on St.-Privat, lay without cover in the open field and heard nothing
> but the whistle of bullets and the beating of their own hearts, which
> throbbed anxiously but stoutly against the soil of Lorraine, at that
> moment Alsace-Lorraine was ours. It was the discipline of Frederick
> William I and the categorical imperative of Kant that recaptured
> Metz and Straßburg. Phrases would never have done it. . . . Now we
> *have* Alsace and Lorraine and can, without any particular loss, give
> up one thing in return: our old world position as general leaseholder
> on morality.[39]

At the very least, Fontane insisted, writers of plays that were set
in the past, whether or not their dramas were intended to inspire patriotism, must have a sense of history. Unless the characters they created moved and spoke as if they lived in the period represented rather
than in their own, then all verisimilitude was lost, and they were
engaged only in presenting an entertainment in fancy dress. On the
other hand, the playwright must remember that he was not a historian
but an artist, who had the right to interpret the character and actions
of the historical figures in his dramas and to invent fictional ones for
the purpose of the story he was telling. In the course of this, there
would be historical omissions and small mistakes. These were tolerable, but what could not be condoned, Fontane wrote in a review of
Gottschall's *Pitt and Fox* in 1878, was the insertion of modern allu-
sions and stereotypes in order to curry the favor of the audience. "It
is this manner of sneaking oneself in in these *impermissible* ways,"
he wrote, "that annoys me in so many comedies and plays of the late
and modern period. The harmless historical blunders, the easy evasion

of the question of correctness seem to me of late to be irrelevant, and only historical *distortion*, with the purpose, thereby, of reaching by the back stairs what cannot be achieved by the broad perron of art—only this betrayal for personal advantage angers me now as ever.''[40]

These faults sometimes took the form of a deliberate implausibility practiced at the expense of the most gullible members of the audience. Karl Gutzkow's *Uriel Acosta* (1846) was an enormously popular verse tragedy about a young freethinker whose book is banned by the leaders of his Jewish community. For the sake of his mother and his love for the Jewish girl Judith, he recants his views and undergoes a humiliating penance. But his mother dies, and his sweetheart, under family pressure, marries another. He then withdraws his recantation, Judith poisons herself, and Uriel commits suicide. Gutzkow was a master of theatrical effect, and, with a good cast, this melodramatic piece made a tremendous impression upon an audience. But after one of the first performances, Arnold Ruge said that he could never persuade himself that the pistol with which Uriel Acosta shot himself was ever really loaded, and the question of plausibility could also be raised about the extravagance of Judith's behavior and the violence of her speeches. Was it really likely that members of Jewish communities in the seventeenth century acted like Gutzkow's characters?

In a review of a performance in January 1879, Fontane made it clear that he did not think so. The tone of the whole play, he wrote, was that of the evangelical liberalism of the 1840s, which had believed that the existing system could be dethroned and a better time ushered in by empty phrases:

> Freedom in the morning, freedom at noon, freedom in the evening. The time when we, after the fortunate completion of our March days, were proud of the fact that we were the freest people on the face of the earth because we had one more freedom paragraph than all of the other nations. Not the slightest concern over the fact that the days were already imminent when the value of those paper paragraphs in terms of freedom would be no greater than the monetary value in their day of the *Assignats*.

All that was past now, Fontane wrote, and serious people no longer used those big words, either because they had seen how dangerous it was to play with fire or because they had begun the earnest work needed to turn words into deeds. But, unfortunately, between the parties that had educated themselves and were alone to be reckoned with politically was what Platen once called ''a happy little people of dear idlers,'' still caught in their youth or retarded by lack of knowledge, still believing in the power of fine words and ready to be driven by them in this or that direction, and as long as this was true there would always be a thankful and credulous audience for *Uriel Acosta*. It was, in the last analysis, ''a tendentious piece, couched in the nebulous phrases of an outdated epoch. It is intended to support opinions and advance aspirations; and therefore, like most tendentious pieces . . . it lacks the stamp of historical truth.''[41]

Fontane was apt to be less rigorous than this in his critical judgments when his Prussian heart was touched. This was true in the case of Heyse's *Kolberg* in 1871, as it was again in the case of the greatest theatrical triumph of 1888. This was Ernst von Wildenbruch's *Die Quitzows*, first staged in the Berlin Opera House in November of that year and achieving its hundredth performance a year later. A four-act play in verse and prose, it told the story of how the Quitzows, a family of robber barons in league with the dukes of Pomerania, laid waste the March of Brandenburg in the fifteenth century until the burgrave of Nuremberg, Frederick of Hohenzollern, was elected margrave of Brandenburg and brought their depredations to an end.

Fontane was well acquainted with the previous work of Wildenbruch, a prolific and successful dramatist, but had no very high opinion of it. Indeed, his long review of the playwright's *Die Carolinger* in December 1883 damned Wildenbruch with faint praise, saying that the play was better than its recent predecessors *Harold* and *Opfer um Opfer* but suffered from the same faults, particularly its continual and extravagant striving after effect, which set both art and common sense on their heads.[42] In the case of *Die Quitzows*, however, he declared that, whatever the other critics might say to diminish the public acclaim that greeted the play, he was for his part striking his weapons and happily declaring himself conquered. Perhaps incautiously, he argued that *Die Quitzows* was not simply a Berlin or a Brandenburg play but a truly German one that would ''make its triumphant way far beyond the territories between the Havel and the Spree and victoriously overcome all particularistic feelings, including the provincial patriotism of our old Prussian provinces.''

On second thought, however, he hedged this bet, as well he might at a time when new forms of particularism, especially in southern Germany, were beginning to disturb political observers, like the historian Heinrich von Treitschke, who feared that the achievement of 1871 was endangered by them. *Die Quitzows* might have a strong appeal to Berliners and their cousins from the Prussian provinces, but this was less likely to be true in Bavaria and Saxony, and Fontane realized this, although he preferred to say that it was only the weak construction of the second half of the play and its excess of melodrama that would probably deny it a place in the national literature.

Even so, he insisted on the solid merits of Wildenbruch's drama, and it was less his Prussian *pietas* than his deep knowledge of Prussian history that led him to do so. He praised Wildenbruch's ''daring realism,'' which he did not hesitate to compare with that of the other reigning theatrical figure of the day, the Norwegian Ibsen, his powers of invention—pointing out how Wildenbruch had seized upon two lines in an old Pomeranian ballad and from them created one of the most convincing characters in the drama, the apprentice smith Köhne Finke—and, above all, his powers of composition, which were based on an astonishing ability to divine the main outlines and the spirit of the age of the Quitzows without being distracted by the monotonous and confusing events that were characteristic of it. There was nothing more boring, Fontane wrote, than the repetition of the same stories in different settings—Bötzow and Köpenick, Pomerania and Sachsen-herzog, raids and cattle rustling, the killing of schoolmasters, sieges and escapes, chivalry and the right of private warfare, more cattle with tocsins and kyrie eleisons and the *Donnerwetter* and damn-it-alls of assorted of brave *Märker*, noble or not, in between.

But in this miserable swamp Wildenbruch has not gone astray. He has not got stuck in it at all, but instead, exercising a really brilliant art of discrimination, has known how to reduce this whole colossal mess to a few definite lines and points . . . and achieved something that cannot but elicit enough admiration from anyone who has a historical and dramatic understanding of what is presented here.[43]

It was not enough to say that it was easy for him because he simply fitted the material to his taste. Like the story of the egg of Columbus, anyone could do it afterward and prove that it wasn't much. But it was much.

That the play had its weaknesses, Fontane was willing to admit. But he insisted that it was an outstanding example of what could be done by means of the reduction of the confusion of the past to an intelligible form by a combination of historical and dramatic instinct. "The whole is and remains a thing that we can heartily rejoice in."[44]

IV

In 1821 the English critic William Hazlitt, beginning his account of the drama for the previous year and looking back to the turn of the century, saw no signs of deterioration but some of healthy change. The *semper varium et mutabile* of the poet, he wrote, could also be applied to "the inconstant stage—it has its necessary ebbs and flows, from its subjection to the influence of popular feeling, and the frailty of the materials of which it is composed. Its own fleeting and shadowy essence cannot be expected to remain for any great length of time stationary at the same point, either of perfection or debasement."[45]

In nineteenth-century Germany, however, the theater bade fair to contradict Hazlitt's words, showing little inclination to change at all. During Fontane's years as a critic, the classics were produced as they had been since the beginning of the century, hence Fontane's complaints about unimaginative productions of *Iphigenie auf Tauvis*. At the same time, pieces from the 1840s, like Birch-Pfeiffer's *Dorf und Stadt* and Heinrich Laube's *Die Karlsschüler*, remained in the repertory; and even Iffland's *Die Jäger*, a moralizing play written in 1783, was apt to make an occasional appearance, as it did, to Fontane's considerable annoyance, in January 1878. In an acerbic review, he wrote:

> The tone that sounds through the whole piece is that of sentimentality. That was the tone of the eighteenth century in which the piece originated; hence its great effect in and for its time, but that time is long past, and as surely as we have emerged from the witches sabbaths of the sixteenth and seventeenth century, so have we left behind the sentimentalities of the eighteenth. . . . We have either advanced a great deal or we have fallen greatly behind, and either is

an advantage. Only the philistine with his eternal tendency to sit
between two stools, will find his direction as always in this play,
for as good as it is in its way, it has had its day.[46]

By philistines Fontane meant the average middle-class theatergoers,
who cultivated the arts as long as they were emphatically moralistic
and did not threaten their materialistic philosophy. And it was their
taste that found its theatrical models in the past rather than in the
future and in the drama of sentiment rather than that of realism.

Still, Hazlitt was right in feeling that no art dependent upon public
feeling could be expected to remain stationary indefinitely, and at the
end of the 1880s the so-called Naturalist rebellion ushered in an era
of profound change in painting, literature, and the theater. In Berlin
this was a throwback to the Young German movement of the 1830s,
scorning everything that was classical or imitative of classicism, re-
pudiating Goethe and Schiller and elevating Börne and Heine to their
places in the pantheon, and focusing its attention on contemporary
social problems, such as the subordination of women in society and
the plight of the urban poor. In the theater, its leaders were Heinrich
and Julius Hart, who founded the journal *Kritische Waffengänge* in
1882, and Maximilian Harden, Paul Schlenther, and Otto Brahm, who
with the Hart brothers founded the Verein Freie Bühne in 1889, an
event of great importance in the history of the Berlin theater. It put
an end to the parochialism of the Berlin stage by bringing to it the
works of Ibsen and Strindberg and encouraging German dramatists to
turn to the same themes that engaged them.

That this change was met with much opposition goes almost without saying, and Fontane commented on this in his review of a performance of Ibsen's *Ghosts*, which was the first production of the
Verein Freie Bühne. We will now, he wrote, hear a lot about how the
theater of the previous age, while emphasizing the ideal, understood
better how to lift the hearts of audiences and teach them how to live
happy lives. This is doubtful but, even if true, does not hide the fact
that the achievements of the past no longer interest the present generation. Indeed, Fontane wrote, ''For some time now classical productions have been the counterparts of empty churches. Pretentious
productions are a sorry kind of stopgap. And in this emergency realism sprang into existence, seeking the welfare of art by opposed

means. If it could no longer be paradise, then it should in place of that be a garden of life." The roads leading in that direction will often run into the desert, but in the end, Fontane wrote, he was sure that beauty would be discovered and that it would be more clearly delineated than before because our eyes will have learned to see more clearly.[47]

From the beginning Fontane was sympathetic with the new movement. This did not mean that he was an inveterate admirer of Ibsen. Much that the Norwegian dramatist wrote he found overstated and wearying; he criticized him for worrying over problems until they became boring to his auditors; and he described one of Ibsen's greatest heroines, Nora in *A Doll's House*, as "the greatest *Quatschliese* who has ever spoken to an audience from the stage" and predicted to Paul Schlenther that in about thirty years Ibsen would have become the object of comedy.[48] Ibsen's strength lay in his ability to reach into the very heart of human life, the novelty and daring of the problems he posed, the simplicity of his language, his gift of characterization, and his economy and consequentiality in carrying the action to its logical conclusion,[49] and these were all qualities that Fontane felt enriched the German theater when they were taken as models.

But greater than Ibsen, in Fontane's view, was Gerhart Hauptmann, whose play *Vor Sonnenaufgang* had its premiere on 20 October 1889. Hauptmann, he wrote to Friedrich Stephany of the *Vossische Zeitung*, was the robber captain, whereas Ibsen was merely the cadet. He had all of Ibsen's strengths without any of his weaknesses, and people like Stephany, who disliked the movement he represented, should guard against believing that he could write only *Schnaps*-dramas. "It is quite false to assume that realism is once and for all married to ugliness. It will be wholly genuine only when it is married to beauty and when the accompanying ugliness, which is a part of life, is transformed." Meanwhile, in all of these new plays, there was something that the old ones didn't have and that made them look undernourished or even dead.[50] As for Hauptmann, it was nonsense to fob him off as someone with a little talent: "In a man who can write something like [*Vor Sonnenaugang*] there is more than in the whole gang that only squint after their royalties."[51]

Fontane finished his long service with the *Vossische Zeitung* in the first months of 1890. His interest had by this time shifted from the Royal Theater, which did not produce any of the exciting new plays, and he had become more and more deeply involved with the Verein Freie Bühne and was fast friends with both Paul Schlenther and Otto Brahm. It was utterly appropriate, therefore, that his distinguished career as a critic should come to an end with a series of reviews devoted to the productions of the Verein's epoch-making 1890 season. In addition to Ibsen's *Ghosts* and Hauptmann's *Vor Sonnenaufgang*, these were *Henriette Maréchal* by Edmond and Jules de Goncourt, a play that had caused a scandal at its Paris premiere in 1865 but now, despite its literary and technical brilliance, seemed old-fashioned to those who were already hailing Hauptmann as the wave of the future; Björnstjerne Björnson's *A Glove*, which posed the question of whether a woman could demand the same premarital moral integrity from her fiancé that he demanded of her; Leo Tolstoi's *Power of Darkness*, a realistic drama of peasant life that was filled with illicit love, babes born out of wedlock, and violence and death; Ludwig Anzensgruber's *Das vierte Gebot*, a Viennese folk play about the reciprocal duties of parents and children, whose impressive theatricality had made it a resounding success at its premiere in 1877; *Die Familie Selike* by Arno Holz and Johannes Schlaf, a new play whose picture of the unrelieved misery among the Berlin poor went, in Fontane's view, far beyond Hauptmann and Tolstoi in breaking with conventional views about what was acceptable on the stage; Arthur Fitger's *Von Gottes Gnaden*, an old-fashioned drama about the abuses of divine right, which Fontane attacked for having no historical plausibility and no relevance to the new movement; and, finally, Hauptmann's *Das Friedensfest*, a family comedy of errors with a tragic end, which showed that the judgments of the author's first play were not mistaken, although it was charged with less of its daring and genius. In a final note on the season as a whole, Fontane wrote that its future-looking spirit and its sense of social conscience were to be commended, but that it was worth remembering that, when one sets sail looking for islands in an uncharted see, one must be prepared to find Calibans as well as Mirandas.[52]

In his great biography of Fontane, Hans-Heinrich Reuter has written that one would have to go back to Lessing's *Hamburgische Dramaturgie* to find anything comparable to this series of reviews. [53] This is perhaps a happy exaggeration. Fontane's reviews were rarely part of a larger argument, nor were they here, and they were never grounded on philosophical principles, as Lessing's theatrical writings were. The difference can be seen in Lessing's treatment of Shakespeare's *Richard III* in the *Hamburgische Dramaturgie*, where he argues on the basis of Aristotle that the play is not a true tragedy, and Fontane's reviews of performances of the same work in 1873, 1877, and 1879, where he is more interested in its theatricality.[54] Nor did Fontane have particular targets, as Lessing did in the drama of Voltaire. Nevertheless, his modernism recalls Lessing's defense of the *Bürgerliche Trauerspiel* against the unnatural restrictions of the past, and in felicity of style and energy of argument he had much in common with the great eighteenth-century critic.

He would probably have been quite uncomfortable to find himself being compared with Lessing. Shortly after his retirement as the *Vossische Zeitung*'s theater reviewer, he wrote to his daughter:

> I have never regarded myself as a great critic and realize that in knowledge and acuteness I stand far behind a man like Brahm. I have always admitted that, but yet, for ordinary people, my scribblings must have been a great comfort because anyone can divine from them the answer to the questions "White or black?" and "Gold or lead?" I had a clear and definite opinion and expressed it stoutly. *This* courage at least I always had. I said to Wildenbruch, "Look, it won't work. It's talented but nonsense," and when he came out with *The Quitzows*, I said with the same plainness, "See, the old Wildenbruch is raging and ranting here too, but there is so much genius in it that I shall grant him indemnity for his foolishness." No one among the modern critics can gird himself up to such round judgments. They are like the shades in the underworld; they waver to and fro and look at you sadly. They are definite only when they grasp an outspoken enemy (who is generally a miserable little doctor) by the hair in order to scalp him before the assembled people. They do that quite nicely.[55]

7

The Historical Novels

To claim that Fontane's first novel deserves to be placed in the very top rank of his fiction would be considered quixotic by most readers. By the critics *Vor dem Sturm* tends to be disregarded, and it is virtually unknown abroad. At the time of its publication, even so sympathetic a reader as Julius Rodenberg, an admirer of Fontane's articles on the theater, confided to his diary that it was a "silly book"—"I ask myself continually, what's coming next? Will they travel into the countryside again (with the ponies)? Will they sit down at the table again? Will they go to sleep again?" Most of those who noticed the book at all seemed to be confused by its relaxed style and slow pace, by the large number of characters who were described with a detail that bore no relation to their importance in the story, and by the fact that, in a novel set in Prussia's heroic time, the years 1812–1813, all of the patriotic actions described failed miserably.

It was not until after the Second World War, when Germans were tired of heroism and, as Heinz Ohff has written, nostalgic for a piece of their own history that was not burdened by the crimes of Hitler, that the book was rediscovered.[1] It began then to be perceived that what had formerly been considered its weaknesses were, in reality, its strengths, and that in its description of life in Berlin and the Oderbruch during the first phase of the rising against Napoleon, of the way in which the nobility on the land and the peasants in the villages lived, of the atmosphere of the court and the university, and of how the great events that were shaking the world influenced the private fortunes of ordinary people in all walks of life, whether they were carpet-makers in Berlin or village mayors in the Mark, Fontane had brought a part of Prussia's history to life with a richness, completeness, and fidelity to reality that made it the only German novel that could be mentioned in the same breath as the undeniably greater achievement of Tolstoi in *War and Peace*. It is also a work that breathes liberality of spirit, and is a great pleasure to read.

Among Fontane's other historical fictions the most distinguished is *Schach von Wuthenow*, a short novel that is set in Berlin on the eve of the collapse of Frederician Prussia in 1806. Notable principally for Fontane's presentation of the mood of the capital on the eve of the defeat of Jena, which is based upon much research in original sources, *Schach* also demonstrates a further development of the critique of Prussia first voiced in *Vor dem Sturm* by the Polish patriot Count Bninski and, in this respect, is the first example of Fontane's use of his fictional work to comment on contemporary politics. As such, it represents a significant step forward to his novels of society.

I

In 1866, writing to Wilhelm Hertz about his plans for the book that was to become *Vor dem Sturm*, Theodor Fontane showed a degree of vagueness that must have exasperated the publisher. He had never, Fontane admitted, asked himself whether the book should be a novel or not or, if so, what rules it should follow. On the contrary, he wanted to write a work according to his own inclination and individuality, without any particular model. Dispensing with murders and fires and stories of great passion, he had the idea of simply presenting a great number of figures from the Mark Brandenburg—that is, persons of mixed German and *wendisch* blood, which would give the book a special character—and to show how the events of 1812 and 1813 affected them. His intention would be to demonstrate the effect of a great idea upon quite simple people, without striving after sensation and éclat. "Amusing, gay, and, when possible, intellectual talk [*Geplauder*] . . . is the main thing in the book."[2]

One recognizes here the author of the *Wanderings*, reminding himself that his gift of light conversation had in the past helped him avoid many an arid stretch of historical exegesis and that it might be useful again. Indeed, in the same letter to Hertz, he wrote, "One must not want to say *everything*, for that suspends the activity of the reader's fantasy and gives birth to boredom."[3] That can hardly have reassured the bookseller, after Fontane's blithe admission that he had not fully considered the question of whether his book would have a story to tell or a hero to give it unity and continuity of plot. Hertz's forbearance when Fontane later decided that he would have to postpone the *märkische* project until he had written his war books may indicate that he had no great confidence in it.

Meanwhile, Fontane himself seems to have reached the conclusion that his first sketch of the book had fundamental weaknesses and that a pastiche of conversations about how different groups reacted to the imminent fall of Napoleon would be hardly enough to compensate readers for the sensational events and tales of passion of which he was so insistent on depriving them. He appears to have concluded that it might not be a bad idea to consult other writers whose books had dealt with social and political crisis and change in human history. Since he had no high regard for the historical novels of Felix Dahn or Julius Woff or for Gustav Freytag's *Die Ahnen*, all of which he regarded as books for and by backward-turned natures, this inevitably meant going back to the inventor of the modern historical novel, Sir Walter Scott, and looking anew at the principles that had guided the construction of works that had, in the first decades of the nineteenth century, taken Europe by storm.

Scott's general theory of the novel and the impression it made on Fontane have been described in an earlier chapter,[4] and what was said there need not be repeated. One aspect of Scott's technique worth emphasizing here, however, is the special function of his heroes, which was to show both sides of the social and ideological struggles that formed the real subject of his tales without betraying, at the outset, a preference for either. Edward Waverley in the novel of that name and Francis Osbaldistone in *Rob Roy* were nothing like the heroes of the sentimental romances of Scott's time and later, who dominated the action, won all the battles single-handedly, and, in the end, carried off the princesses. On the contrary, they tended to be young men of good social class and average gifts, honorable, decent, courageous but not given to passionate commitments, whose political views were loosely held and never clearly articulated, welcome in every company without making much of an impression when they were present, helpful when help was required and always good listeners. By family connection, they were often related to both sides in the social or political struggle that was the novel's subject; with unprejudiced ear, they listened to both sides of the ideological dispute; and on occasion their middle position enabled them to bring representatives of the contending sides into contact with each other, resulting in confrontations and debate over their differences. Thus, while their own fortunes created a plot that aroused the interest of readers (Edward's unwitting treason and his pardon because of courageous action in the battle of Prestonpans; Francis's persecution by his malevolent cousin Rashleigh and his love for the high-spirited Diana Vernon), they also provided a sense of the broader historical development that was Scott's true theme.

If we compare the final form of *Vor dem Sturm* with the sketch in the 1866 letter to Hertz, Fontane's debt to Scott is clear, for the end product has a unity and a true relationship with the historical process that were not originally foreseen. Its story has been given shape and energy by being identified with the fortunes of a Scott-like hero, Lewin von Vitzewitz, who is romantic in disposition, idealistic, and almost as naive when we meet him as Edward Waverley, and it has also acquired a greater ideological dimension by the insertion of several confrontations and debates of the kind that Scott used as a literary device. In the elaboration of the action, Fontane has also been faithful to other rules that Scott observed: namely, that real historical persons (kings, warlords, heads of state) are better talked about than seen and should not become principal characters in the action; that in describing military affairs an author is well advised to restrict himself to what is manageable for him and clear to his readers, opting for the description of small actions rather than whole battles or campaigns; that supernatural occurrences and persons endowed with magical powers can be counted on to titillate the fancies of some of the author's readers but must in the interest of realism be treated with the most extreme skepticism by the author himself and those who speak for him in the story; that the common people in the story—whether Scottish clansmen or the inhabitants of *märkisch* villages—should on occasion be allowed, in the interest of verisimilitude, to speak their own languages, but that this should not be carried so far as to confuse the reader and that, as a general rule, when Lewin's coachman addresses his master in *märkisch*, the latter should reply in German. Not all of the principles of Scott's art were perhaps as fully absorbed by Fontane as these, but on the whole it is clear enough that he had studied Scott closely.

Equally important as an object of study, although the lessons learned were for the most part negative ones, was Willibald Alexis, the author in the middle years of the nineteenth century of a string of "patriotic novels" about the Prussian Mark, two of which, *Ruhe ist die erste Bürgerpflicht* and *Isegrimm*, were set in the period and the locality in which Fontane planned to place his own historical fictions. In the early 1870s, Fontane reread all of Alexis's novels and wrote an article on him that appeared in Julius Rodenberg's *Salon für Literatur, Kunst und Gesellschaft* in 1872.

Willibald Alexis is now almost completely forgotten, except perhaps for his ballad "Fridericus Rex, unser König und Held," which includes the splendid lines delivered by the king as he leaves for the field,

Nun adieu, Lowise, wisch ab das Gesicht,
Eine jede Kugel, die trifft ja nicht.
Denn träf jede Kugel apart seinen Mann,
Woher nähmen die Kön'ge ihre Soldaten dann?

Die Musketenkugel macht ein kleines Loch.
Die Kanonenkugel macht ein weit größeres noch.
Die Kugeln sind alle von Eisen und Blei,
Und manche Kugel geht manchem vorbei.

[Well, adieu, Luise, wipe your face off,
Every single bullet doesn't hit its target.
For if every bullet, contrary to reason, hit its man,
Where would the kings get their soldiers then?

The musketball makes a little hole,
The cannonball makes a much bigger one.
The bullets are all made of iron and lead,
And many bullets miss many people.]

The oblivion into which his prose works have fallen does not do justice to Alexis's energy and imagination, the thoroughness of his historical research, his gift for drawing character, and his great skill in describing landscape. Born in Breslau in 1798, as Georg Wilhelm Häring, he moved to Berlin with his family after his father's death, was educated in that city, and, while still a schoolboy, became a volunteer in the Colberg Grenadiers and participated in the battle of Waterloo. When peace was restored, he studied law at the universities of Berlin and Breslau and then passed the state examinations for the higher civil service. From the beginning, he was more drawn to a career in literature and began to experiment in various forms, finding the historical novel most congenial to him and in the mid-1820s he actually published two novels, *Walladmor* and *Schloß Avalon*, which purported to be "translated from the English of Walter Scott." His considerable success with the public began with a series of *vaterländische Romane* composed between 1832 and 1856, when illness brought his active literary career to a halt, although he lived until 1871.

The first of his patriotic novels, and the first of his books to be published under the name Willibald Alexis, was *Cabanis* (1832), a story of the time of Frederick the Great that deals with the fortunes of an aristocratic family in the French colony of Berlin. This was followed by *Der Roland von Berlin* (1840), set in Berlin and Cölln and the surrounding Mark Brandenburg in the years between 1442 and 1448 and treating the conflict between the first Hohenzollern and the leaders of the *Bürger* of the twin cities; and *Der falsche Waldemar* (1842), dealing with the appearance in 1347 of someone claiming to be Waldemar, margrave of Brandenburg, who died in 1317. More successful, and still the most likely of Alexis's works to be found in secondhand bookstores, was *Die Hosen des Herrn von Bredow* (1846–1848), which is set in the time of the rebellion of the petty nobility in Prussia at the beginning of the sixteenth century. It was followed by *Der Wärwolf* (1848), which treated the fortunes of some of its characters in the struggles of the early Reformation. Finally, *Ruhe ist die erste Bürgerpflicht* (1852) took as its theme the decline of public virtue and political integrity in the two years before the battle of Jena in 1806; and *Isegrimm* (1854) had as its background the regeneration of Prussia after Jena, the wars of liberation, and the country's development in the period before 1848.

In his essay in Rodenberg's *Salon*, Fontane wrote of Alexis's life and career with great sympathy but also with some fundamental criticisms that are of interest in the light of his own later work. Of the novels he rejected only one—*Der falsche Waldemar*—as being completely unsatisfactory, largely because the motivation of the principal character was so romanticized, and basically so unpersuasive, as to be bereft of any credibility to a critical reader. But he pointed out that all of the novels set in medieval times showed a disproportion between the energy expended by the author and the material that was its object. When you come right down to it, he asked of *Der Roland von Berlin*, are the events described either so interesting or so important as to justify Alexis's labors? Few writers have been able to make the Middle Ages come alive (Fontane was inclined to believe that Viktor Scheffel, the author of *Ekkehard* [1955][5] was a lonely exception), and Alexis's limited knowledge of life in Berlin at the beginning of the fifteenth century makes him incapable of drawing his characters as individuals They are all typical figures and, as such, have no more power to seize upon our imagination that those portrayed in the Death Dance in St. Mary's Church in Berlin. As for the importance of the historical story he tells, Alexis has a tendency to see fifteenth-century Berlin as a model of liberty and civic virtue, which it almost certainly was not. He probably knew that his picture was false but persisted in it with

the ethical purpose of giving the bourgeoisie of 1840 an impetus for the better by telling them a historical fairy tale about the freedom and magnificence of the Berlin councilors of 1440. What was at first a political slant finally became (as it always does) a conviction. The

artificial picture stepped into the place of reality and carried the artist
away. He made an enthusiast of himself.[6]

In the other novels dealing with the Middle Ages, the energy of
Alexis's style and his considerable powers of description were also
wasted in constructing a picture of society that was basically untrue.
Fontane made a partial exemption in the most durable of Alexis's
works, *Die Hosen des Herrn von Bredow*, where he praised Alexis's
comic gift and the skill with which he related the political story to
the fortunes of the elk-leather trousers of Herr von Bredow; but even
here the failure to individualize the characters was a serious problem,
and it was even worse in *Der Wärwolf*, its sequel, which suffered
from the further fault that it was difficult to say why the book was
called as it was, unless it was merely to arouse curiosity.

Fontane was even more critical of *Cabanis*, Alexis's novel of the
reign of Frederick II. He recognized the author's careful research on
the history of the French colony in Berlin and found the novel excellent as a picture of Berlin manners and morals in its time. But he
pointed out that it was much too long, and that the characters kept
repeating themselves and never seemed to develop. So also in *Ruhe
ist die erste Bürgerpflicht*, where readers are confronted with too many
characters too quickly, with no clues from the author to help them
determine at the outset which of them are going to be key players in
the story and which will have subsidiary roles.

As has been noted previously, *Ruhe ist die erste Bürgerpflicht* and
its sequel, *Isegrimm*, dealt with themes that would stand in the fore-
ground of Fontane's own historical fiction—the decline and destruction of Frederician Prussia and its subsequent regeneration—and his
judgments of them are particularly interesting. On various occasions,
he was quoted as saying that one or the other of them was his favorite
Alexis novel, and in his essay for Rodenberg's *Salon* his praise of
them is, if anything, excessive. He does, however, admit that, as in
Der Roland von Berlin, Alexis's liberal political opinions tended, in
both these late novels, to romanticize the actuality described by seeing
everything as lighter or darker than it actually was. This was particularly true of his description of the civic and moral decline of Prussia
in the years before 1806. Fontane admits that his own picture of those
years was not as dark as Alexis's, which would not be especially

important if it were not for ''the excess of psychological attention that [Alexis] pays to the morally repulsive.'' This showed a lack of proportion that distorted reality, and it also posed a question of taste. Alexis, Fontane wrote, ''gives the ugly more space, and dwells upon it longer and more lovably, than is justified in a novel that has to be judged in the first instance according to aesthetic standards. . . . Literature has other standards of truth than history.''[7]

Leaving this aside, Alexis was never destined to enjoy the popularity of Scott, nor did he deserve it. His research was too detailed, his period pieces too complicated, and his dialogue too interminable to enable him to retain public attention and affection. Above all, Fontane pointed out, he lacked a sense of humor.

> Wrapped in his tartan plaid, Scott rode over the Grampian hills of his homeland, and the castles and the huts, the kings and the crofters all lay before him, each in its place, and life held nothing that he could not treat, in his fictional forms, with gaiety and superiority. His prejudices merely heightened the effect. He was the great humorist because he was so great and free as a person. In those places where Willibald Alexis tries to assume a similar position, he remains as a child of his time and his country, stuck in irony. He mocks; he ridicules; but his soul never achieves Olympian laughter. He was just no Olympian.[8]

As he brought his first novel to conclusion, Theodor Fontane probably spent little time wondering about his own Olympian qualifications. But he had wanted to write a novel that he himself would be pleased with, and to achieve that he had sought to avoid the mistakes of the writer who had sometimes been called the *märkische* Scott while trying to emulate the virtues of the real one.

The novel was finished during a painful period in Fontane's personal life. In 1876 he had accepted a position as first secretary of the Prussian Academy of Arts, largely, one supposes, to please his wife, who longed for the security that a bureaucratic position would bring and dreamed of her husband becoming a *Geheimrat*.[9] Almost immediately, he discovered that he had made a grievous mistake, that his new colleagues had no respect for his literary achievements and, indeed, treated him *de haut en bas* and seemed to expect servility in

return. He reacted by submitting his resignation, which posed awkward problems of protocol, since his appointment had been signed by
the emperor, and took a lot of time before it was effected, and which
also came close to destroying his marriage.[10] The book, to which he
turned with an almost defiant energy, helped him cope with these
difficulties. He wrote to his friend Mathilde von Rohr:

> Yes, the novel! In these times, so comfortless for me, it is my only
> happiness, my only means of recuperation. In busying myself with
> it, I forget what is troubling me. When it really appears, I shall,
> looking back on the time in which it emerged, have to say: a child
> of sorrow. But it bears no signs of that. In many passages it is gay,
> and nowhere is it sicklied over with misery. I believe that I ought
> to say that it will please *you*, and that the hopes that you have always
> had for it will not be wholly unfulfilled. As I work on it, I feel that
> I am *only* a writer and that only in this fine profession—however
> the jumped-up culture mob [*aufgeblasene Bildungs-Pöbel*] may
> laugh at the thought—I can find my happiness.[11]

III

It would never have occurred to Fontane to refer to *Vor dem Sturm*
as a "patriotic novel." He had, as we have seen, distanced himself
from the heightened nationalism that had overcome Germany in the
seventies, and his war books, not only *Der Krieg gegen Frankreich*
but also *Kriegsgefangenen* and *Aus den Tagen der Okkupation*, had
shown such forbearance toward the former enemy that his son, an
army captain, had remonstrated with him. At the time of publication
in the winter of 1878, he wrote to his publisher, expressing the wish
that reviewers would perceive the book's true intentions. It was, he
wrote,

> the expression of a determined world and life philosophy; it takes a
> stand for religion, morality and the fatherland, but it is full of hatred
> of the "blue cornflower" and "With God for King and Fatherland,"
> that is to say, of caricaturing that trinity or smothering it in phrases.
> I dare say—and I feel this as strongly as I live—that I have put

down something in this book that lifts it far above the usual nov-
elistic rubbish, and not merely in Germany.[12]

The story opens in December 1812 with its hero, Lewin von Vitzewitz, going home for Christmas to the village of Hohen-Vietz in
the Odenbruch between Frankfurt am Oder and Küstrin. The family
estate, situated here since the reign of the Ascanians, is currently pre-
sided over by Lewin's father, Berndt von Vitzewitz, a vigorous representative of the country nobility with good connections at court but
a melancholy man, brooding over the death of his wife six years earlier, during the turbulent days that followed the defeat of Jena, when
she was insulted by an officer of the French occupation force, whom
Berndt subsequently killed in a duel. The mistress of Hohen-Vietz is
now Lewin's sister Renate, whose quiet existence is relieved by the
endless gossip of her companion Aunt Schorlemer, who once lived in
a Herrnhüter community in Greenland, her amused interest in the archaeological researches of the local pastor, Seidentopf, and her friendship with the orphan Marie, the daughter of a wandering player who
died in the village, and who is now the ward of the village mayor
Kniehase. Not far away, at Guse, lives Berndt's eldest sister, Amelie,
whose husband was an officer in the army of Frederick the Great who
took retirement after the battle of Leuthen, because of what he considered to be an unjust reprimand by the king, and became a member
of the court of Frederick's brother Henry. Long widowed, Aunt Ama-
lie maintains an island of French culture at Guse, attended by the older
members of the local nobility who still venerate the spirit of Frederick.
    Lewin is a student in Berlin and the member of a society of young
army officers, civil servants, and fellow students called Kastalia,
whose members cultivate the arts in the same way as Fontane's own
Tunnel did in the forties. One of the members of Kastalia is Tubal
Ladalinski, member of a Polish noble family which, after the last
Polish partition, shifted its allegiance to the Prussian crown. Lewin is
a frequent visitor to the Ladalinski home in Berlin, as Tubal is to
Hohen-Vietz, and, as the ties between the two houses grow stronger,
Tubal and Renate are brought together, and Lewin falls in love with
Tubal's sister Kathinka.
    This network of relationships, which was soon to be changed be-
yond recognition by events in the great world, Fontane describes at

length and with an unhurried attention to detail and a willingness to sacrifice pace to anecdote and historical retrospection. It is easy to imagine that many of his contemporaries felt as Julius Rodenberg did and found it difficult to understand why Aunt Schorlemer is allowed to talk quite so much about Greenland as she does or why Fontane described with such gusto the debates between Pastor Seidentopf and his friend the Frankfurt legal counselor Turgany over the Germanic or Slavic origins of their archaeological findings. But such scenes— and even others more peripheral to the main story, like the description of the evening party of Frau Hulen, Lewin's Berlin landlady, and the scene in the Berlin pub in which Corporal Klemm gives a wrong-headed lecture on military strategy to a quartet of Berlin *Bürger*—are justified by Fontane's determination to give as complete a picture of Prussian society as he can, as they are also by the spirit and humor of the telling and the considerable skill in character delineation. Fontane's later novels, while much more disciplined, profited from the experiments he made in *Vor dem Sturm*.

The moving force in Fontane's novel is Napoleon Bonaparte, whose waning fortunes affect both the policies of the Prussian state, tied to him in alliance, and the private fortunes and ambitions of its citizens, high and low. On 26 December 1812, two days after Lewin goes home for the holidays, the *Berlinische Zeitung* prints reports of the emperor's fateful battle on the Berezina, and this event, which is the occasion of Corporal Klemm's lecture in the pub on the Windmühlenberg a week later, convinces Berndt that the time is ripe for a general rising of the eastern provinces against the French occupation forces. He tells his son on Christmas Day, "It is easy to bury people in the snow. Only no mercy! Few of them will get across the Nieman, but none must be allowed to cross the Oder!"[13]

Neither Lewin nor Prince Hardenberg, the king's chief minister, whom Berndt sees in Berlin the next day, approves of this plan. Lewin tells his father that he is no lover of what is now called the Spanish way of war, and that taking a demoralized army in the rear is something that he, the son of a French mother, could not condone. Prince Hardenberg informs him that the king has no intention of breaking the French alliance and will authorize no anti-French action by provincial leaders.

Events are now, however, slipping out of government control. On 30 December the commander of the Prussian contingent in the Napoleonic army, General York von Wartenberg, concludes a convention at Tauroggen with the advancing Russians, pulls his forces out of the French line, and assumes a position of neutrality. Lewin hears about this at a ball in the Ladalinski home in Berlin, in circumstances that, although he does not realize it at the time, foreshadow the frustration of his romantic dreams of winning Kathinka's heart. The announcement of York's action so infuriates the Polish Count Bninski, a suitor of Kathinka and an admirer of Napoleon, that he inveighs against Prussian loyalty in a way that induces her to see him with different eyes and to begin to question the Prussian loyalties of her father.

Meanwhile, York's action electrifies public opinion and encourages the thought of imminent liberation from French control. In the university, the philosopher Fichte presents a lecture, "The Concept of Real War," to a crowded audience and thoughts of battle subvert the usual program of the Kastalia society, where talks on Borodino and the war in Spain became the order of the day and a new friend of Lewins, named Hansen-Grell, arouses enthusiasm by reading a ballad about Frederick's marshal Seydlitz:

Sie reiten über die Brücken,
Der König scherzt: "Je nun,
Hie Feind in Front und Rücken,
Seydlitz, was würd Er tun?"
Der über die Brückenwandung
Setzt weg, halb links nach vorn,
Der Strom schäumt auf wie Brandung—
Ja, Calcar, das ist Sporn.[14]

[They ride over the bridges,
And Frederick jokes, "Well now,
If the enemy were in our front and rear,
Seydlitz, what would you do?"
Over the bridge's wall
he spurs, half-left and forward,
The stream foams up like surf—
Ja, Calcar, das ist Sporn.]

Finally, as a culmination of all this martial enthusiasm, there is a grand expedition by sleigh to Kloster Lehnin, where the members and their guests dine while counterfeit monks produce a spectral Bonaparte amid cries of *"Pereat!"* It is during the homeward ride from this extravaganza that Lewin admits to Kathinka that he loves her and wishes to marry her, only to be told, "You are a child." A few days later, Tubal sends word to him that she has fled with Bninski. Shattered by this news, Lewin returns to Hohen-Vietz in a state of collapse and, after he has been nursed back to health by his sister, commits himself almost despairingly to the rising against the French garrison in Frankfurt that his father has been planning since the beginning of the year.

It is notable that, in describing the evolution and execution of this project, Fontane nowhere subscribes to the temptation of taking the easy way and describing it as a grand patriotic enterprise. His emphasis is rather on the moral issues involved, the question of loyalty, and the questionability of Berndt's motivation. In a passage that Scott might have written, these issues are debated by Berndt, the village mayor, Kniehase, and the assistant director of the Frankfurt school, Othegraven. Berndt begins by referring to a rash of recent break-ins and robberies, which he attributes to deserters from the Grande Armée, although Kniehase, rightly as it turns out, says they have been committed by local riffraff. Berndt insists that, before these grow out of control completely, a *Landsturm* must be organized, village by village, which, in dealing with the smaller problem, will be prepared to deal with the larger, when the bulk of the French army attempts to cross the Oder. When Kniehase answers that this will require a command of the king, to whom they all owe their loyalty, Berndt replies that he recognizes his loyalty to the king, but that there is another loyalty that binds both ruler and subject and that is to the soil: "The king is there for the sake of the land. If he separates himself from that, or lets himself be separated from it through weakness or false counsel, then he breaks his oath and absolves me from mine."[15]

Kniehase answers that without the king's command nothing can be done, since the king is everything to the peasants, who owe the draining of the Oderbruch and their churches and homes to the crown; and he remains unmoved when Berndt gives way to an impassioned speech about the sacredness of the soil, made all the more so to him because his wife, dead because of the crimes of the French, is buried in it: "I have learned what earth is. There must be blood in it. And everywhere hereabouts it is fertilized with blood. At Kunersdorf there is a place called the 'red field.' And should all that be given up because a king is not strong enough to resist weak counsellors? No, Kniehase, *with* the king as far as it goes; *without* him if that must be."[16]

Berndt appeals to the *Konrektor* to support him, and Othegraven, a deeply religious man, shifts the focus of the argument to one of values. Prussia has always been a royal land, he says, and one deeply loyal to its rulers. But it would be an abomination to make blind obedience a people's highest virtue. That place belongs to freedom and love. Trusting in these, and in the hope that no lasting break will come between the king and his people, his subjects must have the determination to act, while showing the king that they are for him even if their actions seem to say the opposite. It is a matter of the heart. "It is more difficult to decide than to obey—more difficult and often more loyal."[17] Schill and Hofer knew that their rulers were forced to opt for inactivity, but their hearts told them that they themselves must act for the country.

Fontane's characters generally speak for themselves rather than for him, and he was certainly aware of the shortcomings of this argument. But it is enough to persuade Kniehase to give up his opposition, and the plans for the rising go forward. Yet none of Berndt's expectations is fulfilled. The French deserters, against whom an elaborate operation is mounted, turn out to be a couple of thieves from a neighboring village. A plan to ambush regiments of Oudinot's corps who are bivouacking at Schloß Guse and to seize the war chest they are reportedly carrying is foiled by the foresight of their commander, who senses the danger and leads his troops to safety before the trap is sprung. Finally, when the attack is launched upon the French troops in Frankfurt, they turn out to be not the demoralized rabble that Berndt expects but a well-trained reserve unit that reacts quickly and drastically. His peasant detachments are forced to retreat with significant losses. Hansen-Grell is killed in the fighting, Othegraven taken and executed by the French, and Lewin captured and placed in prison in Küstrin to await a similar fate.

It is at this point that Fontane, a stern critic of the exaggerated patriotism of his own time, has Berndt von Vitzewitz examine his own motives with a pitiless eye:

> Berndt, don't deceive yourself, don't lie to yourself. What was it? Was it fatherland and sacred vengeance, or was it pride and vanity? Was the decision up to *you*, or did you want to shine? Did you want to be the first? Tell me the answer. I want to know it, I want to know the truth. . . . Poor, petty human nature! And I thought I was greater and better! Yes, fancying that I was better, that's what it was. Pride goeth before a fall, and what a fall! But I am punished, and this hour prepares my reward.[18]

Major General von Bamme, the diminutive Ziethen hussar, who is a member of Aunt Amelie's circle at Guse, and as a professional soldier was chosen to lead the assault on Frankfurt, also experiences a revelation as a result of the fighting there. He has always had a tendency to think of his own kind as a superior race, and he confesses to Berndt that that faith has been severely shaken.

> There is nothing to this stuff about two kinds of people. One thing at least we thought we had taken a lease on, courage. Then along comes this albino rabbit Grell and dies like a hero with a saber in his hand. About the *Konrektor* I won't speak at all: a death like his can make an old soldier ashamed. And where does it all come from? You know. West wind. I make nothing of these windbags of French-men, but in all their stupid stuff there is a pinch of truth. Nothing much will come of their fraternity, nor of their freedom. But there is something in what they have stuck in between. Because what does it mean in the end but *Mensch ist Mensch*.[19]

Here, certainly, Fontane is speaking through Bamme, and this speech is the clearest validation of his claim that *Vor dem Sturm* is an expression of his "world and life philosophy."

The novel comes to its end with a dispatch that is in sharp contrast to the meandering pace of its earlier chapters With the aid of Hoppenmariecke, a figure who might have appeared in a novel by Scott, a "kobold," as Othegraven calls her, who is feared by some people as a witch and suspected by others as a thief but has always been protected by Levin, a way is found to get intelligence to him in his prison cell in Küstrin, which alerts him to the preparations being made to effect his escape. In the execution of this escape, however, Tubal is fatally wounded and dies after the return to Hohen-Vietz. The novel ends, then, with Berndt chastened by the results of the action he insisted upon; Renate deprived of her destined mate; and Lewin and Marie coming together in a union that will presumably renew the fortunes of the Vitzewitz house. In what is the weakest part of his book, Fontane deals with these events in an almost cursory fashion, telling his readers that Lewin loves Marie without allowing them to see this for themselves or giving them any way of imagining what their future life together will be like.[20] So too Renate, an attractive and interesting woman in the earlier chapters of the book, is allowed to fade away with deplorable suddenness into an old lady in a cloister, keeping a diary.

Still, the novel itself is an impressive performance, and it is necessary to ask why. Writing of *Vanity Fair*, a work that Fontane greatly admired (and which, incidentally, also had a botched ending), the critic F. R. Leavis once noted caustically that it had "nothing to offer the reader whose demand goes beyond the 'creation of characters' and so on."[21] This charge has also been made against Fontane, but in his case, as in Thackeray's, it is singularly unjust In reality, Fontane's first novel was a model of what a historical novel should be. It created a credible world filled with credible characters. To nineteenth-century readers of Prussian stock, it said, "This is what we were once like." To non-Germans it offered an interesting picture of another culture in all its variety in a time of crisis. To anyone interested in Napoleon, it gave a new appreciation of how his ambitions impinged upon the lives of ordinary people living not in the centers of power but in the byways of history, where nevertheless great decisions were made that had some effect upon his fall. To provide all that, and a good story as well, was no small achievement.

In Fontane's own career, *Vor dem Sturm* marks the emergence of a new spirit of criticism of the Prussia that Fontane had idealized in his ballads and in the *Wanderings*. This was induced in part by his concern about the spirit of arrogant nationalism that had been one of the results of the victory over France, although it may have been influenced also by his unpleasant experience with Prussian bureaucracy during his brief career in the Prussian Academy and his lingering resentment over the lack of recognition shown him for his war books. In any event, during the last stages of the composition of *Vor dem Sturm*, his mind was never entirely free from reflection on the more unpleasant aspects of Prussianism.

This did not, to be sure, obtrude upon the text of the novel, but it was not entirely absent either. Count Bninski, Kathinka's suitor, may be considered the voice of this side of his author, the Polish patriot and admirer of Napoleon who, after Tauroggen, rails against Prussia's lack of loyalty,[22] and later, in an emotional conversation with Kathinka, describes Prussia as a predatory and greedy land:

> All that flourishes here is class and petty formality, number and routine, and along with it that hateful poverty that breeds, not simplicity, but only cunning and wretchedness. Scant and frugal, that's the motto of this land. . . . A simulation of existence—appearance and cunning—and with them a deep-seated conception of being something special. And why? Because they have that joy in fighting and robbing that always goes with poverty. It is never satisfied, this people; without polish or form or anything that does good or pleases, it has only one desire: always more. . . . A people of pirates who make their raids on land. But always with Te Deums and for the sake of God and the highest values! For it has never been short of inscriptions for its banners.[23]

On the eve of the onslaught upon Frankfurt, these sentiments are echoed by the Prussian lieutenant Hirschfeldt, who is acting as Bamme's chief of staff, in a talk with Tubal Ladalinski. He says:

> I was abroad for a long time, and one learns about oneself when abroad. Anyone who comes back is surprised by nothing as much as by the naive belief, which he finds here on every side, that in the land of Prussia everything is the best. The big, the small, the whole and the single. The best, I say, and, above all, the most honorable. And yet precisely here lies our weakest point. What kind of politics have we made for the last twenty years! Nothing but deceit and betrayal, and we will have to go to ruin because of it. For it's all the same, state or individual, whoever wavers and shifts, whoever

is unreliable and unsteady, whoever breaks vows, whoever, in short, does not keep his word, is doomed.[24]

IV

Such passages, which reflected Fontane's increasingly pessimistic reflections about contemporary social and political tendencies in Germany, were to become more frequent in Fontane's next major historical fiction, the short novel *Schach von Wuthenow*. Set in Berlin in the autumn of 1806, this is, for all of its careful historical construction, a parable for Fontane's own time, an interesting forecast of *L'Adultera, Unwiederbringlich*, and the other novels of contemporary life that were to follow. In constructing a picture of aristocratic life in Berlin in the months before the disaster of Jena, Fontane was counting upon his readers' memories of what happened in historical time after the end of his story to make the connection between the private tragedy described in the book and the national one that followed and might well be repeated.

In *Schach von Wuthenau*, the historical setting is described with great economy in the opening chapter, in which Frau von Carayon and her guests discuss the recent attempt of the Prussian foreign minister Count von Haugwitz to appease Emperor Napoleon of France, who, since his overwhelming victory over Austria and Russia at Austerlitz in December 1805, has been accusing Prussia of breaches of neutrality and has been encroaching upon Prussian territory. Haugwitz's mission has apparently been successful, and has assured the future cession of Hannover to Prussia, but it has been highly unpopular with Prussian patriots and the Prussian military, who are agitating for war. In the discussion at the Carayon reception, however, Haugwitz is strongly supported by a former staff captain named von Bülow, recently returned to Prussia from abroad, where, like Lieutenant Hirschfeldt in *Vor dem Sturm*, he has learned a lot about his own country, particularly that everything of significance in the world does not have to happen between Nuthe and Notte, and that Mirabeau was not mistaken when he likened Prussia to a fruit that was already rotten before it was ripe.[25] A provocative and incisive critic, whose role in the novel is to outrage others by means of drastic formulations whose truth they are unwilling to face, Fontane's Bülow is based upon the historical figure Freiherr Dietrich von Bülow, a military publicist of great talent, an admirer of Napoleon, whose victory at Austerlitz he considered the new Actium, and a bitter critic of his own country for failing to appreciate this or to see that it required profound changes in the Frederician system. Overly assertive and paranoid, he was eventually declared to be insane and died in confinement in Riga in 1807.[26]

Bülow shows his colors at the Carayon reception when a new guest, Rittmeister Schach von Wuthenow, brings the news that a street mob has been besieging the Haugwitz residence, howling and throwing stones in protest against the treaty. His fellow officer Alvensleben complains that this will be blamed on the Regiment Gensdarmes, whose opposition to the Haugwitz policy is well known. This elicits from Bülow the retort:

> And rightly so. . . . Why do these gentlemen, who every day become smarter than the king and his ministers, use this kind of language? Why do they make politics? Leaving aside the question whether an army may make politics in any case, when they do so they should at least make sense. At last we are on the right path, at last we are standing where we should have been from the beginning, at last His Majesty is listening to the precepts of reason, and what happens? Our officer class, whose every third word is of the king and their loyalty, . . . indulge themselves with an opportunism that is as dangerous as it is naive, and, through their insolent activity and more insolent language, invite the anger of the emperor, who has only just been appeased with difficulty.[27]

These words are hotly contested by Schach, and the eruption of a political debate between the two is avoided only by the adroitness of their hostess, who changes the subject of the conversation.

But it is not the antagonism between Bülow and Schach that is the center of Fontane's novel, although there are other brushes between the two, which Fontane uses to throw light on the conventionality of Schach's political views. Rather, it is the relationship between Schach and the two women of the story, Josephine von Carayon, a handsome widow of thirty-seven of established social position and great charm, and her attractive and idealistic daughter Victoire, whose beauty would have matched her mother's were it not for the fact that she suffered disfigurement by smallpox at the age of fifteen. Schach, a handsome and socially accomplished man, is a frequent visitor at the Carayon receptions, and it is widely believed that he hopes to marry Josephine, although he seems to be in no haste about this. Victoire herself favors this match, although she herself is drawn to Schach. But in a conversation with Bülow and other officers at the wine restaurant Sala Tarone, Alvensleben advances the theory that Schach is a person so obsessed with externals that such a wedding is out of the question, since he would consider Victoire to be unpresentable in society, and would be embarrassed to have to introduce her to persons of high position as his daughter. The thought that the match is impossible brings an expression of satisfaction from Bülow, who has come to admire Josephine for possessing the charm of truth and naturalness, but regards Schach as being pedantic and pompous as well as

> the embodiment of that Prussian narrowness that has only three articles of faith: first, "the world rests no more securely on the shoulders of Atlas than the Prussian state on those of the Prussian army"; second, the Prussian infantry attack is irresistible; and, third and last, "a battle is never lost until the Regiment Garde du Corps has attacked." Or naturally the Regiment Gensdarmes, for they are brothers, twin brothers. I detest such expressions, and the time is near when the world will recognize the hollowness of such boasting.[28]

Shortly thereafter Schach takes mother and daughter and their old aunt by carriage to Tempelhof—on one of those country excursions that now became a regular feature in Fontane's novels—where they book a table in the restaurant and then walk through the fields to view the village church. Coming back, Schach accompanies Victoire, and they talk about the chivalric order of Knights Templar and its founder, Philippe le Bel, which leads her to say artlessly that all historical figures with this nickname are unsympathetic to her. "I hope not out of envy," she adds. "But beauty, which must be true, makes one egoistic, anyone who is egoistic is thankless and untrue."[29] Schach tells himself that this remark was not intended to be directed at him but feels that it was spoken out of "a dark presentiment." As they reach the village, he waits until the other couple joins them, and then changes his partner, reentering the restaurant with Josephine, as if corroborating both Alvensleben's theory and Victoire's remark.

Victoire guesses the reason for his behavior but is paradoxically attracted more strongly to him. Schach, too, finds that she is much on his mind. At a *Herrenabend* to which he has been invited by Prince Louis Ferdinand (who, as most of Fontane's readers would have known, was to die at Saalfeld only a few months later after Napoleon opened hostilities against Prussia), the prince, who has had much experience with women, is intrigued by what he hears about the Carayons and remembers seeing Victoire when she was young and being impressed by her beauty. When Schach tells him that this has been much diminished, he refuses to believe it and gives a Schach a lecture on feminine beauty. He speaks of a *beauté du diable*, which conceals fire, energy, and passion beneath a superficial ugliness, a higher form of beauty because it has "gone through the fire." He expresses the desire to resume his acquaintance with the Carayons and says that his friend Pauline will visit them and arrange a meeting.

A few days later, after a great review of the army on Tempelhof Field, which one observer with premonitory foresight called the "farewell review of the Frederician army," Schach visits the Carayon residence and finds Victoire alone. He tells her of the pending invitation but warns her that Louis Ferdinand is "alternatively a heroic prince and a prince of debauchery" and is perhaps not an acquaintance to be cultivated. She answers that she is not in a position to judge the morals of society and that, in any case, her disfigurement gives her a freedom to make her own decisions. Schach suggests that she is taking her ideas from the book she is reading, which he supposes is a volume of Rousseau. She answers that it is rather her favorite author, Mirabeau, who was, like her, a victim of smallpox and that, if she could, she would make his name part of her own. She speaks these words with a passion and bitterness that transfigure her, and Schach, thinking of the prince's description of *beauté du diable*, loses his composure and finds himself holding her hand and uttering endearments. Victoire gives herself to him.

In the days that follow, however, Schach reverts to his reserved and distant manner, and it is apparent to Victoire that he recognizes no change in their relationship. She then confesses to her mother, and

Josephine, in one of the most brilliant passages in the book for what it reveals about Schach's character and her own, accosts Schach and, after saying, in a friendly manner, that she has no intention of making a scene or delivering a moral sermon, says that Victoire has told her the truth but asked her to be silent, expressing the romantic desire to bear all of the blame, private and public, for what happened in order to spare the man she loves. Josephine continues:

> Weak as my love for Victoire makes me, I am not so weak that I am ready to support her in this comedy of generosity. I belong to society and obey its rules. That's the way I was brought up, and I have no desire to sacrifice my social position for a sacrificial whim of my beloved daughter. In other words, I have no desire to go into a cloister or to play the role of a saint withdrawn from the world, even for Victoire's sake. And so I must insist on the legitimation of what has happened. That, *Herr Rittmeister*, is what I had to say to you.

Recovering his composure with difficulty, Schach answers that he realizes that everything in life has its natural consequences, and that he has no desire to avoid these.

> He had had the wish to remain unmarried, and to say good-bye to an idea that he had held so long caused for the moment a certain confusion. But he felt no less certainly that he had to congratulate himself on the day that would shortly bring this change in his life. Victoire was her mother's daughter, and that was the best assurance of his future, the promise of real happiness.

Josephine notes the coolness of this answer, and is wounded by the absence from it of either love or a sense of guilt. She answers pointedly that he himself must feel that his assent might have been more wholehearted and natural, but that it is nevertheless acceptable. What she wants now is a formal engagement in the cathedral and a gala wedding. After that events can take their course.[30]

After he has left her, however, all of Schach's doubts about marriage, and especially about marriage to Victoire, return. He says to himself:

I am helplessly given over to the scorn and witticisms of my comrades, and the ridiculousness of a happy country marriage, which
blooms like a violet in the shade, looms before me in model form.
I see exactly how it will be: I'll quit the service, take over the
running of Wuthenau again, plow, improve the soil, raise rape or
turnips, and devote myself to wedded bliss. What a life, what a
future! On this Sunday, a sermon; on the next, the Gospel or Epis-
tles; and in between whist *en trois*, always with the same pastor.
And then, once in a while, a prince comes to the nearest town,
perhaps Prince Louis in person, and changes his horses, while I
appear either at the gate or the hotel. And he looks me over in my
old-fashioned coat and asks how things are going with me. And as
he does so, every muscle in his face is saying, "My God, what three
years can do to a person!" Three years—and perhaps it will be
thirty![31]

Nevertheless, he makes the wedding arrangements with the Carayons,
including plans for an extended honeymoon in Italy. But now his
worst fears are realized. He receives in the mail a caricature called
"Le choix de Schach," showing him as a Persian shah between two
female forms, recognizable as Josephine and Victoire von Carayon.
Other caricatures follow and find their way into the public, and
Schach, humiliated, takes leave and retires to his estate without in-
forming his betrothed or her mother.

The story now moves quickly to its conclusion. Feeling that her
daughter has been betrayed, Frau von Carayon goes to Paretz, where
the royal couple are in residence, and appeals to the king for help. In
a personal interview with Schach, he insists that he keep his promise.
Schach obeys; the marriage takes place; but, immediately thereafter,
he shoots himself. The last word is spoken by Bülow, in a letter to
his publisher from Königsberg. He writes:

There you have the essence of false honor. It makes us dependent
upon the most vacillating and arbitrary thing that exists, the judgment of society, even although it is based upon quicksand, and it
sees to it that we sacrifice the most sacred commandments and our
finest and most natural impulses to these social idols. And to this
cult of false honor, which is nothing but vanity and eccentricity,

Schach too has succumbed, and greater things than he will follow. Remember these words. We have stuck our heads in the sand like the ostrich, in order not to hear or see. But this ostrich-like precaution has never worked. When the Ming dynasty went into decline, and the victorious Manchu army had already penetrated into the palace garden in Peking, messengers and envoys continued to arrive with news of victory after victory for the emperor, because it was against the manners of high society and the court to speak of defeats. Oh this good form! An hour later an empire was in ruins, and a throne overturned. And why? Because everything artificial becomes a lie, and everything that is not true leads to death.[32]

Schach von Wuthenow is a more polished and disciplined production than its predecessor, but less impressive and less rewarding for its readers. It lacks the epic sweep, the attempt to see the whole of society, and the richness and variety of *Vor dem Sturm*. Fontane has limited his characters severely: two aristocratic women, a prince, a handful of army officers, a military publicist who talks too much and does too little, and some minor figures who make cameo appearances (King Frederick William III, for example, and Queen Luise). No members of the lower classes are seen except Schach's groom and his family retainers at Wuthenow, and no bourgeois, except the musician Dussek, who seems to have been inserted in the story to give Fontane an opportunity, through Bülow, to make a remark about "your whole *Bürgertum* which doesn't want to create a new class of freedom but only, with vanity and jealousy, to incorporate itself with the old privileged classes."[33]

None of these, moreover, with the exception of Josephine von Carayon, is fully developed by the author. Consider the case of Aunt Marguerite, with her insistence on pronouncing "i's" as "ü's" (*Kürche*) and her zeal for imparting well-known information (*"Sieh, Victoire, das sind Binsen."*).[34] She is such a pale shadow compared with Aunt Schorlemer in *Vor dem Sturm* that we are almost persuaded that Fontane doesn't have his heart in what he is doing. A more serious failure in this respect, and certainly one felt by many readers, is Fontane's failure to make Schach himself a credible figure. His fellow officers, even when criticizing him, are apt to insist that he is not to be underestimated: "He is nevertheless one of our best."[35] But Fontane gives us no reason to believe this or, for that matter, to explain why it is that two attractive and intelligent women are fascinated by him. Schach is handsome and has good manners, but he is of mediocre intelligence, with an instinctive suspicion of new ideas. He appears also to be completely humorless. There is much speculation in the book about "le choix de Schach," but it turns out in the end that he is not sexually drawn to either Josephine or Victoire; he just wants to go to their parties and to remain uncommitted. He is, in everything that he does, more *Schein* than *Sein*, and this being so is not of the stuff to be an effective tragic hero or to be attractive to the ordinary reader.

If the personal drama that is the center of the story is weakened by these deficiencies, the historical novel suffers from a lack of historical description. The tragedy of *Schach von Wuthenow* is presumably set in a society in moral decay and on the verge of destruction but, while we are told that this is so through the monologues of Bülow, which become a bit of a bore, we never see any actual signs of it, except perhaps in the public demonstration of officers of the Regiment Gensdarmes against Iffland's production of the Reformation drama *Weihe der Kraft*. This spectacle, which comes in the wake of Victoire's surrender to Schach and so disgusts her that it prompts her confession to her mother, consists of a sleigh ride on the salt-strewn streets of the city and represents

> contempt for everyone and everything. First, debauched nuns with a witch of a mother superior at their head, howling, drinking, and playing cards, and then in the middle of the column the principal sled, rolling on cylinders and from the excess of its gilt decoration designed apparently as a triumphal chariot, in which Luther and his famulus sat and, on the barbette, Katharina von Bora.

In his comments on *Ruhe ist die erst Bürgerpflicht* in his essay on Willibald Alexis, Fontane criticized Alexis severely for the emphasis that he placed on the moral decay of Berlin in 1806 and for dwelling on the uglier aspects of this "longer and more lovingly" than was necessary.[36] Yet for all its other faults, Alexis's extensive descriptions in *Ruhe ist die erste Bürgerpflicht* of his heroine's temptations in the salons of high society and of the seamy side of Berlin politics convey a more convincing picture of a society in dissolution than is to be found in *Schach von Wuthenau*. Partly out of prudery, perhaps, Fontane preferred to rely upon symbolism and analogy rather than description,[37] but readers can be expected to read only so much into a couple of references to Mirabeau or the description of the prank of some bored army officers.

Still, Fontane was feeling his way, and the techniques with which he experimented in *Schach von Wuthenow* were to be used more effectively in his novels of society.

8

The Novels of Society

It has often been noted that, in contrast to the situation in Great Britain and France, the national literature of Germany was not in the nineteenth century rich in works of social realism or authors who combined high aesthetic standards with gifts of political and social analysis. There were no Thackerays and Stendhals, nor Flauberts and Dickenses among the prose writers of the decades before unification and, indeed, the German writers who made any pretense of dealing with contemporary and social subjects before 1870—Jean Paul, E. T. A. Hoffmann, Karl Immermann, Gustav Freytag—rarely ventured beyond the realm of the idyllic or the fantastic or the parochial. Their works seldom awaken any shock of recognition among non-German readers and in general have an antiquarian flavor that may be charming but is usually remote from the realities of the modern world.[1]

The explanation often given for this is that Germany was, in two senses, a retarded nation. Long after the Western countries had become powerful nation-states, it had continued to be fragmented into dozens of separate political entities, and the resultant lack of a cultural capital like London or Paris, where artists might gather and exchange ideas, had necessarily led to a narrowness of focus, a provincial perspective, and a lack of the urbanity that characterized the literature of the West.[2] Moreover, the effects of political disunity upon economic development, the relative slowness of industrial growth and of the rise of a strong middle class, and the late arrival of such concomitant features of industrial society as urbanization, the proletarianization of the lower classes, and the disintegration of inherited social categories and values deprived German writers of the kinds of themes that challenged their colleagues in countries that were more advanced economically.

There is much to be said for this explanation, but it is not entirely satisfactory, else how would we account for the fact that, even after 1871, when the creation of the empire put an end to Germany's political divisions and the country experienced a surge of economic development that transformed it within a generation into one of Europe's leading industrial producers, German writers still, on the whole, avoided social and political themes? It was not until the 1880s, with the coming of the naturalist movement, that writers and dramatists showed any appreciable interest in such subjects as social justice, sexual discrimination, and the plight of the poor; and, even when they did so, their attention lacked persistence and was often disingenuous, for they tended to concentrate on prostitution, the more lurid aspects of urban crime, and other subjects that were likely to titillate the palate of the middle-class reading public.[3] In the underlying values of society the naturalists had little interest, and in its politics none; and by the end of the 1890s, when the vogue of naturalism was past, German writers were little more concerned with serious problems of contemporary life than before 1871. There was a good deal of talk in artistic circles in the 1880s about the need to imitate Émile Zola and write sociological novels—this was the stock-in-trade of Michael Georg Conrad and the group in Munich that founded the journal *Die Gesellschaft* in 1885[4]—but, in fact, few German imitators appeared.

The causes of this lack of social engagement must be sought, therefore, not in the slowness of the country's political and economic development but in German views of the proper function of literature.

It had long been a strongly rooted prejudice that writers worthy of respect, true *Dichter*, should concern themselves with transcendental themes and spiritual values, that the problems and politics of contemporary society were no business of theirs, and that anyone who persisted in dealing with such questions was automatically deprived of his artistic status and relegated to the company of mere scribblers or *Literaten*.[5]

Erich Auerbach has suggested that this odd differentiation owes much to the towering figure of Goethe, whose interest in the actualities of social development was minimal, who found such things as the growth of industry and the increasing evidence of social mobility distasteful, and whose own novels were set in static social contexts, the actual conditions of life serving merely as immobile backgrounds against which the drama of Goethe's own ideological growth unfolded. To the emerging structure of life Goethe paid little attention, and such was his authority, Auerbach suggests, that his exclusive concentration on individuality and ideas came to be regarded as the criterion of art as opposed to mere literature.[6]

Whether or not Goethe was responsible for it is less important than the fact that the double standard prevailed. It is notable that Heinrich Heine, a writer of whom one would think any nation in the world would be proud, has never received his due recognition in the land of his birth, in part because political and social criticism was never far below the surface of anything he wrote.[7] This confirmed bias against present-mindedness has doubtless served as a warning to countless writers with aspirations to lasting fame. In our own century, Thomas Mann, who certainly had the talent to write social novels, seemed uncomfortable with the genre and once confessed, "Social problems are my weak point [although] this puts me to some extent at odds with my art form itself, the novel, which is propitious to the examination of social problems. But the lure of . . . individuality and metaphysics simply happens to be ever so much stronger in me. . . . I am German. . . . The Zolaesque streak in me is feeble."[8]

The inhibition imposed by literary tradition was reinforced by a concern for what the reading public would tolerate. Authors like to be read, and German writers after 1871 could not but be aware that a reading public that had made Heinrich von Treitschke's *Deutsche Geschichte im XIX. Jahrhundert* a best-seller was hardly likely to welcome books that criticized the social foundations or political practice of the new Reich of which they were so proud. The educated middle class of the Bismarck and Wilhelmine years was excessively preoccupied with its own social status and prestige, which were its substitutes for the political power that it did not possess. Its jealous regard for its position, which it felt was threatened by the rising class of technicians and functionaries, made it vulnerable to a process of ideological feudalization and robbed it of its intellectual independence.[9] Increasingly more conservative as the period advanced, this *Bildungsbürgerhtum* expected from the authors of its novels and dramas entertainment or moral elevation. It did not want to be told by them that there were things in the world that ought to be put right and that its duty was to correct them, and it had the power to make its disapproval felt. It took a determined writer to disregard this.

Of those who did disregard it,[10] the most successful and the most lasting in his influence was Theodor Fontane.

I

In turning to the novel of society, Fontane was not motivated by any desire to indoctrinate his readers. It was rather his historical instinct that inspired him to begin his series of Berlin novels. He was fascinated by the changes that had taken place in Berlin during his lifetime, particularly by the accelerated mutations of social relations and mood that occurred after the war in France had united Germany and made Berlin the capital city, the shifts in values that took place as considerations of power and money began to bulk larger in German thinking and social justice and civility less. He was interested in writing about these things not in the abstract sense but in the particular, and certainly without any ideological presuppositions or intentions. Discussing the origins of *L'Adultera*, the first of the novels, with Paul Lindau, he said that he had been ''principally interested in giving a picture of Berlin life and society; the circumstantial and the scenery was the main thing.''[11]

For this purpose he was, of course, superbly equipped, for, in addition to his long experience as a writer, he was a Berliner by choice and inclination. In his old age, to be sure, he sometimes denied this.

On Fontane's seventieth birthday, when Maximilian Harden wrote a commemorative essay about him in his journal *Die Zukunft*, he expressed his gratitude to Harden for having described him as an old Fritz grenadier. This, he wrote, was "sublime," adding, "Also what you say about my descent. I am a *Märker* but still more a Gascon."[12] But this sort of thing was greatly exaggerated. The fact that Fontane's family came from France hardly made him a Gascon; his command of the French language was merely competent, and his Frenchness found expression largely in the commemorative odes that he composed (in German) for annual gatherings of the French colony in Berlin.[13]

His self-identification with Mark Brandenburg was somewhat more substantial—he was born, after all, in Neuruppin—but almost equally sentimental, the product of the extensive research, archival and ambulatory, that was the basis of his travel books. In any real sense, leaving the question of origins aside, Fontane was a Berliner. Except for his long absence in England in the 1850s, he lived in Berlin for almost all his life, from the time when it was a sleepy residential capital enclosed within a wall whose circumference could be traversed by foot in four hours[14] until the days when it had become a *Weltstadt* that, with its suburban villages and towns, covered an area thirty miles across. It was in the Berlin of the 1840s that Fontane had his beginnings as a writer, and the tumultuous growth of the city (its population had grown to 862,341 by 1871 and to 1,315,287 within the next fifteen years) contributed to the development and maturation of his literary skills, changing his perspective, honing his critical capacities, and supplying him with ever new themes and problems. It was with this dependence on the city in mind that he wrote to Paul Heyse in June 1860:

> In the course of the years, and particularly since my stay in London, it has become a necessity for me to live in a great middle point, in a center where decisive things happen. However one may mock at Berlin, and however willing I am to admit that now and then it deserves this mockery, at bottom the fact is undeniable that what happens or does not happen here has a direct effect upon the great events of the world. It has become a necessity for me to hear such

a balance wheel whirring close to me, even at the risk of its becoming now and then the well-known mill wheel.[15]

This feeling did not change with the years, despite his frequent complaints about the city and its inhabitants. To be sure, he conceived the idea that *Berliner Luft*, which the novelist Conrad Alberti once described as "nervous, endlessly quivering, [working] upon people like alcohol, morphine, cocaine, exciting, inspiring, relaxing, deadly: the air of the world city,"[16] was injurious to his health and that the smell of the Landwehr Canal affected him with a kind of malarial fever, but he was always nervous about his health, and such worries were also a rationalization for his long working holidays in resorts like Thale in the Harz and Krümmhubel in the Silesian mountains.[17] He was also a constant critic of the volubility, the lack of urbanity, and the dowdiness of the Berlin middle class, particularly when away from home, and portrayed them as figures of fun (as in the case of the two Berlin tourists in the novel *Cécile*)[18] or, less kindly, as a "society of cockiness, larking-around, gossip and belittling" (*Schnoddergesellschaft von Ulk, Klatsch und Kleinmacherei*).[19] In his more pessimistic moods, he was apt to drift into reflections about the corrupting effect of the city upon creative ability ("As a rule I am firmly convinced that the big city makes people nimble, quick and agile, but it makes them shallow, and from anyone who does not live in seclusion it drains away his higher powers of production"), although his own life disproved the generalization, or into moralizing complaints about the pervasive materialism of the metropolis: "The big city hasn't time to think, and—what is even worse—it hasn't time for happiness. What it creates, hundred and thousandfold, is merely 'the pursuit of happiness,' which is the same as unhappiness."[20]

Perhaps such passages merely underline Fontane's Berlinness, for self-criticism was always a Berlin trait, as he once admitted to his friend Friedländer:

The more *berlinisch* one is, the more one rails or jeers at Berlin. That this is so is due not only to the critics and jeerers. It lies also in their object, in our good Berlin itself. Just as our Junkers remain ineradicably the same, small, very small people who take themselves for historical figures, so the Berliner remains an egotistical, narrow-small-town person. The city grows and grows, the millionaires increase tenfold, but a certain shoemaker's mentality remains, which expresses itself above all in the belief that "mother's dumplings are the best." But at the same time nothing here—for one cannot cite Bismarck and Molke all the time, who were not even Berliners—nothing is the best; in Berlin there is only imitation, good average, respectable mediocrity, and all clever Berliners feel that as soon as they are outside Berlin.[21]

All the same, he never left Berlin and, even at his gloomiest, never wavered from the sentiments that he expressed in an eloquent letter to Theodor Storm in 1853, in which he praised the egalitarian instincts, the sound morality, and the readiness to sacrifice of the ordinary Berliner, reminding him that in 1813, during the war of liberation, the city had raised not only several regiments of troops of the line but ten thousand volunteers, out of a population of only 180,000. He told Storm: "The people here have a genuine and true joy in sacrifice—even the educated. Yes, even the *'Berliner Kinder'* (who are in large part a disagreeable sort) provided *that it amounts to something.*"[22]

There was an implication here that the Berliner was a model for the rest of the German nation that, indeed, to use a phrase that Fontane used in another connection,[23] before God everyone was really a Berliner. However that may be, for the common people of Berlin, their ability to rise to any occasion, their unflappability and their devastating capacity for repartee, and their use of the inexhaustible resources of their wit to give order to their often difficult lives, Fontane had a deep affection, as he had for their songs, their jokes, and their preferred amusements. In March 1886, as a member of a committee giving awards for new poetry, he insisted that a special prize be given to the author of a song that had taken Berlin by storm:

Mutter, der Mann mit dem Koks is da!
Mädel, sei stille, ick seh et ja.
Ick hab keen Jeld, du hast keen Jeld.
Wer hat den Mann mit dem Koks bestellt?[24]

Gassenhauer, he said, sometimes deserved more respect than more formal expressions of the muse. "It is always something to have put a particular word or song into the mouth of a city of millions for four weeks."[25]

Fontane loved Berlin speech and acquired a perfect ear for its cadences and rhythms, as for the love of exaggeration and the subtle antithetical constructions that characterized it. This is manifest in his letters, but most of all in his novels, where—to cite only one example—the scene in *Der Stechlin*, where the dying insurance secretary Schikaneder talks with his wife about their years together and tells her how to order her future is so natural that it goes beyond literature.[26] Combined with his talent for penetrating the psychology of situations and the persons caught up in them, Fontane's command of the local idiom repeatedly produces small miracles of verisimilitude, as in the penultimate scene in *Stine*, when Pauline Pittelkow, trying to rally the heroine after the death of her lover, says:

> Go on and cry, Stinechen, go on and really cry. When it really pours again, it's already half over, just like the weather. And now drink another cuppa. . . . Olga, where are you? I bet the girl is in the kip again. . . . And next Sunday is Sedan Day and we'll all go off to the Finkenkrug and ride on the carousel and throw the dice. And then you'll throw the double six again.[27]

He was no less skillful in reproducing the vocal mannerisms of the upwardly mobile middle class, which combined the wit and volubility of Berlin speech with floods of quotations, gleaned perhaps from Büchmann's *Geflügelte Worte*, that remarkable work that first appeared in 1863 and afforded an easy way of adding embellishment, if not distinction, to spoken style.[28] Not that the use of citation as a conversational gambit or badge of culture was an exclusively middle-class trait. If Van der Straaten in *L'Adultera* and Kommerzienrat Treibel in *Frau Jenny Treibel* are accomplished, if excessive, in its use, this is no less true of Professor Schmidt in the latter novel. No century before or since was ever so obsessed with education as the nineteenth, and in Germany, where *Bildung* became the expression of universal culture, it was perhaps only natural that the citation should become a

means of communication and identification in daily life as in scientific
and literary circles. Among German novelists Wilhelm Raabe was
known for his extensive use of the quotation, not for vanity's sake or
to display his learning but to emphasize recollections, experiences,
epiphanies, and intimations of meaning or truth.[29]

As Fontane refined his style, he relied less and less on narrative
and description and more and more on conversation. Speech, he believed, was the key to a man's character and capacities, and in speaking with others individuals revealed their differences, as well as their
integrity or unreliability, their moral convictions and social prejudices,
and the way they reacted to their times.[30] Conversation was the sovereign instrument of self-disclosure as it was the best defense against
it. In *Unwiederbringlich* Count Holk, worried lest his privacy be betrayed, is advised by a friend that the best defense is a "free manner,
unaffectedness and lots of talk. Talking a lot is a pleasure anyway and
at times the true diplomatic wisdom, for it prevents things from being
ascertained precisely and, even better, one thing nullifies another."[31]
Finally, conversation is rarely disciplined and restricted to discrete
subjects but tends to drift here and there, revealing as it does a lot of
miscellaneous information about the participants and their society.
Writing about the seventh chapter of *Irrungen, Wirrungen*, Walter
Killy has observed that, if we had nothing of the novel except this
chapter, we should still have some interesting historical information,
as well as a fascinating cultural-historical document.

> One could deduce from it that lobster and chablis would be on the
> menu at such a gathering, that parsons who started as house tutors
> and ended in the position of *pastor loci*, were apt to have property
> disputes with landlords, that a respectable estate like that of Botho's
> father could be ruined by gambling and unwise economy, that it was
> still common in the landed nobility to make early arrangements for
> the marriage of their children, and—an apparent bagatelle—that
> charming ladies of rank went to Norderney for the baths.[32]

While most readers are charmed by the wit and charm of Fontane's conversation, opinions have been divided on its effectiveness
as a tool of social realism. Russell Berman talks of Fontane's "dissolution of reality in conversation" and argues that it is his way of

arguing that there is no objective reality beyond what people say of it and that order and privilege in society can only be upheld as linguistic fabrications of arbitrary meanings.[33] Fontane, who always believed in the primacy of the word in human intercourse, while admitting the gap between the word and the truth, would probably not have wished to push things quite so far. Certainly, he made neither political nor philosophical claims for his experiments with the social novel. Of *Der Stechlin* he wrote:

> At the end an old man dies and two young people get married,— that is just about all that happens in 500 pages. Of complications and solutions, of conflicts of the heart and conflicts in general, of excitement and surprises there is virtually nothing. In an old-fashioned *märkische* estate; on the one hand, and a new-fashioned ducal residence (Berlin) on the other, various people meet and talk about God and the world. All talk, dialogue, in which the characters tell the story. Naturally I don't claim that this is the best way of writing a contemporary novel but it is the one that is called for.[34]

If we apply this kind of radical reductionism to them, not much more happens in Fontane's other novels than in *Der Stechlin*. In *Irrungen, Wirrungen* (1888), a young aristocrat who is deeply in love with a daughter of the people is informed by his uncle that his family will lose its estate unless he marries a wealthy young woman of his own station. He does what he considers to be his duty and leaves his sweetheart. In *Frau Jenny Treibel* (1892), a gymnasium professor's daughter sets her cap for the son of Frau and Kommerzienrat Treibel but is balked by the young man's mother, who, driven by social ambition, arranges for his marriage to the daughter of a Hamburg commercial firm. The professor's daughter marries a young scholar and goes off to excavate Troy. In *Die Poggenpuhls* (1896), a Prussian aristocratic family lives in genteel poverty in Berlin, trying desperately to preserve their social position and that of two officer sons. In the end, the death of an uncle in Silesia brings a legacy that modestly increases their income. In *Mathilde Möhring* (1906), a young woman is responsible for the successful political career of her husband but, when he suddenly dies, is forced to return to her former position and to begin all over again.. There is, of course, more to these stories than these bare scenarios, which would hardly attract readers to them. The real stories lie in the talk.

That having been said, it should be noted that the stories are often affected by critical happenings that take place off stage. In *Quitt* (1890), an awkward book whose story occurs partly in the Silesian mountains and partly in an America that no American will recognize, there is a murder. *Stine* (1890), *Cécile* (1887), and *Unwiederbringlich* (1891) end with suicides; and in *Cécile* and *Effi Briest* (1895), there are duels with fatal consequences. Indeed, there is also a duel in *Irrungen, Wirrungen*, although one that took place before the story began. When the lieutenant Botho von Rienacker is confronted with the necessity of terminating his love affair with Lene Nimpsch and marrying a woman of his own social class, he goes on a lonely ride in the Tiergarten to the place where Frederick William IV's all-powerful police president Carl Ludwig von Hinckeldey had been killed in a duel in 1856, because of an affair in which honor seemed to require that he act as he did. Botho seems to be seeking reassurance from Hinckeldey's example for the hard choice that he will have to make.[35]

The importance that he attributes to the duel is one of several indications of how clearly Fontane realized the extent to which violence, and the mental constructs (*Hilfskonstructionen*) that human beings used to justify it, like the concept of honor, regulated society and, pace Berman, was the real force maintaining order and privilege within it.[36]

II

In June 1862 Fontane wrote to his wife:

> Your little reprimand about Counts and Excellences is really pretty undeserved. I should have thought that I had explained myself enough in my letter. It is, to be sure, true that I come more into contact with the nobility than with the *Bürgertum*, but that is partly the result of my métier (poet and writer of the *Wanderungen*), and partly a consequence of my political direction. Poets and artists in all ages traffic almost exclusively with princes, nobles and the patriciate; it is really quite natural. Today, indeed, when the *Bürger-*

stand (in the widest sense) has an outstanding significance and in
part is precisely the recipient of the advantages that otherwise were
unique to the nobility and the clergy, that doesn't *have* to be so any
longer, but someone who fights in the camp of the "feudals" must
make do with them.[37]

When Fontane wrote this letter he was working for the *Kreuzzeitung*, which is what he means by his "political direction." But the
opinions of that paper did not represent his political or social philosophy. He was an old forty-eighter, and the liberal-democratic views
he had held at that time had been strengthened by his long years of
residence in England. There is a strong intimation in his letter that he
believed that the time was coming when the Prussian-German middle
class would become as dominant in the country as its counterpart in
England, and that when that happened it would inherit the nobility's
political, social, and cultural role in society. In which case, he might
not have to offend his wife's social predilections so often.

In 1862 there was every reason to be confident in that result. The
middle-class liberals had apparently recovered from their defeat in the
year of revolution and were beginning a new assault upon the privi-
leges of the crown, this time striking at its control over the military.
But their efforts were defeated by the political resolve and tactical
skill of Otto von Bismarck, and their political will dissolved in the
wave of nationalism that swept over the country in the wake of the
victories over Austria and France. During the 1870s the so-called National Liberals tried to convince themselves that their support was
essential to the government; by the end of the decade it was clear that
this was not true, and that the German bourgeoisie was dead as an
independent political power. Henceforth, it gave itself over to mon-
eymaking, to attempts to effect a social symbiosis with the ruling
aristocratic class, and to cultural activities

Fontane watched this process with growing alienation. In the days
when, as he said in 1873, to be a *Bürger* meant to possess three things,
"property, respect for the law, and the feeling that flows from the
first two,"[38] he had had high hopes for the bourgeoisie. As the years
passed he became a harsh critic of the materialistic traits and the
parvenuism of parts of the new German middle class, hating "the
Bourgeoishaft with an emotion," as he once wrote, as if he were a

"sworn Social Democrat."[39] Still, he did not abandon his own bourgeois credentials. Even in his last year of life, he could write:

> I am always happy when I read names like Lisco, Lucä, Gropius,
> Persius, Hänsel, Thaer, Körte, Dieterici, Virchow, Siemens, because
> as I do so I am aware that in these blooming families, now in their
> second and third generations, a new nobility, even if without the
> "von," is growing up, in which the world really has something,
> models for the new age (for that is nobility's real function), who
> can challenge the world and not see their life task in the egotistical
> pickling of dead things.[40]

He was well aware, however, that such names now represented only
a tiny minority of the *Bürgertum* and that the old bourgeois spirit had
died in the wake of the victory over France and the easy prosperity
of the *Gründerzeit*.

But this was not all that had changed. The nobility, for which he
had always had a tendresse—he wrote his wife late in life that "*märkische* Junker and country pastors remain my ideals, my secret
loves"[41]—was no longer as easy to admire. He had always been aware
that the Prussian legacy to a united Germany would be ambiguous;
and, in the very year of unification, in a curiously veiled passage in
one of his war books, he had written of the spirit of Potsdam as
consisting of "an unholy amalgamation . . . of absolutism, militarism,
and philistinism." and said that "a breath of unfreedom, of artifici-
ality, of the contrived . . . blows through it all and oppresses any soul
that has a greater need to breathe freely than to get in line."[42] In the
years that followed, he became increasingly convinced that it was this
kind of Prussianism that had captured the country, which was now
being ruled by and for a nobility that no longer had the qualities that
justified such a monopoly of power. Increasingly he felt that

> the Junker, our most characteristic type of nobility, has become un-
> appetizing. A frightful mixture of dim-wittedness, vanity, and prej-
> udice.[43]

> Prussia—and indirectly all Germany—suffers from its East Elbians.
> We must recover from our nobility; we can visit them, like the
> Egyptian Museum, and bow before Ramses and Amenophis, but to

rule the country for their sake, in the delusion: *this nobility is the country*, that is our misfortune, and as long as this condition persists any development of German power and German reputation abroad is unthinkable. Where the Emperor sees columns are only feet of clay.[44]

As an artist, Fontane was aware that the aristocratic always had an aesthetic charm that appealed to readers. His own work had profited from the contacts with the landed nobility that he had forged during the period of the *Wanderings*, and his long friendship with Mathilde von Rohr of Dobbertin, whom he called "a *Prachtnummer*, . . . a masterpiece of an old *märkisch* noble lady," and who had supplied him with much information and served as his confidante in difficult times.[45] He retained a sneaking admiration for the Junkers, unappetizing as their behavior had been in recent years, and wrote that they "remained interesting as figures of art, and historians and *Dichter* could take pleasure in the fact that such people had existed and still did; they had a fascination like everything that is sharply etched." [46] Fontane preferred to give his novels aristocratic settings, and to introduce into them figures like Botho von Rienacker's's uncle from the country with his hatred of Berlin ("Damned nest! One can't breathe!") and Effi's father, old Briest, and the general who came to Berlin to visit his relatives the Poggenpuhls and to attend a performance of "The Quitzows," and, in his last novel, Count Barby and the *domina* aunt Adelaide, and old Dubslav. These were all relics of a former age rather than representatives of the new Germany, and Dubslav was so idealized that it is difficult to think of him as ever really existing. But the late novels would be the weaker for their absence, and Fontane did not greatly offend against realism by their inclusion. For, after all, it cannot be argued that he neglected the darker side.

Indeed, through all of his Berlin novels there runs a steady stream of careerists and adventurers and restless and ambitious men, beginning with Rittmeister von Schach in *Schach von Wuthenow* (1883), including the retired colonel St. Arnaud in *Cécile* (1887) and Landrat von Instettin in what is perhaps Fontane's most successful novel of society, *Effi Briest* (1895), and ending with Ministerialassessor Rex in *Der Stechlin*. Intent upon their own ends and insensitive to the feelings of others, these representatives of the new Prussia were quick to resort to violence when they supposed that this was required by their sense of honor, that old military concept which had, in civilian life, been translated into a cruel and unnatural code of etiquette that imprisoned the upper classes in a moral straitjacket.

Fontane wrote of the tyranny of honor in two of his novels. In *Cécile* he told the story of a young civil engineer named Leslie-Gordon, attached to the Prussian army, who becomes acquainted, during a stay in a fashionable hotel in Thale in the Harz, with a retired colonel of a Guards regiment, St. Arnaud, and his lovely but mysteriously melancholy wife, Cécile. Gordon is powerfully attracted but scrupulously proper in his behavior toward her. Their acquaintance is continued when they meet again in Berlin, and here Gordon discovers Cécile's secret, that with the connivance of her mother, she was for some years mistress to an old prince. After her protector's death, she returned to her family home in a small regimental town, where St. Arnaud met and became engaged to marry her. On the eve of the wedding, he received from the officers of his regiment a letter saying that the projected marriage would be unsuitable, and promptly called out the officer who had acted as spokesman for the others and killed him in a duel, for which he was forced to retire.

This information, while arousing Gordon's sympathy for Cécile, also inflames his desire, and in his attempts to see her he becomes importunate. This comes to the attention of St. Arnaud, who immediately challenges Gordon to a duel, less because of the affront to his wife than because of the insult to him. He tells himself:

> It wasn't the love affair as such that aroused his anger at Gordon, but the thought that the fear of *himself*, the man of fixed purposes, had not been enough to frighten him off. To be feared, to frighten, to make felt at every moment the superiority that courage gives you, that was really his passion. And this merely average Gordon, this blurred Prussian first lieutenant, this man of cables and international wire-pulling, he had believed he could play his game with him. This presumption![47]

He kills Gordon and travels to the Riviera, expecting Cécile to follow him, but she commits suicide.

In *Effi Briest*, the theme is handled with greater penetration and sophistication. The Prussian bureaucrat von Instettin marries Effi, a young woman of aristocratic family, still scarcely more than a girl, and takes her away to live in a small seaside town where she has no friends. Intent on pursuing his own career—he has attracted the favorable attention of Bismarck and spends long periods of time at the chancellor's estate at Varzin—he neglects his young wife, while at the same time exploiting her nighttime fears in order to discipline her. Her loneliness makes Effi amenable to the attentions of a Major von Crampas, who lives nearby, and they have a brief affair. Six and a half years later, Instettin learns of this from some old letters. Although it is clear that Effi has had no relations with Crampas during that time, and although he dearly loves her, Instettin challenges the major to a duel and kills him, and then drives Effi from his home and takes her child from her. As an intelligent man, he is well aware that his conduct is not rational, but in order to render his doubts ineffectual he tells a close friend, Baron von Wüllersdorf, of the affair, thus making it, as he sees it, impossible for him not to go forward with his drastic course of action. In what has been called "the greatest conversation scene in the German novel,"[48] and certainly Fontane's most searching analysis of the moral hollowness of German society in his time, Instettin says:

> We're not isolated individuals, we belong to society, and we must continually take society into account; we are dependent upon it. If one could live in isolation, I could let this go. I would then be bearing a burden that I had agreed to accept. . . . But with people living all together, something has evolved that exists here and now, and we've become accustomed to judging everything in accordance with its rules, other people and ourselves as well. And to violate that doesn't work. Society would scorn us and, in the end, we would scorn ourselves and not be able to stand it, and would shoot a bullet through our heads.

In any case, he adds, there's no keeping the secret now. He has to go ahead. If he does not, then one day, when someone has suffered an affront, and he suggests that allowances should be made because no real harm has been done, he will see a smile pass, or start to pass, over Wüllersdorf's face and will imagine him thinking, "Good old

Instettin! He's never been able to discover anything that smells too strong for him!'' Wüllersdorf, who has been trying to dissuade him, now strikes his guns. ''I think it's dreadful that you're right,'' he says, ''but you *are* right. . . . The world is simply the way it is, and things go, not the way we, but the way others, want them to. All that high-flown stuff about a judgment of God is, of course, rubbish, and we don't want any of it. On the other hand, our cult of honor is a form of idolatry, and yet we must submit to it, as long as the idol is allowed to stand.''[49]

Fontane's view that the nobility had submitted to a kind of totemism convinced him that it was fast losing its originality, spontaneity, and moral energy and was ceasing to be a vital force in German life, a conviction that he expressed in *Die Poggenpuhls* (1896), the story of a noble family that lives on the memories of what they once were. But it had meanwhile corrupted other sections of society, the educational establishment and the clergy, which repeated and sanctified its prejudices, and the once self-reliant middle class. The portraits of the *Besitzbürgertum* (propertied middle class) that Fontane gives us in his novels are increasingly unflattering, reprobating both their money-grubbing and their parvenuism.

Fontane had less success with his middle-class figures than with his aristocratic ones, partly because, as Peter Demetz has suggested, he did not really believe that people from the world of business or specialists in any field were capable of arousing the interest and sympathy of his readers.[50] He tried to compensate for this in various ways. His scholars, for instance—like Eginhard aus dem Grunde in *Cécile* and Professor Cujacius in *Der Stechlin*—are treated as comic figures, dressed in bizarre ways and shown as advocating theories that can only be described as fantastical. Even Professor Schmidt in *Frau Jenny Treibel* does not entirely escape this fate. In *The Prelude*, Wordsworth differentiated between the kinds of professors he met at Cambridge: on the one hand,

> . . . old men,
> Old humourists . . .
> . . . men unscoured, grotesque
> In character, tricked out like ancient trees

Which through the lapse of their infirmity
Give ready place to any random seed
That chooses to be reared upon their trunks,

and, on the other,

... those with whom
By frame of academic discipline
We were perforce connected, men whose sway
And known authority of office served
To set our minds on edge[51]

The self-educated Fontane knew nothing of academic discipline, and
we cannot imagine his gymnasium professor Schmidt—who is certainly not unscoured but almost tediously an old humourist—in any
academic setting. In general, artists come off better in Fontane's novels. The singer Marietta Trippelli in *Effi Briest* is a credible figure,
with all of her eccentricities,[52] and the same must be said Pauline
Pittelkow's actress friend Wanda in *Stine*, who entertains her guests
with a miniature Judith and Holofernes drama played with potatoes.[53]
Fontane understood the world of the theater and always believed, with
Pauline Pittelkow, that "everybody from the theater has something
and gets a *chic*, and can speak."[54] With his portraits of businessmen,
however, he had greater difficulty.

Fontane's first attempt to portray the life of the *Besitzbürgertum*
was *L'Adultera* (1882), set in the *Gründerjahre*, the boom period that
followed the war against France. Kommerzienrat van der Straaten is
a financier and highly successful speculator, married to Mélanie de
Caparoux, a woman less than half his age. He is a self-confident,
ebullient Berliner, with some pretensions to culture, but with a streak
of vulgarity that he does not attempt to hide. This increasingly grates
upon his wife's nerves and helps attract her to a young businessman
named Ebenezer Rubehn, whom van der Straaten has brought into
their home, perhaps to test his wife. She falls in love with Rubehn
and runs away with him, eventually returning to Berlin with her new
husband and learning to live happily outside of society, which has
now repudiated her. As this drama unfolds, van der Straaten remains
magnanimous and forgiving, ready apparently to take Mélanie back,

a fact that only confirms her original conviction that she could no longer remain with him.

This story, awkward at best, was made even more so by Fontane's decision to make both van der Straaten and Rubehn converted Jews. Fontane always had a problem with the Jewish question, and, although he had many close Jewish friends and correspondents (Georg Friedländer, the intimate of his old age, for one) and although he often said that the Jewish middle class was infinitely more cultivated and intellectually stimulating than the non-Jewish, he fretted over the long-term cultural effects of a growing Jewish population and became increasingly pessimistic in his letters about the success of assimilation.[55] Why he should have introduced the theme here is puzzling, unless it was, as Peter Demetz has suggested, because he lacked the confidence to describe the working out of his love triangle in autochthonous society and was trying to ease his problem by marginalizing his characters. But this, of course, weakened the novel as a critique of German society, and Fontane all but acknowledged this by fleeing into sentimentality in the book's last chapters.[56]

Ten years later, Fontane wrote another story of life among the propertied middle class, *Frau Jenny Treibel*. Its point, he wrote in a letter to his son Theodor, was to show "the hollow, wordy, deceitful, arrogant, hard-hearted nature of the bourgeois point of view, which talks about Schiller and means Gerson [Bleichröder]."[57] In the novel, Counselor of Commerce Treibel, who has made a fortune from manufacturing Prussian blue, the dye used for army uniforms, has been assiduously copying the politics of the aristocratic classes and has now decided to become a candidate for a conservative seat in a rural district, while cultivating decayed gentlewomen in the hope that they will help his candidacy. One of them is bewildered by his ambition and lectures him on the politics of social stratification. She says to him: "Aristocratic estate-owners are agrarian conservatives; professors belong to the National Liberal party; and industrialists are Progressives. Become a Progressive! What do you want with a royal order? If I were in your place I would go in for municipal politics and seek bourgeois distinction!" That is not the kind of advice Treibel wants to hear, and he answers that conservatism suits him better, especially since he is a *Kommerzienrat*, "a title of fragmentary character" that cries out for augmentation.

Factories in general incline toward bourgeois distinction; factories in particular, however—and my own inclines most decidedly in that direction—constitute the exception. Your expression tells me you want proof of this. Well then, I'll try to give it to you. I ask you, can you think of a market gardener who—let's say on the Lichten-berger or Rummelsburger boundary—grows cornflowers *en gros,*—cornflowers, that symbol of royal Prussian sentiment—and is at the same time a *pétroleur* or dynamiter? You are shaking your head and that confirms my denial. And now I ask you further, what are all the cornflowers in the world compared with a Berlin Blue factory? In Berlin Blue you have the symbolical Prussia, so to say, in its highest potency, and the more certain and indisputable that is the more imperative is my remaining on the side of conservatism. The augmentation of the Commercial Counsellor's title signifies in my special case a natural assumption . . . in any case more than a bour-geois distinction.[58]

All this is said with great joviality, but Treibel is deadly serious, and believes in what he says. So does his wife Jenny, as ruthless a social climber as Proust's Madame Verdurin. As a friend says, Jenny "really imagines that she has a sensitive heart and a feeling for higher things, but she has a heart only for the ponderable, for everything that can be weighed and pays interest."[59]

Treibel's electoral plans come to nothing because he chooses as his agent a reserve lieutenant named Vogelsang, whose reactionary pronouncements alienate the press, the newspapers, and the central committee of the Conservative party. Fontane was here hitting out at a major feature of the militarization of the German middle class after 1871. The expanding army found it impossible to maintain the tra-ditional monopoly of the officer corps by the nobility and had to admit young men of the middle class as reserve officers. It guarded against any significant ideological change within the army by submitting the new officers to what might be called a process of feudalization, in which they were indoctrinated in the manners, ideas, and vices of the existing establishment. This was not difficult. In imperial Germany the possession of a commission was an important sign of social ac-ceptability, and it was eagerly sought after. In Zuckmayer's *Der Hauptmann von Köpenick*, a new reserve officer dilates upon the im-portance of the uniform and listens approvingly as his tailor says:

"*Na*, so you have managed to become a reserve lieutenant—that is the chief thing—that is the thing you must be these days—socially, professionally, in every connexion! The doctorate is the visiting card, but the reserve commission is the open door—that's the essential thing these days."[60] Middle-class social gatherings were awash with uniforms, and Mélanie van der Straaten, reading the visiting card of a caller, sighs, "Lieutenant in the Reserve of the Fifth Dragoon Regiment. . . . I detest these everlasting lieutenants! Are there no human beings any more?"[61] Vogelsang's uniform doubtless impressed old Treibel but in the end cost him the election.

Finally, in his gallery of bourgeois types, Fontane shows us, in the figure of the mill owner Gundermann in *Der Stechlin*, the kind of person who has squandered so much of himself to acquire an aristocratic title that he has forfeited all respect and is generally regarded as a mean-spirited intriguer and sycophant. "Gundermann is a bourgois and a parvenu," someone says, "therefore, just about the worst thing anyone can be."[62]

III

It was the effect of a society increasingly dominated by Instettins and Gundermanns on class relationships that most concerned Fontane. As early as January 1878, in a letter to Mathilde von Rohr, he wrote:

> When I look around me in society, I encounter in the upper strata of our people, among the aristocracy, the officials, the dignitaries, the artists and the scholars, a merely moderate decency. They are narrow, covetous, dogmatic, without a sense of form and propriety; they want to take and not to give; they respect the appearance of honor rather than honor itself, and, to an unbelievable extent, they lack nobility of mind, generosity, and the gift of forgiveness and sacrifice. They are self-seeking, hard and unloving.[63]

A society whose upper classes were like this was unlikely to have much understanding of, or sympathy for, its most vulnerable members.

It has often been pointed out that Fontane's range of social vision was limited and that he did not write, for example, about the problems of the poor. This is true enough, but he did pay more attention than most of his contemporaries to another and larger group of victims of society—namely, women, who are the main characters of all but the first and last of his novels.[64] This was not because he held theoretical or doctrinaire views on the subject of women's rights, although he knew, of course, that this was becoming a subject of lively debate, and he was acquainted with August Bebel's widely read *Woman and Socialism* (*Die Frau und der Sozialismus*), which was published in 1883. For his time, Fontane had a singularly emancipated attitude toward women, for he liked them and credited them with qualities— intelligence, courage, independence of spirit—that other men did not see. His closest advisers and friends were women, above all his wife, with whom he had many difficulties but never failed to take into his confidence, as some of his most interesting and revealing letters show, his daughter Martha (the model for Corinna Schmidt in *Frau Jenny Treibel*, and Mathilde von Rohr. He was also fascinated by their moods and inconsistencies, and once wrote, "If there is a person who has a passion for women and loves them almost twice as much when he encounters their weaknesses and confusions, the whole enchant- ment of their womanhood [*Evatum*] in full flight, that person is I."[65] This accounts both for the care he lavished on the women who ap- peared in his stories and for their rich diversity—one thinks of Frau Captain Hansen in *Unwiederbringlich* ("a remarkable mixture of *frou- frou* and Lady Macbeth")[66] or Melusine's charming blend of grace and advanced political views in *Der Stechlin*. His observations of German life convinced him that the current condition of women was a distressing commentary on the moral state of the country.

His approach to the problem is illustrated by his reaction to the protests against the serialization of *Irrungen, Wirrungen* in the Vos- sische Zeitung, which took the form of letters demanding the termi- nation of "this dreadful whore's story." He wrote to his son:

> We are sticking up to our ears in all sorts of conventional lies and should be ashamed of ourselves for the hypocrisy that we practise and the crooked game we play. Are there, aside from a few afternoon preachers, into whose souls I should not like to peep—are there aside from a few of these questionable existences—still any edu- cated and generous people, who become really morally outraged

over a *Schneidermamsell* who has a free love relationship? I don't
know any and can add that if I did I would avoid them as a dangerous people. . . . What is outrageous is the behavior of several
newspapers whose number of illegitimate children goes far over a
dozen (the chief editor always with the lion's share) who now take
pleasure in teaching me good manners. Poor wretches! But one can
always find privy counsellors, and not only subaltern ones, who will
agree with such hypocrisy.[67]

It was this disingenuousness that he sought to attack in his novels,
exposing the double standard of morality that tolerated infidelity and
sexual license on the part of males (in *Stine*) but outlawed women
who acted similarly (in *L'Adultera*, for example, and *Effi Briest*). In
two of his most interesting but least read stories, *Quitt* and *Cécile*,
and again in *Effi Briest*, he dealt with the tendency in upper-class
society to educate women only in such things as would make them
attractive to men and secure them good marriages, a practice he found
shameful and degrading, since it deprived them of the opportunity for
full development of their talents and depersonalized or reified them
by turning them into commodities in the male market or, as in the
case of *Cécile*, into odalisques.

Typical of male attitudes toward women in the nineteenth century
was Adelbert von Chamisso's "Frauen-Liebe und Leben," a cycle of
nine poems published in 1830. Recounting a woman's life from her
first love through marriage and childbearing to widowhood, these
graceful verses were often set to music, most notably by Robert Schumann, a circumstance that has led Henry and Mary Garland to write
tartly, "The tenderness of Schumann's music disguises the masculine
egotism underlying the cycle."[68] Not many people today would be
inclined to disagree, for Chamisso's heroine expresses an adoration of
her husband and a willing subordination to him that offends modern
sensibilities:

> Du Ring an meinem Finger,
>   Da hast du mich erst belehrt,
> Hast meinem Blick erschlossen
>   Des Lebens unendlichen Wert.
>
> Ich werd ihm dienen, ihm leben,
>   Ihm angehören ganz,

Hin selber mich geben und finden
　　Verklärt mich in seinem Glanz.

Du Ring an meinem Finger,
　　Mein goldnes Ringelein,
Ich drucke dich fromm an die Lippen,
　　Dich fromm an das Herze mein.

[Oh Ring upon my finger,
　　You have taught me for the first time,
And revealed to my eyes
　　The endless value of life.

I will serve him and live for him.
　　And belong to him utterly,
Give myself to him and find
　　Myself transfigured in his brightness.

Oh Ring upon my finger,
　　My little golden ring,
I press you devoutly to my lips
　　And devoutly to my heart.][69]

In the nineteenth century the sentiments voiced here would have been considered commendable. Society was intent upon keeping women in a state of dependence, partly in their own interest (the philosopher Schopenhauer had argued, after all, that they were inferior beings and without the intellectual gifts necessary to support themselves) and partly because public morality depended upon it. Once married, they no longer had any control over their own financial resources, which were now controlled by their husbands, and, in case of incompatibility, divorce was difficult, if not impossible. The possibility of escaping from the home into other activities was severely limited. Charitable activities of a religious nature were always possible, but nothing more ambitious, for women were denied basic civic rights (the right to vote and to belong to political organizations and trade unions) and were excluded from any share in the government, on either the state or community level. Their part in the nation's cultural life was limited, in comparison with France, for example, by antiquated social codes and taboos. And, until the very eve of the First

World War, they were denied the educational opportunities that would have opened new careers to them.

Since so much was made in the nineteenth century about the female's natural dependence on the male, it is interesting to note how sharply Fontane's fictional heroines contradicted that. In the relationship between Mélanie and Rubehn in *L'Adultera*, Stine and Woldemar in *Stine*, Lene and Botho in *Irrungen, Wirrungen*, and Matilde and Hugo in *Mathilde Möhring*, it is the woman who is the stronger, the more resilient in time of trouble, and in every sense the educator of the man. Even so, her strength is nothing against the accumulated weight of social custom and moral hypocrisy. Stine and Lene both lose their lovers because society forbids their union; Mélanie forfeits her position in society when she leaves her husband, and Matilde hers when her husband dies. The cruelest case of this kind of deprivation is that suffered by the heroine of *Effi Briest*, a novel that, in the incisiveness of its social analysis and its psychological insight into the predicament of women in the nineteenth century, bears comparison with *Madame Bovary* and *Anna Karenina*.[70] After she has been put aside by her husband because of an ancient infidelity, Effi receives a letter from her mother, who is no less a prisoner of social convention than he. It reads:

And now about your future, my dear Effi. You'll have to fend for yourself, and you may be sure of our support as far as material circumstances are concerned. You will do best to live in Berlin (these things are best got over in a big city) and so you'll be one of many who are deprived of fresh air and clear sunlight. Your life will be lonely and, if you can't put up with that, you'll probably have to move out of your social class. The world in which you've been living will be closed to you. And the saddest thing for us, and for you (if we are correct in thinking that we know you), is that your parents' house will be closed to you too. We can't offer you a quiet place in Hohen-Cremmen, a refuge in our home, for that would mean closing this house to all the world, and we are certainly not prepared to do that. Not because we are all that dependent on the world or that we would find it absolutely intolerable to bid farewell to what is called society. No, not for that reason, but simply because we have to show our colors and to make clear to everybody our—I cannot spare you the word—our condemnation of your behavior, the behavior of our only child, whom we loved so.[71]

The society that can punish poor Effi for a mistake made when she was hardly out of her childhood was capable of turning a blind eye to forms of sexual exploitation committed against the vulnerable classes of society. One of Fontane's most brilliant creations is Pauline Pittelkow in *Stine*. A handsome woman with a ready wit, she has decided that, in order to bring up her daughter decently, she will become the mistress of an upper-class protector rather than go to work in the factory. She tells Stine that she is not proud of this but sees no other way out:

> It's this way, they're all worthless, and yet it's good this way, at least for people like us (with you it's different) and for everyone who is stuck so deep in it and doesn't know how to get in or out. For how in the end is one to live?
>
> From work.
>
> *Ach Jott*, work! You're young, Stine. Sure, work is good, and when I roll up my sleeves I always feel at my best. But, you know, then one gets sick and miserable, and Olga must go to school. And where are you going to get it then? *Ach*, that is a long chapter.[72]

And so Widow Pittelkow does what she thinks she has to do, but not at the cost of her self-respect, and when her protector offends her dignity by toasting her at a party as "my queen of the night," she is quick to respond, "*Na, Graf*, not like that, not so boisterous! I don't like that. And before all the others! . . . Queen of the night. *Is nich zu glauben.*"[73]

IV

In a letter to his daughter in 1883, Fontane wrote that he might have become a Zola or a Turgenev had he not been less interested in portraying society as a whole than he was in individuals and the way they reacted to the pressures society placed upon them. His own writing, he said, was in any case "completely free from two things: from exaggerations especially and, above all, from excesses in the direction of ugliness. I am not a pessimist and don't pursue melancholy; and busy myself much more with leaving everything in the same relationships and averages that life gives to its appearances."[74]

The typical Fontane novel was not a broad-gauged analysis of social life in a particular age but the story of how a particular group of individuals in society reacted to the circumstances in which they had to live. Trollope's title *How We Live Now* could have suited them all admirably, whether they told the sad story of Botho and Lene or recounted the tragic end of the love affair between Stine and Waldemar. Nor did Fontane waste time arguing that things should be different or calling for basic reforms that would alleviate injustice and inequality. His critical mode was one of detachment and irony.

The result of this personal reticence was, of course, that the message that came through was sometimes ambiguous. What, for instance, are we to make of the novel *Mathilde Möhring*? Are we to sympathize with its heroine because her ambitions are balked by a male-dominated society or regard her as a somewhat obsessed representative of the age's passion for social climbing? Are we to regard her husband as a weakling or see in him a lover of culture to which his wife is impervious?[75] These questions Fontane leaves for the reader to decide.

This explains why the cultural and educational establishment of Fontane's own time was almost completely deaf to his strictures, apparently finding it impossible to regard the man who had written the *Wanderings* as anything but a loyal subject, true to king, nobility, and the existing social order. It was only after the publication of his correspondence that it was realized that this was far from being the case, causing a small revolution in German studies.[76] That this was so, and that the reading public of his own time read his stories with no deeper discomfort than an occasional twinge of moral outrage over his frankness in dealing with the relations between the sexes, gives some substance to the charges of critics like Georg Lukács who have written that, with all of his social sensitivity, Fontane never sought to explain the basic causes of the ills that he revealed or to suggest any solutions for them. In novels like *Effi Briest*, Lukács has written, Fontane was really predicting that the Bismarckian-Wilhelmine Reich was headed for another Jena. But "it was really a passive, a skeptical-pessimistic prophecy. The forces of German renewal lay outside his literary horizon.''[77]

This last sentence is perhaps not wholly fair. Fontane's weakness, if that is what it was, was not so much a lack of analytical depth as it was one of choice. He believed that it was the function of the novelist not to tell his readers what to think but, rather, to explain to them the way things were. ''The task of the modern novel,'' he once said, ''seems to me to be that of portraying a life, a society, a circle of people who are an undistorted reflection of the life we lead.'' If one can do that, with the clarity, perspicuity, comprehension, and feeling that are demanded of the artist, then readers should be able to understand their society and their lives better. Whether they will want to change them is really up to them.

We know now that the people for whom Fontane was writing didn't want to change them and that, partly because of that, the Bismarckian-Wilhelmine Reich went to its doom. But Fontane's novels remain, and today he has more readers, both in his own country and abroad, than he ever had before. The writer who dreamed as a boy of becoming a historian has in the years since his death become precisely that, for his novels are a basic source both for professional students of nineteenth-century Germany and for Germans who read him out of nostalgia and a desire to know what their country was like before the long time of the troubles began in 1914. But that is surely not the only reason for his continuing popularity. The bulk of his new readers, one likes to think, is composed of those who have discovered on their own that Fontane is clearly the greatest German novelist before Thomas Mann, a master of construction, an incomparable stylist, and the creator of unforgettable portraits, especially of women who combine personal integrity and moral courage with beauty, wit, and discernment.

NOTES

INTRODUCTION

1. William Hazlitt, *The Spirit of the Age, or Contemporary Portraits* (1825), (Chelsea House edition, New York, 1963), pp. 285 f.

2. Hans-Heinrich Reuter, *Fontane*, 2 vols. (Berlin, 1968).

3. Ernst Kohn-Bramstedt, *Aristocracy and Middle Class in Germany: Social Types in German Literature, 1830–1890* (London, 1937).

4. Ibid., pp. 1–2.

5. Theodor Fontane, *Tagebücher 1852, 1855–1858*, ed. Charlotte Jolles in collaboration with Rudolf Muhs, 2d ed. (Berlin, 1995), pp. 151–152. Fontane was reading the end of chapter 6 of Macaulay's *History of England from the Accession of James the Second*.

1. HISTORY

1. "Geschwisterliebe," *Der junge Fontane: Dichtung, Briefe, Publizistik*, ed. Anita Golz (Berlin, 1969), pp. 23–56.

2. Theodor Fontane, *Sämtliche Werke*, Nymphenburg edition (Munich, 1967), XV, 11 (*Von Zwanzig bis Dreißig*, ed. Kurt Schreinert and Jutta Neuendorff-Fürstenau). Fontane's memory was faulty, as Charlotte Jolles has shown. The publication of the story began not on the day of the examination but earlier, on 14 December 1839. Moreover, the poems alluded to were not published until January–March 1840. See ibid., p. 460.

3. Helmut Richter, "Nachwort," in *Der junge Fontane*, p. 643.

4. *Der junge Fontane*, p. 248 ("Kleinigkeiten aus Berlin").

5. For an excellent survey of Fontane's politics in the early years, see Charlotte Jolles, *Fontane und die Politik* (Berlin, 1983).

6. *Sämtliche Werke*, XIV, 124 f. (*Meine Kinderjahre*).

7. Theodor Fontane, *Briefe* (Munich, 1976 ff.), I, 375 (to Theodor Storm, 14 February 1854).

8. *Achim und Bettina in ihren Briefe*, ed. Werner Vortriede, with an introduction by Rudolf Alexander Schröder, 2 vols. (Frankfurt am Main, 1981), II, 661, 665.

9. "Mein Erstling: Das Schlachtfeld von Groß-Beeren," in *Sämtliche Werke*, XIV, 189–191 (*Meine Kinderjahre*).

10. Ibid, XIV, 216 ff. (*Christian Friedrich Scherenberg und das literarische Berlin von 1840 bis 1860*) XV, 149 ff. (*Von Zwanzig bis Dreißig*).

11. Ibid., XIV, 292 (*Scherenberg und das literarische Berlin*).

12. Ibid., I, 112–114 (*Vor dem Sturm*, chapter 17).

13. Ibid., XX, 747 (*Balladen und Gedichte*, ed. Edgar Gross and Kurt Schreinert).

14. Ibid., XV, 163 (*Von Zwanzig bis Dreissig*).

15. *Das ewige Brunnen: Ein Volksbuch deutscher Dichtung*, ed. Ludwig Reiners (Munich, 1958).

16. *Sämtliche Werke*, XX, 79–81 (*Balladen und Gedichte*).

17. *Briefe*, I, 117 (to Gustav Schwab, 18 April 1850).

18. *Briefe*, III, 538 (to Pol de Mont, 24 May 1887).

19. Fontane was a great admirer of Derfflinger. See his remarks about his role in rehabilitating the Oderbruch after the Thirty Years' War in the Schloß Guse chapter of his novel *Vor dem Sturm*. *Sämtliche Werke*, I, 116–117.

20. *Sämtliche Werke*, XX, 104–105 (*Balladen und Gedichte*).

21. Ibid., XX, 214–216.

22. *Briefe*, III, 558 (to Pol de Mont, 24 May 1887). See also III, 579–580 (to Pol de Mont, 13 January 1888).

23. Ibid., III, 60 (to Malthide von Rohr, 5 January 1880).

24. Ibid., I, 327 (to Friedrich Witte, 4 December 1852); and 324 (to Bernhard von Lepel, 6 November 1852).

25. *Sämtliche Werke*, XIV, 298 (*Scherenberg und das literarische Berlin*).

26. Ibid., p. 311.

27. *Briefe*, 1, 50 f. (to Bernhard von Lepel, 17 November 1848).

28. *Sämtliche Werke*, XIX, 53–124 (*Politik und Geschichte*, ed. Charlotte Jolles and Kurt Schreinert).

29. For Fontane's strong feelings on this subject, see his article of 19 March 1850 in the *Dresdener Zeitung*. Ibid., p. 110.

30. *Briefe*, I, 193 f. (to Ryno Quehl, 24 October 1851).

31. Ibid., p. 194 (to Bernhard von Lepel, 30 October 1851).

32. Hans Heinrich Reuter, *Fontane*, 2 vols. (Berlin, 1968), I, 262.

33. Ibid., pp. 300–308.

34. Jolles, *Fontane und die Politik*, pp. 123–125.

35. See *Sämtliche Werke*, XIX, 129–148 (*Politik und Geschichte*).

36. Theodor Fontane, *Tagebücher*, I, 1852/1855–1858, ed. Charlotte Jolles with the assistance of Rudolf Muhs; II, 1866–1882, 1884–1898, ed. Gotthard Erler with the assistance of Therese Erler (Berlin, 1994), I, 9 April 1856.

37. Ibid., 19 August 1856.

38. Ibid., 4 June 1857.

39. Jolles, *Fontane und die Politik*, pp. 138–139.

40. *Briefe*, I, 654 f. (to Paul Heyse, 15 February 1859); 657 f. (to Wilhelm von Merckel, 5 March 1859).

41. Ibid., pp. 660–662, (to Emilie Fontane, 15 and 18 March 1859); 663–664 (to Wilhelm von Merckel, 19 and 25 March 1859); 669 (to Paul Heyse, 2 May 1859).

42. Ibid., pp. 708 f. (to Paul Heyse, 28 June 1860).

43. Ibid., II, 21 ff. (to Wilhelm Hertz, 11 January, 22 February 1861).

44. "Vaterländische Reiterbilder aus drei Jahrhunderten" (1879), *Sämtliche Werke*, XIX, 619 ff. (*Politik und Geschichte*).

45. "Die Märker und die Berliner und wie sich das Berlinertum entwickelte," 1889). Ibid., pp. 719 ff.

46. Ibid., VIII, 173 f. (*Der Stechlin*).

47. Werner Kaegi, *Jacob Burckhardt: Eine Biographie* (Basel, 1956) VII, 137.

48. *Briefe*, II, 59 (to Wilhelm Hertz, 12 February 1862).

49. See *Tagebücher*, I.

50. Pierre-Paul Sagave, *Theodor Fontane. Schach von Wuthenow. Text und Dokumentation* (Frankfurt am Main, 1966).

2. SCOTLAND

1. J. D. Mackie, *A History of Scotland*, 2d ed. (Harmondsworth, Middlesex, 1976), pp. 20–22.

2. The term *Caledonian Antysyzygy* was used by C. Gregory Smith to denote the combination of opposites in the Scottish character; Scottish Lit-

erature (London, 1919), pp. 4, 35. When Goethe had Faust say, "Zwei Seelen wohnen, ach! in meiner Brust," he was denoting something similar.

3. The part played by this theme in German life and literature is so well known that it requires no comment. It has been a staple of Scottish politics from the time of the Union to the rise of the Scottish National Party, as well as a major theme in modern Scottish literature. See, for example, MacDiarmid's "The Parrot Cry" and "A Drunk Man Looks at the Thistle," in *The Complete Poems of Hugh MacDiarmid*, 2 vols. (London, 1985), I, 81 ff., 192 ff.; and Tom Scott's "Fergus," in *The Penguin Book of Scottish Verse* (London, 1970), pp. 490 ff.

4. *Goethes Werke*, Hamburger Ausgabe, IX, 10th ed. (Munich, 1982), 582 (*Dichtung und Wahrheit*, Dritter Teil, 13. Buch).

5. This was the plant celebrated during the Second World War in the German soldier song "Auf der Heide blüht ein kleines Blümelein/ Und das heißt Erika!"

6. Johann Peter Eckermann, *Gespräche mit Goethe in den letzten Jahren seines Lebens* (Munich, second ed., 1984), p. 407.

7. Ibid., p. 252.

8. Rudolf Schenda, *Volk ohne Buch: Studien zur Sozialgeschichte der populären Lesestoff, 1770–1910* (Frankfurt am Main, 1988), pp. 205, 208.

9. *Briefe*, 5 vols. (Munich, 1970), II, 203 f. (to Emilie Fontane, 20 May 1868).

10. *Sämtliche Werke*, XV (*Von Zwanzig his Dreissig*), 138.

11. *Sämtliche Werke*, XXI/1 (*Literarische Essays und Studien*), 419.

12. *Sämtliche Werke*, XX (*Balladen und Gedichte*), 737.

13. On Frederick William IV, see the excellent book by Walther Bußmann, *Zwischen Preußen und Deutschland: Friedrich Wilhelm IV, Eine Biographie* (Berlin, 1990).

14. *Sämtliche Werke*, XX, 465 f.

15. On all this, see Mackie, *History of Scotland*, pp. 159–165.

16. *Sämtliche Werke S. W.*, XX, 135 f.

17. See Antonia Fraser, *Mary Queen of Scots* (London, 1969), pp. 359 f.

18. *Sämtliche Werke*, XX, 130–133.

19. Fraser, *Mary Queen of Scots*, pp. 236, 251–253.

20. *Sämtliche Werke*, XX, 463 f. In reality, he seems to have died in a Danish prison.

21. Ibid., pp. 129 f.

22. Friedrich Schiller, *Maria Stuart*, act III, scene 4.

23. *Sämtliche Werke*, XX, 133–35.

24. Ibid., p. 737.

25. See, for instance, Fraser, *Mary Queen of Scots*, pp. 311–317.

26. *Sämtliche Werke*, XXI/1, 497–499 (*Literarische Essays und Studien*).

27. Ibid., I, 329 f. (*Vor dem Sturm*).

28. Ibid., XX, 119 (*Balladen und Gedichten*).

29. *The Poems of Robert Burns*, (London, 1935), p. 488.

30. *Sämtliche Werke*, XX, 357 (*Balladen und Gedichte*).

31. Ibid., XV, 163 (*Von Zwanzig bis Dreißig*).

32. Ibid., pp. 59, 61 (to Lepel, 22 November 1848).

33. Ibid., pp. 75, 81 (to Lepel, 16 July, 16 August 1849).

34. Ibid., p. 92 (to Lepel, 24 October 1849).

35. See above, chapter 1.

36. *Sämtliche Werke*, XX, 188 (to Lepel, 29 August 1851).

37. *Sämtliche Werke*, XVII (*Aus England und Schottland*), 261–262 (*Jenseit des Tweed:* "Ein Gang nach St. Anthony' s Chapel").

38. Ibid., p. 198. (*Jenseit des Tweed*: "Johnston's Hotel. Erster Gang in die Stadt").

39. Ibid., 388 f. (*Jenseit des Tweed*: "Von Oban bis Loch Lomond").

40. *Briefe*, IV, 451 (to Georg Friedländer, 6 May 1895).

41. *Sämtliche Werke*, XVII, 229 (*Jenseit des Tweed*: "High-Street und Canongate").

42. Ibid., p. 523 (*Englische Tagebücher*).

43. Ibid., pp. 355 f. (*Jenseit des Tweed*: "Der Kaledonische-Kanal").

44. Ibid., p. 206 (*Jenseit des Tweed*: "Holyrood-Palace").

45. Ibid., p. 235 (*Jenseit des Tweed*: "City-Cross und Old-Tolbooth").

46. Ibid., p. 280.

47. *The Oxford Book of Scottish Verse*, chosen by John MacQueen and Tom Scott (Oxford, 1966), p. 337.

48. *Sämtliche Werke*, XVII, pp. 276–283. (*Jenseit des Tweed*: "Floddenfield").

49. *Sämtliche Werke*, XVII, p. 347 (*Jenseit des Tweed*: "Culloden-Moor").

50. Ibid., pp. 284–86. (*Jenseit des Tweed*: "Von Edinburg bis Stirling").

51. Ibid., pp. 418–427 (*Waltham-Abbey, Lochleven Castle, Oxford*).

52. Ibid., IX, 5 (*Wanderungen durch die Mark Brandenburg*, I. *Die Grafschaft Ruppin*).

53. Ibid., XIX, 472, 868 f. (*Politik und Geschichte*).

54. Ibid., XXII/1, 233 (*Causerien über Theater*).

55. See Hugh Trevor-Roper, "The Highland Tradition of Scotland," in *The Invention of Tradition*, ed. Eric Hobsbawm and Terence Ranger (Cambridge, England, 1983).

56. *Sämtliche Werke*, IV, 178 f., 214, 219 (*Cécile*).

57. See Walter Müller-Seidel, *Theodor Fontane: Soziale Romankunst in Deutschland* (Stuttgart, 1975), p. 108.

58. *Sämtliche Werke*, XXI/1, p. 208 (*Literarische Essays und Studien*).

59. See Reuter, *Fontane*, pp. 534, 565 ff. Cf. Peter Demetz, *Formen des Realismus: Theodor Fontane* (Munich, 1964), pp. 60 f.

60. Ibid., p. 31.

61. Müller-Seidel, *Fontane*, p. 137.

62. Georg Lukács, *Studies in European Realism* (New York, 1964), p. 70.

63. Georg Lukács, *Deutsche Realisten des 19. Jahrhunderts* (Berlin, 1959), p. 279.

64. *Briefe*, II, 211 (to Emilie Fontane, 2 September 1868).

3. WANDERINGS

1. Boswell, *Life of Johnson* (Oxford Standard Authors edition, (London, 1969), pp. 955–957.

2. *Briefe*, II, 25 (to Wilhelm Hertz, 26 February 1861).

3. Ibid., p. 98 (to Wilhelm Hertz, 21 May 1863).

4. Ibid., p. 110 (to Heinrich von Mueller, 2 December 1863).

5. Ibid., p. 15 (to Ernst von Pfuel, 18 January 1864).

6. Wolf Jobst Siedler, *Wanderungen zwischen Oder und Nirgendwo:* (Berlin, 1988), pp. 74 f.

7. Ibid., p. 64.

8. Theodor Fontane, *Wanderungen durch die Mark Brandenburg*, ed. Martin Hürlimann (Zurich, 1960).

9. *Sämtliche Werke*, XIII, 385 ff. (*Fünf Schlößer*).

10. Kleist, *Prinz Friedrich von Homburg*, act V, scene 10.

11. *Sämtliche Werke*, XI, 165 (*Havelland.*).

12. On the earlier history, see Wolf Jobst Siedler, *Auf der Pfaueninsel: Spaziergänge in Preuens Arkadien* (Berlin, 1987).

13. On the collaboration of Karl Friedrich Schinkel and Linné, see Gordon A. Craig, "The Master Builder," *New York Review of Books*, 11 June 1992, p. 40.

14. *Sämtliche Werke*, XI, 187.

15. *Briefe*, I, 286 (to Emilie Fontane, London, 20 July 1852). For the tenacity of the memory, see *Tagebücher, 1852, 1855–58*, ed. Charlotte Jolles and Rudolf Muhs, 2d ed. (Berlin, 1995), p. 108.

16. *Sämtliche Werke*, XI, 193–196 (*Havelland*).

17. *Sämtliche Werke*, XX, 399 f. (*Balladen und Gedichte*).

18. Eva von Freeden and Jürgen Fischer.

19. *Sämtliche Werke*, X (*Das Oderland*), 359 ("Der Blumenthal").

20. Ibid., p. 287 ("Küstrin: Die Katte Tragödie").

21. Ibid., XI (*Havelland*), 314 ff. ("Paretz").

22. Ibid., p. 324.

23. Ibid., p. 309.

24. "Modern history gives no comparable example of purity, brightness, and guiltless endurance, and we would have to go back to the days of the early Middle Ages to find someone of equal loveliness (and then only within the church). But Queen Luise stood within the midst of life, without life having cast a shadow on her." Ibid., IX (*Die Grafschaft Ruppin*), p. 479 ("Granson").

25. Erwin Strittmatter, *Ole Bienkopp: Roman* (Berlin, 1963), p. 213.

26. *Sämtliche Werke*, IX (*Die Grafschaft Ruppin*), 252 ("Rheinsberg").

27. Ibid., VIII (*Der Stechlin*), 5.

28. Ibid., XI (*Havelland*), 42 f. ("Kloster Lehnin"). See also ibid., X (*Das Oderland*), p. 141 ("Friedland").

29. Ibid., XI (*Havelland*), 35 ff. ("Die Zisterzienzer in der Mark").

30. Ibid., pp. 95–97 ("Kloster Chorin").

31. Ibid., pp. 42–71 ("Kloster Lehnin").

32. Ibid., I, 409 ff. (*Vor dem Sturm*, chapter 51).

33. See Gisela Heller, *Unterwegs mit Fontane in Berlin und der Mark Brandenburg*(Berlin, 1983) pp. 175–177, 216–219.

34. Siedler, *Wanderungen zwischen Oder und Nirgendwo*, p. 78.

35. *Sämtliche Werke*, XI (*Havelland*), 378 ("Kaputh").

36. Eva von Freeden, Berndt Fischer, and Philip Bade of the *Frankfurter Allgemeine Zeitung's Magazin*.

37. *Briefe*, III, 319 (to Emilie Fontane, 14 May 1884).

38. *Sämtliche Werke*, III, 144 ff. (*Irrungen, Wirrungen*, chapters 11, 12)

39. Ibid., XX (*Balladen und Gedichte*), 249 ("Herr von Ribbeck auf Ribbeck in Havelland").

40. Ibid., XII (*Spreewald*), 151 ff. ("Buch").

41. Ibid., IX, 361 f. (*Die Grafschaft Ruppin*).

42. Ibid., pp. 12–13 ("Lehde").

43. Ibid., p. 13.

44. Ibid., p. 15.

45. Ibid., X, 22–23. (*Das Oderland*).

46. Ibid., XII, 401 n. (*Spreewald*).

4. WAR

1. Charles Oman, *On the Writing of History* (New York, n. d.), pp. 159 f.

2. Herbert Roch, *Fontane, Berlin und das 19. Jahrhundert* (Berlin, 1962), pp. 149 f.

3. *Sämtliche Werke*, XIX, 281–560 (*Politik und Geschichte*).

4. Theodor Fontane, *Der Krieg gegen Frankreich 1870–1871*, 4 vols. (Zurich, 1985).

5. *Briefe*, II, 269 (to Wilhelm Hertz, Berlin, 11 August 1866).

6. See Clausewitz's famous chapter ''Friction in War,'' in Carl von Clausewitz, *On War*, edited and translated by Michael Howard and Peter Paret (Princeton, 1976), pp. 119 ff.

7. See, for example, *Briefe*, II, 192–194 (to Franz von Zychlinski, 22 November 1867).

8. Hans-Heinrich Reuter, *Fontane*, 2 vols. (Berlin, 1968), I, 386.

9. Theodor Fontane, *Reisebriefe vom Kriegsschauplatz Böhmen 1866*, ed. Christian Andree (Frankfurt am Main, 1973).

10. See Gordon A. Craig, *The Battle of Königgrätz* (Philadelphia, 1964), pp. 53f.

11. Fontane, *Reisebriefe*, p. 52. Compare his later account of the firefight in Theodor Fontane, *Der deutsche Krieg von 1866*, 2 vols. (Berlin, 1871), I, 154–163.

12. *Sämtliche Werke*, XIV, 119 (*Meine Kinderjahre*).

13. Theodor Fontane, *Der Schleswig-Holsteinsche Krieg im Jahre 1864* (Berlin, 1866), pp. 84 f.

14. Fontane, *Der deutsche Krieg*, pp. 610–626.

15. Hans Scholz, *Theodor Fontane* (Munich, 1978), p. 204.

16. See Karl Heinrich Hoefele, *Geist und Gesellschaft der Bismarckzeit, 1870–1880* (Göttingen, 1967), pp. 449 f.; and *The Wagner Companion*, ed. Peter Burbidge and Richard Sutton (New York, 1979), p. 28.

17. Fontane, *Der Schleswig-Holsteinsche Krieg*, p. 348.

18. *Briefe*, II, 325 (to Karl Zöllner, Warnemunde, 23 July 1870).

19. Ibid., p. 326 (to Emilie Fontane, Dobbertin, 5 August 1870).

20. Ibid., pp. 326 f.

21. *Sämtliche Werke*, XX, 265 (*Balladen und Gedichte*).

22. Ibid., p. 266.

23. Fontane, *Der Schleswig-Holsteinsche Krieg*, p. 52.

24. Ibid., pp. 160, 162, 199 f.

25. Ibid., pp. 183 f.

26. The film was called *Why Worry?* (1923).

27. Fontane, *Der Schleswig-Holsteinsche Krieg*, p. 199.

28. Ibid., p. 252.

29. Ibid., pp. 203 f.

30. Ibid., p. 217.

31. Ibid., pp. 310 ff.

32. Ibid., pp. 265 ff.

33. Fontane, *Der deutsche Krieg* I, 110, 364 f.

34. Ibid., p. 316.

35. Ibid., pp. 338 f.

36. Ibid., pp. 62 ff.

37. Ibid., p. 448. Cited by Christian Andree in the afterword of Fontane, *Reisebriefe*, p. 94.

38. Fontane, *Der deutsche Krieg*, I, 247–248.

39. Fontane, *Reisebriefe*, p. 62

40. Fontane, *Der deutsche Krieg*, I, 563.

41. Ibid., pp. 241–243

42. Ibid., II, 335.

43. Friedrich Nietzsche, *Unzeitgemäße Betrachtungen* (1873), in *Sämtliche Werke* (Stuttgart, 1964), p. 3.

44. *Sämtliche Werke*, XVI, 7–158 (*Kriegsgefangenen*); Reuter, *Fontane*, I, 450.

45. Ibid., pp. 485 f. (*Aus den Tagen der Okkupation*).

46. Ibid., p. 69.

47. Fontane, *Der Krieg gegen Frankreich*, I, p. 340.

48. Ibid., p. 287.

49. Reuter, *Fontane*, I, 456.

50. *Briefe*, II, 549–50 (to Mathilde von Rohr, Berlin, 30 November 1876).

51. Ibid., p. 550.

52. Reuter, *Fontane*, I, 456.

5. BISMARCK

1. *Briefe*, IV, 101 (to Emil Friedrich Pindtner, 26 February 1891).

2. Otto von Bismarck, *Briefe an seine Frau und Gattin*, ed. Fürst Herbert Bismarck (Stuttgart, 1900), p. 27.

3. *Sämtliche Werke*, XVI (*Aus den Tagen der Okkupation*), 7–153 ("Kriegsgefangen").

4. *Briefe*, IV, 350 (to August von Heyden, 6 May 1894).

5. Hans-Heinrich Reuter, *Fontane*, 2 vols. (Munich, 1968), I, 448–450.

6. On all of this, see Otto Pflanze, *Bismarck*, 3 vols. (Princeton, 1963 ff.), II, 38 ff.

7. *Briefe*, II, 282 (to Emilie Fontane, 3 December 1869).

8. Thomas Mann, "Der alte Fontane," *Aufsätze, Briefen, Essays*, I (1983), 198 f.

9. *Bismarck-Briefe*, selected and with an introduction by Hans Rothfels (Göttingen, 1955), p. 13.

10. *Briefe*, IV, 41 (to Georg Friedländer, 1 May 1890).

11. Mann, *Aufsätze*, I, 183.

12. Otto von Bismarck, *Die gesammelten Werke* (Berlin, 1924 ff.), IX, 48 (conversation with Sidney Whitman, Varzin, October 1891).

13. Ibid., XIV (1), 4 (to Gustav Scharlach, Kniephof, 7 April 1834).

14. Ibid., p. 415 (to Leopold von Gerlach, Frankfurt, 15 September 1855).

15. Ibid., XIV (2), 845 (to Albrecht von Roon, Varzin, 13 December 1872).

16. Ibid., p. 709 (to Alexander Andrae-Roman, Varzin, 26 December 1865).

17. Mann, *Aufsätze*, I, 199.

18. *Briefe*, I, 609 (to Wilhelm von Merckel, London, 18 February 1858).

19. Ibid., III, 447 (to Mathilde von Rohr, Berlin, 9 January 1886).

20. Ibid., p. 457 (to Georg Friedländer, Berlin, 2 March 1886).

21. Ibid., pp. 461 f. (to Moritz Lazarus, Berlin, 29 March 1886).

22. Ibid., IV, 159 (to Georg Friedländer, Berlin, 4 October 1891).

23. Ibid., III, 706 f. (to Emilie Fontane, Bayreuth, 28 July 1889).

24. Ibid., IV, 520 (to the *Norddeutsche Allgemeine Zeitung* [draft], middle March, 1876).

25. *Sämtliche Werke*, XX, 245 (*Balladen und Gedichte*).

26. Ibid., p. 272.

27. Reuter, *Fontane*, I, 470.

28. *Sämtliche Werke*, XX, 246 (*Balladen und Gedichte*).

29. *Ibid.*, pp. 53 f.

30. Ibid., XVI. 170 (*Aus den Tagen der Okkupation*).

31. Briefe, IV, 336 (to Maximilian Harden, 4 March 1894).

32. *Sämtliche Werke*, IV, 25–27 (*L'Adultera*).

33. Ibid., pp. 242–243 (*Cécile*).

34. Ibid., III, 121–125 (*Irrungen, Wirrungen*).

35. Ibid., IV, 319 (*Die Poggenpuhls*).

36. Ibid., VII, 284–285 (*Der Stechlin*).

37. Bismarck, *Die gesammelten Werke*, XI, 289 f.

38. *Briefe*, II, 405 (to Mathilde von Rohr, Berlin, 17 March 1872).

39. Ibid., pp. 581 f. (to Emilie Fontane, Berlin, 5 June 1878).

40. Ibid., III, 25 (to Emilie Fontane, Berlin, 8 June 1879).

41. Ibid., p. 125 (to Philipp zu Eulenburg, Berlin, 12 March 1881).

42. Ibid., p. 303 (to Martha Fontane, Berlin, 16 March 1884).

43. Ibid., p. 131 (to Philipp zu Eulenburg, Potsdam, 23 April 1881).

44. Ibid., p. 516 (to Georg Friedländer, Berlin, 26 January 1887).

45. Ibid., pp. 592 f. (to Martha Fontane, Berlin, 14 March 1888).

46. Ibid., p. 674 (to Georg Friedländer, Berlin, 7 January 1889).

47. Ibid., p. 710 (to Guido Weiß, Berlin, 14 August 1889).

48. Ibid., IV, 41 (to Georg Friedländer, Berlin, 1 May 1890).

49. Jacob Burckhardt, *Über das Studium der Geschichte: Der Text der "Weltgeschichtliche Betrachtungen,"* edited by Peter Ganz, on the basis of preliminary studies by Ernst Ziegler (Munich, 1982), p. 378.

50. *Briefe*, IV, 82 (to Friedrich Witte, Berlin, 4 January 1891).

51. Ibid., p. 41 (to Georg Friedländer, Berlin, 1 May 1890).

52. Ibid., p. 328 (to Georg Friedländer, Berlin, 1 February 1894).

53. Ibid., p. 440 (to Martha Fontane, 1 April 1895).

54. Ibid.

55. Ibid., p. 644 (to Georg Friedländer, Berlin, 5 April 1897).

56. Ibid., p. 386 (to Otto Brahm, Berlin, 27 September 1894).

57. Heinrich Mann, "Theodor Fontane," in *Fontane und Berlin*, edited by Hans-Dietrich Loock (Berlin, 1970), p. 85.

6. THEATER

1. *Briefe*, II, 284 f. (to Emilie Fontane, Berlin, 4 December 1869).

2. Heinz Ohff, *Theodor Fontane: Leben und Werk* (Munich, 1995), pp. 227 f.

3. *Sämtliche Werke*, XV, 400 (*Kritische Jahren—Kritiker-Jahren*).

4. See *Tagebücher*, I, 104 ff. (London, 9 April 1856).

5. See Gerhard Wahnrau, *Berlin, Stadt der Theater* (Berlin, 1957), pp. 268–269.

6. *Briefe*, II, 431 f. (to Maximilian Ludwig, Berlin, 2 May 1873).

7. Marcel Reich-Ranicki, *Die Anwälte der Literatur* (Stuttgart, 1994), p. 122.

8. Herbert Roch, *Fontane, Berlin und das 19. Jahrhundert*, p. 282.

9. *Sämtliche Werke*, XV, 390 (*Kritische Jahre—Kritiker-Jahre*).

10. Gottfried Riemann, "Schinkel's Buildings and Plans for Berlin," in *Karl Friedrich Schinkel: A Universal Man*, ed. Michael Snodin (New Haven, Conn., 1991), p. 20.

11. Walter Bussmann, *Zwischen Preußen und Deutschland: Friedrich Wilhelm IV, Eine Biographie* (Berlin, 1990), p. 322.

12. Georg Brandes, *Berlin als Reichshauptstadt: Erinnerungen aus den Jahren 1877–1883*, 1989), p. 52.

13. *Sämtliche Werke,*. XXII/2, 509–511 (*Causerien über Theater*).

14. Ibid., XXII/1, 7–8.

15. Ibid., XXII/2, 527.

16. Gordon A. Craig, *The Triumph of Liberalism* (New York, 1988), p. 163.

17. *Sämtliche Werke*, XXII/2, 90 f. (*Causerien über Theater*).

18. Ronald Berman, *The Rise of the German Novel: Crisis and Charisma* (Cambridge, Mass., 1986), p. 142.

19. *Sämtliche Werke*, XXII/2, 37 f. (*Causerien über Theater*). Cited in ibid.

20. Wahnrau, *Berlin, Stadt der Theater*, p. 472

21. *Sämtliche Werke*, XXII/1, 353–354, (*Causerien uber Theater*).

22. Ibid., p. 604.

23. Ibid., pp. 605 ff.

24. Ibid., pp. 850 f.

25. Ibid., XXII/2, 466 f.

26. Ibid., p. 287.

27. Ibid., pp. 11, 42, 288, 292.

28. Ibid., XXII/1, 887.

29. Ibid., pp. 686, 688.

30. Ibid., pp. 829 f.

31. Ibid., p. 764.

32. Ibid., pp. 302 f.

33. Ibid., XXII/2, 220 f.

34. Ibid., XXII/1, 805.

35. Ibid., p. 270.

36. Ibid., p. 846.

37. Ibid., pp. 9–12.

38. Ibid., 238.

39. Ibid., pp. 240 f.

40. Ibid., pp. 722 f.

41. Ibid., pp. 747–749.

42. Ibid., XXII/2, 264.

43. Ibid., pp. 578–584.

44. Ibid.

45. William Hazlitt, *Essays*, selected and edited by Percy Van Dyke Shelly (New York, 1924), p. 189.

46. *Sämtliche Werke*, XXII/1, 636.

47. Ibid., XXII/2, 708.

48. *Briefe*, IV, 707 (to Friedrich Stephany, Berlin, 22 March 1898).

49. *Sämtliche Werke*, XXII/2, 713 f.

50. *Briefe*, III, 729 (to Friedrich Stephany, Berlin, 10 October 1889).

51. Ibid., p. 732 (to Friedrich Stephany, Berlin, 22 October 1889).

52. *Sämtliche Werke*, XXII/2, 710–743.

53. Reuter, *Fontane*, II, 719 f.

54. *Lessings Werke*, ed. by Georg Witkowski (corrected and expanded ed., 7 vols., Leipzig, o. D.), V, 243–274 (Stücke 73–79); Fontane, *Sämtliche Werke*, XXII/1, 283 ff., 616 ff., 808 ff.

55. *Briefe*, IV, 98 f. (to Marthe Fontane, Berlin, 21 February 1891).

7. THE HISTORICAL NOVELS

1. Heinz Ohff, *Theodor Fontane, Leben und Werk* (Munich, 1995), p. 285.

2. *Briefe*, II, 163 (to Wilhelm Hertz, 17 January 1866).

3. Ibid., p. 162.

4. Chapter 2, pp. 45ff.

5. The best critical treatment of this work is that of Peter Paret, in *Art as History: Episodes in the Culture and Politics of Nineteenth-Century Germany* (Princeton, N.J., 1988).

6. Sämtliche Werke, XXI, pt. 1, 181 (*Literarische Essays und Studien*).

7. Ibid., pp. 200–201.

8. Ibid., p. 212.

9. See Fontane's resigned note, ''Wie sich meine Frau einen Beamten denkt,'' which was probably written in 1876. *Sämtliche Werke*, XV, 445, 681 (*Von Zwanzig bis Dreißig*, ed. Kurt Schreinert and Jutta Neuendorff-Fürstenau.)

10. See *Briefe*, II, 517 ff., 520 ff., 525, 530 ff., 536 ff., 540, 543.

11. Ibid., p. 547 (to Mathilde von Rohr, Berlin, 1 November 1876).

12. Ibid., p. 637 (to Wilhelm Hertz, Berlin, 24 November 1978).

13. *Sämtliche Werke*, I, 29.

14. This is the third of three Seydlitz ballads by Fontane. See *Sämtliche Werke*, XX, 208–212, 747 (*Balladen und Gedichte*).

15. *Sämtliche Werke*, I, 191.

16. Ibid., p. 193.

17. Ibid., p. 195.

18. Ibid., pp. 581 f.

19. Ibid., p. 633.

20. See the criticism in Reuter, *Fontane*, II, 559 f.

21. Quoted in J. I. M. Stewart's introduction to William Thackeray, *Vanity Fair* (Harmondsworth, Middlesex, 1968), p. 23.

22. *Sämtliche Werke*, I, 324.

23. Ibid., p. 424.

24. Ibid., p. 551 f.

25. Ibid., II, 274.

26. See the brief account of his career by R. R. Palmer in *Makers of Modern Strategy: Military Thought from Machiavelli to Hitler*, edited by Edward Mead Earle with the collaboration of Gordon A. Craig and Felix Gilbert (Princeton, N.J., 1943), pp. 68–74.

27. *Sämtliche Werke*, II, 276 f.

28. Ibid., p. 288.

29. Ibid., p. 303.

30. Ibid., pp. 340–342.

31. Ibid., p. 344.

32. Ibid., p. 384.

33. Ibid., p. 316.

34. Ibid., p. 299.

35. Ibid., p. 288.

36. Ibid., XXI, pt. 1, 200–201.

37. On the role of the symbol in Schach von Wuthenau, see Reuter, *Fontane*, II, 602 ff.

8. THE NOVELS OF SOCIETY

1. The first paragraphs of this chapter repeat the introduction of my article "Irony and Rage in the German Social Novel," in *Essays on Culture and Society in Modern Germany*, ed. Gary D. Stark and Bede Karl Lackner (College Station, Tex., 1982), pp. 98 ff.

2. See Goethe's comments on this in *Goethe, Sämtliche Werke: Jubiläums-ausgabe in 40 Bände*, ed. Eduard von der Hellen (Stuttgart, 1902–1907), xxxvi, 139, which are balanced by his insistence that, by promoting

cultural rivalry among German rulers, disunity had its positive side. *Conversations with Eckermann*, 23 October 1828.

3. See R. Hamann and Jost Hermand, *Naturalismus*, 2d ed. (Berlin, 1968), p. 284.

4. Ibid., pp. 278–282.

5. On this, see especially Robert Minder, "Deutsche und französische Literatur—inneres Reich und Einbrüderung des Dichters," in *Kultur und Literatur in Deutschland und Frankreich* (Frankfurt am Main, 1962), pp. 5–43. See also Wolf Lepenies, *Die drei Kulturen: Soziologie zwischen Literatur und Wissenschaft* (Munich, 1985), pp. 265 ff.

6. Erich Auerbach, *Mimesis: The Representation of Reality in Literature* (Princeton, N.J., 1953), pp. 452 ff.

7. See Gordon A. Craig, *The Politics of the Unpolitical* (New York, 1995), pp. 125–142.

8. Nigel Hamilton, *The Brothers Mann: The Lives of Heinrich and Thomas Mann* (New Haven, Conn., 1979), p. 213.

9. See Klaus Vondung, ed., *Das wilhelminische Bildungsbürgerthum: Zur Sozialgeschichte einer Ideen* (Göttingen, 1976), pp. 30–33.

10. Chief among them were Friedrich Spielhagen, in novels like *In Reih' und Glied* (1866) *Hammer und Amboss* (1869), and *Sturmflut* (1876); and Wilhelm Raabe in his late novels *Pfisters Mühle* (1884) and *Die Akten des Vogelsang* (1896). The effect of the former was always weakened by flatness of characterization and shrillness of tone, and it is difficult to read him now. Raabe, a splendid writer, was more interested in psychological problems than social ones, but he had a sense of the future, which many of his contemporaries lacked. See the perceptive book Barker Fairlie, *Wilhelm Raabe: An Introduction to His Novels* (Oxford, 1961).

11. *Briefe*, III, 503 (to Paul Lindau, 28 November 1886).

12. *Briefe*, III, 742.

13. See, for example, *Sämtliche Werke*, XX (*Balladen und Gedichte*), 272 f. ("Prolog").

14. *Geschichte Berlin*, ed. Wolfgang Ribbe, 2 vols. (Munich, 1987), I. 407.

15. *Briefe*, I, 709 (to Paul Heyse, 38 June 1860).

16. Conrad Alberti, *Die Alten und Jungen* (1889), chapter 1. In the 1960s, one could buy, at the newspaper stand at the corner of the Kurfürstendamm and Joachimstaler Allee, little cans that were purported to be full of *Berliner Luft*, which one could mail home as a sovereign specific to one's friends.

17. *Briefe*, III, 389 (to Emilie Fontane, 1 June 1885) and elsewhere.

18. *Sämtliche Werke*, IV, 148, 153 (*Cécile*).

19. *Briefe*, III, 654 (to Friedrich Haase, 8 November 1888); see also 704 (to Moritz Lazarus, 8 July 1889).

20. Ibid., p. 369 (to Georg Friedländer, 21 December 1884).

21. Ibid., IV, 354 (to Georg Friedländer, 14 May 1894).

22. Ibid., I, 142 f. (to Theodor Storm, 2 May 1853).

23. Sämtliche Werke, XVIII *Unterwegs und wieder daheim*, in the section on "Der Berliner Ton." See also Dieter Hildebrandt, "Vor Gott ist jeder ein Berliner," *Die Zeit*, no. 15, 19 April 198.

24. *Der richtige Berliner in Wörtern und Redensarten*, ed. by Hans Mayer and Siegfried Mauermann (Munich, 1996), p. 254.

25. *Briefe*, III, 462 (to Moritz Lazarus, 29 March 1886).

26. *Sämtliche Werke*, VIII, 110ff. (*Der Stechlin*).

27. Ibid., III, 313 (*Stine*).

28. Hermann Meyer, "Theodor Fontane; 'L'Adultera' und 'Der Stechlin,' " in *Theodor Fontane*, ed. Wolfgang Preisendanz (Darmstadt, 1973), pp. 218 f.

29. Georg Büchmann, *Geflügelte Worte*, new ed. by Hans Martin Elster (Munich, 1979), p. 3.

30. See Peter Demetz, *Formen des Realismus: Theodor Fontane* (Munich, 1964), pp. 130–131.

31. *Sämtliche Werke*, V, 67 (*Unwiederbringlich*).

32. Walter Killy, "Abschied vom Jahrhundert: Fontane, 'Irrungen, Wirrungen,' " in Preisendanz, *Theodor Fontane*, p. 270.

33. Russell A. Berman, *The Rise of the Modern German Novel* (Cambridge, Mass., 1986), p. 152.

34. Paul Böckmann, "Der Zeitroman Fontanes," in Preisendanz, *Theodor Fontane*, p. 100.

35. Ute Frevert, *Ehrenmänner: Das Duell in der bürgerlichen Gesellschaft* (Munich, 1991), pp. 194, 324; David E. Barclay, *Anarchie und guter Wille: Friedrich Wilhelm IV. und die preußische Monarchie* (Berlin, 1995), p. 384.

36. See Kevin Mcaleer, *Dueling: The Cult of Honor in Fin de Siècle Germany* (Princeton, N.J., 1994).

37. *Briefe*, II, 69f.

38. Reuter, *Fontane*, I, 92.

39. *Briefe*, IV, 148 (to Martha Fontane, Wyk, 25 August 1891).

40. Kenneth Attwood, *Fontane und das Preußentum* (Berlin, 1970), p. 221.

41. *Briefe*, III, 325 (to Emilie Fontane, Thale, 10 June 1884).

42. *Sämtliche Werke*, XVI, 496 (*Aus den Tagen der Okkupation*).

43. *Briefe*, IV, 352 (to Georg Friedländer, 14 May 1894).

44. *Ibid*., p. 643 (to Georg Friedländer, 5 April 1897).

45. Ibid., III, 727 (to Wilhelm Hertz, 18 September 1889). As an example of the closeness of their relations, see also ibid., II, 533 ff. (to Mathilde von Rohr, 1 July 1876), in which he tells her the reasons for his resignation as secretary of the Academy of Art and describes the resultant difficulties with his wife.

46. Ibid., IV, 352 (to Georg Friedländer, 14 May 1894). See also Böckmann, ''Der Zeitroman Fontanes,'' in Preisendanz, *Theodor Fontane*, pp. 92 f.

47. *Sämtliche Werke*, IV, 278 (*Cécile*).

48. K. Wandrey, *Theodor Fontane* (Munich, 1914), p. 285.

49. *Sämtliche Werke*, VII, 373–375. (*Effi Briest*).

50. Demetz, *Formen des Realismus*, p. 126.

51. *The Poetical Works of Wordsworth* (Oxford 1920), pp. 656–57 (*The Prelude*, Book III).

52. *Sämtliche Werke*, VII, 244–248. (*Effi Briest*).

53. *Ibid*., III, 254–257 (*Stine*).

54. *Ibid*., p. 245.

55. See *Briefe*, IV, 49, 473, 672, 706, and especially 714. Also Reuter, *Fontane*, II, 753 ff.

56. Demetz, *Formen des Realismus*, pp. 154 f.

57. *Briefe*, III, 601 (to Theodor Fontane [son], 22 April 1888).

58. *Sämtliche Werke*, VII, 28 (*Frau Jenny Treibel*).

59. Ibid., p. 71.

60. Carl Zuckmayer, *Der Hauptmann von Köpenick. Ein deutsches Märchen in drei Akten* (Franfurt am Main, 1956), p. 42 (act I, scene 7).

61. *Sämtliche Werke*, IV, 41 (*L'Adultera*).

62. Ibid., VIII, 162 (*Der Stechlin*).

63. *Briefe*, III (to Mathilde von Rohr, January 1878).

64. Reuter, *Fontane*, II, 643.

65. *Briefe*, IV, 405 f. (to Paul and Paula Schlenther, 6 December 1894).

66. *Sämtliche Werke*, V, 68 (*Unwiederbringlich*). See also Demetz, *Formen des Realismus*, p. 168.

67. *Briefe*, IV, pp. 559 f. (to Theodore Fontane [son], 8 September 1887).

68. Henry Garland and Mary Garland, *The Oxford Companion to German Literature* (Oxford, 1976), p. 239.

69. Adelbert von Chamisso, *Sämtliche Werke in Zwei Bänden*, ed. Werner Feudel and Christel Laufer (Munich, 1980), I, 12

70. See J. P. Stern's comparison of the three novels in *Re-inter-pretations: Seven Studies in Nineteenth-Century German Literature* (London, 1964), pp. 315 ff.

71. *Sämtliche Werke*, VII, 391 (*Effi Briest*).

72. Ibid., III, 241 (*Stine*).

73. Ibid., p. 252.

74. *Briefe*, III, 242 f. (to Martha Fontane, 5 May 1883). See also p. 503 (to Paul Lindau, 28 November 1886).

75. On possible readings of the novel, see Walter Müller-Seidel, *Theodor Fontane: Soziale Romankunst in Deutschland* (Stuttgart, 1975), pp. 324 ff.

76. Robert Minder, *Dichter in der Gesellschaft: Erfahrungenen mit deutsche und französische Literatur* (Frankfurt am Main, 1966), p. 151.

77. Georg Lukács, *Deutsche Realisten des 19. Jahrhunderts* (Berlin, 1959), p. 306.

BIBLIOGRAPHY

Kenneth Attwood, *Fontane und das Preussentum* (Berlin, 1970).

Erich Auerbach, *Mimesis: The Representation of Reality in Western Literature* (Princeton, N.J., 1953).

David E. Barclay, *Anarchie und guter Wille; Friedrich Wilhelm IV. und die preußische Monarchie* (Berlin, 1995).

Russell A. Berman, *The Rise of the German Novel: Crisis and Charisma* (Cambridge, Mass., 1986).

Otto von Bismarck, *Briefe an seine Frau und Gattin*, edited by Fürst Herbert Bismarck (Stuttgart, 1900).

Otto von Bismarck, *Die gesammelten Werke* (Berlin, 1924 ff.)

Boswell, *Life of Johnson* (London, 1969).

Georg Brandes, *Berlin als Reichshauptstadt. Erinnerungen aus den Jahren 1877–1883*, edited by Erik M. Christensen and Hans-Dietrich Look (Berlin, 1989)

Georg Büchmann, *Geflügelte Worte* (new edition, Munich, 1979).

Peter Burbidge and Richard Sutton, editors, *The Wagner Companion* (New York, 1979).

Jacob Burckhardt, *Über das Studium der Geschichte: Der Text der ''Weltgeschichtlichen Betrachtungen.'' Auf Grund der Vorarbeiten von Ernst Ziegler nach den Handschriften*, edited by Peter Ganz ((Munich, 1982).

Robert Burns, *The Poems of Robert Burns* (Oxford, London, 1935).

Walter Bußmann, *Zwischen Preußen und Deutschland: Friedrich Wilhelm IV. Eine Biographie* ((Berlin, 1990).

Adalbert von Chamisso, *Sämtliche Werke in zwei Bände*, edited by Werner Feudal and Christel Laufer (Munich, 1980).

Carl von Clausewitz, *On War*, edited by Michael Howard and Peter Paret (Princeton, 1976).

Gordon A. Craig, "The Master Builder," *New York Review of Books*, 11 June 1992.

Gordon A. Craig, *The Politics of the Unpolitical: German Writers and the Problem of Power, 1770–1871* (New York, 1995).

Gordon A. Craig, *The Triumph of Liberalism: Zurich in the Golden Age, 1830–1869* (New York, 1988).

Gordon A. Craig, *The Battle of Königgrätz* (Philadelphia, 1964)

Gordon A. Craig, *The Germans* (New York, 1982)

Peter Demetz, *Formen des Realismus: Theodor Fontane* (Munich, 1964).

Edward Mead Earle, editor. *Makers of Modern Strategy: Military Thought from Machiavelli to Hitler* (Princeton, 1943).

Johann Peter Eckermann, *Gespräche mit Goethe in den letzten Jahren seines Lebens* (Munich, 1984).

Barker Fairlie, *Wilhelm Raabe: An Introduction to His Novels* (Oxford, 1961).

Theodor Fontane, *Der deutsche Kriege von 1866* (2 vols., Berlin, 1871).

Theodor Fontane, *Der Krieg gegen Frankreich 1870–1871* (2 vols., Berlin, 1873: new edition in 4 vols., Zurich, 1985)

Theodor Fontane, *Der Schleswig-Holsteinische Krieg im Jahre 1864* (Berlin, 1866).

Theodor Fontane, *Reisebriefe vom Kriegsschauplatz Böhmen 1866*, edited by Christian Andree (Frankfurt am Main, 1973).

Theodor Fontane, *Sämtliche Werke*, Nymphenburg Edition (Munich, 1955 ff.).

Theodor Fontane, *Tage- und Reisetagebücher*, edited by Gotthard Erler (2nd revised edition, Berlin, 1995).

Theodor Fontane, *Wanderungen durch die Mark Brandenburg*, edited by Martin Hürlimann (Zürich and Freiburg im Breisgau, 1960).

Theodor Fontane, *Werke, Schriften und Briefe*, edited by Walter Keitel and Helmuth Nürnberger (Munich, 1976 ff.)

Antonia Fraser, *Mary, Queen of Scots* (London, 1969).

Ute Frevert, *Ehrenmänner. Das Duell in der bürgerlichen Gesellschaft* (Munich, 1991).

Henry and Mary Garland, *The Oxford Companion to German Literature* (Oxford, 1976)

Johann Wolfgang von Goethe, *Sämtliche Werke. Jubiläumsausgabe in vierzig Bänden*, edited by Eduard von der Hellen (Stuttgart, 1902–1907).

Johann Wolfgang von Goethe, *Werke. Hamburger Ausgabe in vierzehn Bänden*, edited by Erich Trunz (Munich, 1982).

W. P. Guenther, *Preussischer Gehorsam: Theodor Fontanes Novelle "Schach von Wuthenow"; Text und Deutung* (Munich, 1981).

Richard Hamann and Jost Hermand, *Naturalismus* (Berlin, 1968).

William Hazlitt, *Essays*, edited by Percy Van Dyke Shelley (New York, 1924).

William Hazlitt, *The Spirit of the Age, or Contemporary Portraits* (1825) (New York, 1963).

Gisela Heller, *Unterwegs mit Fontane in Berlin und der Mark Brandenburg* (Berlin, 1983).

Dieter Hildebrandt, "Vor Gott ist jeder ein Berliner," *Die Zeit*, 3 April 1987.

Eric Hobsbawm and Terence Ranger, editors, *The Invention of Tradition* (Cambridge, 1983).

Karl Heinrich Höfele, *Geist und Gesellschaft der Bismarckzeit 1870–1890* (Göttingen, 1967).

Charlotte Jolles, *Fontane und die Politik* (Berlin, 1983)

Werner Kaegi, *Jacob Burckhardt. Eine Biographie* (4 vols, Basel und Stuttgart, 1947–1977).

Heinrich von Kleist, *Sämtliche Werke*, edited by Helmut Sembdner (2 vols., Munich, 1961).

Ernst Kohn-Bramstedt, *Aristocracy and the Middle Classes in Germany: Social Types in German Literature, 1830–1890* (London, 1937).

Wolf Lepenies, *Die drei Kulturen: Soziologie zwischen Literatur und Wissenschaft* (Munich, 1985).

Gotthold Ephraim Lessing, "Die Hamburgische Dramaturgie" in *Werke*, edited by Georg Witkowski (7 vols., Leipzig and Vienna, 1882).

Hans-Dietrich Look, editor, *Fontane und Berlin* (Berlin, 1970).

Georg Lukács, *Deutsche Realisten des 19. Jahrhunderts* (Berlin, 1959).

Georg Lukács, *Studies in European Realism* (New York, 1964).

Kevin Macaleer, *Duelling: The Cult of Honor in Fin de Siècle Germany* (Princeton, 1994).

Hugh MacDiarmid, *The Complete Poems of Hugh MacDiarmid*, edited by Michael Grieve and W. R. Aitken (2 vols., London, 1985).

J. D. Mackie, *A History of Scotland* (Harmondsworth, Middlesex, 1976)

John MacQueen and Tom Scott, editors, *The Oxford Book of Scottish Verse* (Oxford, 1966).

Thomas Mann, *Briefe, 1889–1936* (Frankfurt am Main, 1962)

Thomas Mann, *Gesammelte Werke in 12 Bänden* (Frankfurt am Main, 1960 ff.)

Hans Mayer and Siegfried Mauermann, *Der richtige Berliner in Wörtern und Redensarten* (Munich, 1996).

Robert Minder, Dichter in der Gesellschaft: Erfahrungen mit deutscher und französischer Literatur (Frankfurt am Main, 1966)

Robert Minder, *Kultur und Literatur in Deutschland und Frankreich* (Frankfurt am Main, 1962).

Walter Müller-Seidel, *Theodor Fontane: Soziale Romankunst in Deutschland* (Stuttgart. 1975).

Friedrich Nietzsche, *Werke. Kritische Gesamtausgabe*, edited by Giorgio Colli and Mazzino Montinari (Berlin and New York, 1967 ff.).

Heinz Ohff, *Theodor Fontane: Leben und Werk* (Munich, 1995).

Charles Oman, *On the Writing of History* (New York, n. d.)

Peter Paret, *Art as History: Episodes in the Culture and Politics of Nineteenth Century Germany* (Princeton, N.J., 1988).

Otto Pflanze, *Bismarck* (3 vols., Princeton, 1963 ff.)

Wolfgang Preisendanz, editor, *Fontane* (Darmstadt, 1973).

Marcel Reich-Ranicki, *Die Anwälte der Literatur* (Stuttgart, 1994)

Ludwig Reiners, editor, *Der ewige Brunnen. Ein Hausbuch deutscher Dichtung* (Munich, 1958).

Hans-Heinrich Reuter, *Fontane* (2 vols., Berlin, 1968)

Wolfgang Ribbe, editor, *Geschichte Berlins* (2 vols., Munich, 1987).

Helmut Richter, editor, *Der junge Fontane. Dichtung, Briefe, Publizistik* (Berlin und Weimar, 1969).

Herbert Roch, *Fontane, Berlin und das 19. Jahrhundert* (new edition, Düsseldorf, 1985).

Hans Rothfels, editor, *Bismarck-Briefe* (Göttingen, 1955).

Pierre-Paul Sagave, Theodor Fontane. "Schach von Wuthenau". Text und Dokumentation (Frankfurt am Main, 1966).

Rudolf Schenda, *Volk ohne Raum: Studien zur Sozialgeschichte der populären Lesestoff 1770–1910* (Frankfurt am Main, 1988).

Friedrich Schiller, *Werke. Nationalausgabe*, edited by J. Petersen, G. Fricke, and others (Weimar, 1943 ff.)

Hans Scholz, *Theodor Fontane* (Munich, 1978)

Wolf Jobst Siedler, *Auf der Pfaueninsel: Spaziergänge in Preußens Arkadien* (Berlin, 1987).

Wolf Jobst Siedler, *Wanderungen zwischen Oder und Nirgendwo. Das Land der Vorfahren mit der Seele suchend* (Berlin, 1988)

Michael Snodin, editor, *Karl Friedrich Schinkel. A Universal Man* (New Haven, Conn., 1991).

Gary D. Stark and Bede K. Lackner, editors, *Essays on Culture and Society in Modern Germany* (College Station, Tex., 1982)

J. P. Stern, *Re-Interpretations. Seven Studies in Nineteenth Century German Literature* (London, 1964).

Erwin Strittmatter, *Ole Bienkopp. Roman* (Berlin, 1963).

Klaus Vondung, ed., *Das wilhelminische Bildungsbürgertum. Zur Sozialgeschichte einer Ideen* (Göttingen, 1976).

Werner Vortriede, editor, *Achim und Bettina in ihren Briefen* (2 vols., Frankfurt am Main, 1981).

Gerhard Wahnrau, *Berlin: Stadt der Theater* (Berlin, 1957).

Wordsworth, *The Poetical Works of William Wordsworth*. Oxford Edition, edited by Thomas Hutchinson, M.A. (London, 1920).

Edda Ziegler and Gotthard Erler, *Theodor Fontane. Lebensraum und Phantasiewelt. Eine Biographie* (Berlin, 1996)

Carl Zuckmayer, *Gesammelte Werke* (4 vols., Frankfurt am Main, 1960).

INDEX